The Bronx In The Frontier Era
From the Beginning to 1696

by

LLOYD ULTAN

Written in collaboration with The Bronx County Historical Society

KENDALL/HUNT PUBLISHING COMPANY
4050 Westmark Drive   Dubuque, Iowa 52002

THE BRONX IN THE FRONTIER ERA
Copyright © 1993, by The Bronx County Historical Society.
All rights reserved. Printed in the United States of America.
No part of this book may be used or reproduced in any manner
whatsoever without written permission except in the case of brief
quotations embodied in critical articles and reviews.
For information, address:
The Bronx County Historical Society
3309 Bainbridge Avenue
The Bronx, New York 10467

Editor: Gary D. Hermalyn

Library of Congress Cataloging in Publication Data

Ultan, Lloyd, 1938 —

    The Bronx in the Frontier Era: From the Beginning to 1696
By Lloyd Ultan; Written in collaboration with The Bronx County
Historical Society, 1993

250 p. 15 x 23 cm.
Includes bibliographical references p.213- and index p.223.

    1. Bronx (New York, N.Y.) – History. 2. Frontier and pioneer
life – New York (N.Y.) 3. New York (N.Y.) – History – Colonial
Period, ca. 1600 – 1775. I. Bronx County Historical Society. II.
Title.
[FI28.68.B8U582 1993] 974.7'27502–dc20   92-42459
ISBN 0-941980-340   CIP

Book and Cover Design: Dan Eisenstein

ACKNOWLEDGMENTS

This book could not have been written without the kind assistance of a small army of people. I must thank my colleagues at the Edward Williams College of Fairleigh Dickinson University for granting me released time and a sabbatical leave so I could search for documents and other source material. I am grateful to the National Endowment for the Humanities for a grant to perform necessary tasks. To the innumerable people at The Bronx County Historical Society, especially the corps of secretaries and those who labor in the magnificent library, I must give thanks for expert and professional assistance, cheerfully given. I only regret I do not have the space to name them all individually, and am forced to confine my gratitude to a collective, but heart-felt, "thank you." I must, however, single out Gary Hermalyn, the Society's Executive Director, for his constant support of the project, both moral and fiscal. I also thank Stephen Stertz, my able and resourceful research assistant, and Saul Weber, whose voluntary efforts often proved invaluable. Above all, I salute my family for putting up with all the difficulties they had to face because of this project.

THE BRONX IN THE FRONTIER ERA

From the Beginning to 1696

CONTENTS

Introduction		vii
A Note on Time, Names, Measurements, and Money		x
I.	The Advent of Mankind, ca. 10,000 B.C. to 1609 A.D.	1
II.	The Age of Exploration, 1609 to 1638	12
III.	The First European Settlers, 1639 to 1648	21
IV.	The English Farmer and the Dutch Patroon, 1646 to 1655	41
V.	The Rise of the First Village, 1654 to 1664	51
VI.	The Great Land Grab, 1664 to 1673	65
VII.	The Dutch Interlude, 1673 to 1674	87
VIII.	From Riding to County, 1675 to 1683	97
IX.	Rebellion, 1684 to 1691	121
X.	Consequences, 1691 to 1696	143
XI.	Perspective on the Bronx Frontier, 1609 to 1696	171
Notes		185
Bibliography		213
Index		223

INTRODUCTION

The history of The Bronx is the history of the nation in microcosm.

That simple statement is generally true. The Bronx has experienced almost all of the major movements and trends in the history of the United States. These include, but are not limited to, the frontier, independence, industrialization, immigration, and urbanization.

This means that The Bronx can be used as a laboratory to determine whether the interpretations of historians who labor in the field of national history are correct in a local context. If they are not, why not? If not, what interpretation can be offered for the events which happened?

It is the job of a professional historian to offer not only a clear and factually accurate account of the events of the past, but an interpretation of those facts so they have some meaning. In doing so, professionals have concentrated on national and state histories, histories of other countries, diplomatic and intellectual history, histories of business, labor, science, ethnic groups, and so on. They have mined these and other fields, and have made important contributions toward them.

In recent decades, with an increasingly large proportion of the American population centered in cities, historians intensified their investigation of the field of urban history. Generally, they do so in two different ways.

Most urban historians investigate the growth of a city from its historic center outward. The focus is constantly on the center and what growth means to that area. While the approach is a valid one, in the context of New York City, of which The Bronx is a part, it means that urban historians concentrate their attention on the city's borough of Manhattan, and give but passing mention, if any, to the city's four other boroughs: Brooklyn, Queens, Staten Island, and The Bronx. Yet, each of the city's boroughs has a different ambiance, outlook, and history. This creates a tension that is a leitmotif in the city's life that is all but ignored by urban historians who study New York City.

Other urban historians tend to compare and contrast two or more cities to investigate how each tries to solve a series of common problems. This is a very valuable technique, but it tends to ignore some of the very important events leading to the development of any one city which may not have a bearing on the problem or problems under investigation. Thus, part of the story of a given city is left untold.

Today, when people think of The Bronx, they conjure up the image of a place that is the epitome of the urban problems facing the nation. There have been monographs and articles placing The Bronx in this context, and they usually take the sociological or cultural anthropological approach to explain the origin of those problems. A historian, seeing the long view, finds some of the seeds of those problems in the distant past. For instance, throughout its history, the residents of The Bronx, a name which was applied to the area only in 1898, never belonged to their own political entity. At first, they were in territory disputed by the Dutch and the English, then they became part of the North Riding, and later of Westchester County, before having their territory annexed to New York City. Thus, the people of The Bronx have always had a more limited voice in determining their destiny than those who resided in a territory that was also a municipality or a county in and of itself. Through the years, decisions made outside the area have had a profound effect on the development of The Bronx.

This work, then, is not one that fits into the usual mold of urban history. It is, in fact, local history, a field professional historians usually leave to graduate students writing their dissertations, or to amateurs.

Although professionals have some good reasons for shying away from local history as a field of investigation, by doing so, they do themselves and the profession a disservice. While there are several very good amateur historians who have produced works of merit, too often, a person untrained in historical investigation and techniques tends to give credence to unsubstantiated evidence or tries to glorify the locality by overemphasizing the contributions past residents made to national events. Oddly, when a national or state historian has to investigate the local background of a person or an event, he must rely upon such local histories, thus opening his own work to questions of reliability.

This work of local history is written by a professional historian. While it examines the beginnings of The Bronx, it is meant to be one of a series of volumes investigating the history of The Bronx through the years. It will offer interpretations of events within the context of the narrative. Like national histories, it will explore political, social, and economic developments. Wherever possible, the information is based upon evidence surviving from the time period under consideration. Any errors, whether of fact or interpretation, are solely the fault of the author. It is hoped, however, that this work, and those to follow, will inspire other professional historians to investigate the history of The Bronx, and, perhaps, of other localities.

A NOTE ON TIME, NAMES, MEASUREMENTS, AND MONEY

Most of the material in this book deals with events and people in the seventeenth century. To avoid confusion, the reader should be aware of some of the major differences between that era and our own, especially in the areas of time, names, measurements, and money.

In the seventeenth century, the Dutch, under whose auspices The Bronx was first settled, used the Gregorian calendar, the same that we use today. The English, however, still followed the older Julian calendar. Consequently, in dating events, English documents were then a full ten days behind the Dutch, and the English continued to begin the year in March, rather than in January, the way the Dutch and other users of the Gregorian calendar did. This causes some confusion in trying to uncover exactly when an event happened, especially when the two peoples interacted. To avoid confusion, I have dated all events according to the modern, or Gregorian, calendar, even in explaining events that happened after the English conquest of the Dutch colony.

Also, in the seventeenth century, there was no uniform spelling. People wrote down the names of people and places, spelling them the way they sounded to them. This causes some confusion in attempting to locate places and in identifying people, since a Dutchman might hear a word to sound one way, and an Englishman to sound another. Moreover, people of the same nationality would spell names differently, and one person could spell a name one way at one time and a different way at another. To avoid confusing the reader, I have

A Note on Time, Names, Measurements, and Money

attempted to choose one spelling and to use it throughout the book. At times, this process was arbitrary, but no more so than the actions of the people of the seventeenth century who wrote the surviving documents in the first place.

Today, there are only two major systems of measurements in the world: the metric and the English. In the seventeenth century, almost every nation had its own standard of measurement. The Dutch, for instance, measured area in morgens, and the English in acres. A person used to the metric system will not understand either of these measurements. Consequently, for the convenience of readers, I have used the original measurements, whether Dutch or English, and, in parentheses, have added the metric equivalent. I have similarly translated Dutch measurements into the English system as well.

Unfortunately, this procedure cannot be followed in recording monetary transactions. The types of money in use in the seventeenth century came from many jurisdictions and was bewilderingly varied. Moreover, the value of each coin in relation to today's American dollars cannot be accurately ascertained in light of the constantly changing value of modern currency. In addition, the value of wampum or seawan, beaver, and barter goods, although expressed in terms of Dutch guilders or English pounds, did not have the same value as the respective European currency. On top of that, English colonial currency in the colony of New York did not have the same value as the pound sterling of the mother country. This is so despite the fact that both of these currencies were expressed in terms of pounds, shillings, and pence, and were written using the same symbols, namely £ for pounds, s. for shillings, and d. for pence. To avoid compounding the readers' confusion, I simply record the money in terms of the currency used and expressed in the original documents without bothering to find the current value or an equivalent amount in any other currency.

CHAPTER I

THE ADVENT OF MANKIND

ca. 10,000 B.C. to 1609 A.D.

No one recorded the coming of the first human beings to the area that would one day become The Bronx. We do not know who they were, when they came, or why. We do not know what was done the moment the first humans set foot on Bronx soil or even where those first footprints were made. The society to which those people belonged did not develop a written language. Therefore, those who wish to solve the mystery surrounding the first representatives of mankind to live in The Bronx must rely on two imperfect sources. One is the evidence of archaeology; the other is the writing of people alien to the first arrivals and who came on the scene thousands of years later.

Unfortunately, for the modern person doing research, most of the archaeological sites were uncovered when scientific archaeology was in its infancy. The objects uncovered were not catalogued precisely. Thus, there is room for controversy among professionals in interpreting the meaning of the objects collected, especially when they have only a hazy idea of the age of one object in relation to another found at the same site.

The alien writers present other difficulties. They did not readily recognize subtle differences among the various groups of people living in the same area, and, in describing them, they confused the ways of

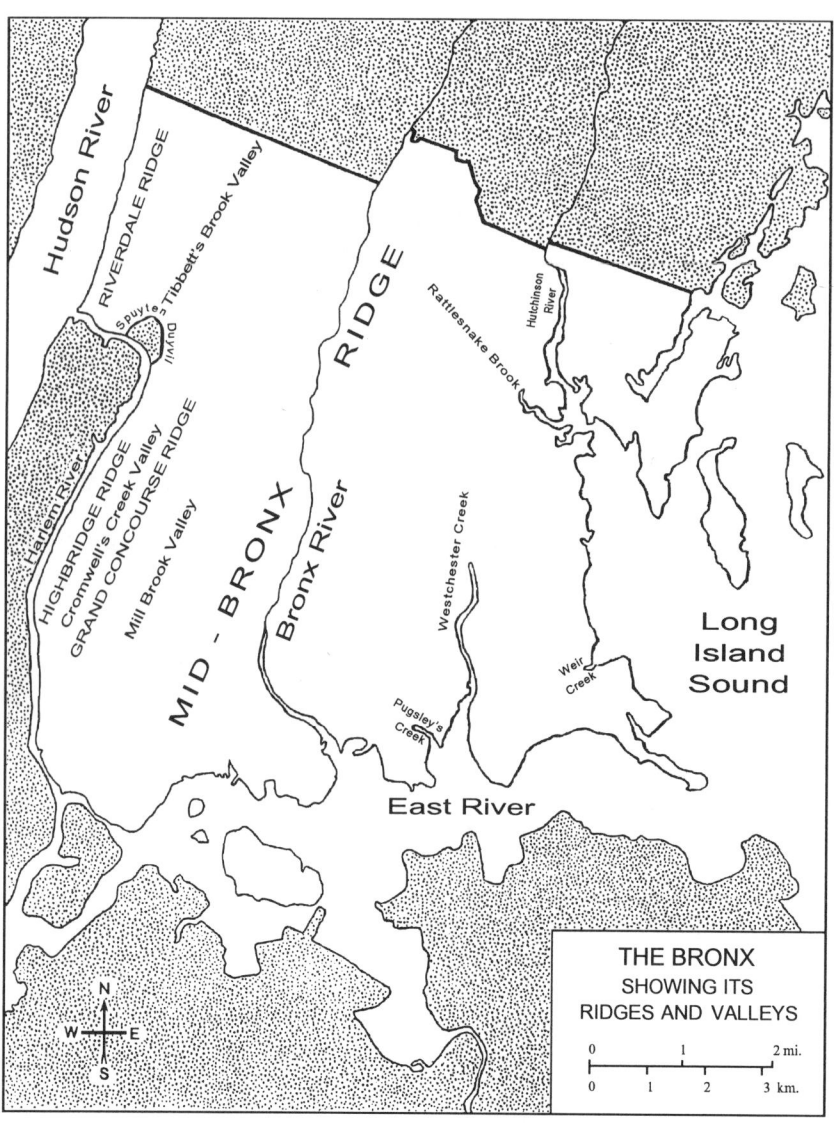

THE BRONX
SHOWING ITS
RIDGES AND VALLEYS

one people with another. Moreover, the alien writers brought the ideas and values of their own cultures with them. In writing about what they saw, they interpreted the inhabitants' actions and habits in terms of the values they knew and understood. The writers did not take these people on their own terms.

Therefore, everything that is said about the first inhabitants of The Bronx is subject to revision and change as some new bits of information are uncovered, or as new interpretations appear to explain the information which already exists.

It is possible that the first person might have come to The Bronx about 10,000 B.C., when the ice of the great glacier that covered a large part of North America was retreating and the climate was far colder than it is today. The landscape was then filled with the sparse vegetation of tundra upon which such large mammals as the mastodon fed. If so, that person could have been a member of an isolated group hunting a mastodon using a spear tipped with a stone fashioned into the form of a fluted projectile. No archaeological site has yet revealed the presence of such a group in The Bronx, however, and such groups were rare in the entire northeastern section of the United States. Nevertheless, such a site was discovered on Staten Island.[1]

The titanic forces gradually changing the face of the earth by minuscule gradations over thousands of years also changed the landscape of The Bronx. By about 8000 B.C., the slow warming of the region allowed the first fir tree to appear, the vanguard of a vast forest of conifers that would dominate the region until approximately 6000 B.C. Such a forest does not support many animals upon which mankind had learned to depend, and there are no traces of humans living in the area that would one day become The Bronx. Geological forces shaping the land were still at work, and the future Bronx gradually assumed the form with which later peoples would become familiar.[2]

By approximately 5000 B.C., a person happening upon the area would behold a place of some variety. The western edge of the territory was defined by the Hudson River valley and the narrower Harlem River, which is really a strait. The former separated the area from New Jersey, while the latter cut it off from Manhattan Island. To the south, the Bronx Kill formed a narrow passageway between the mainland of The Bronx on one side and the Randall's Island on the other. Along the eastern coastline, the boundaries were defined by the East River (really another strait) and Long Island Sound.

There was no natural barrier or boundary to define the northern limits of this mainland area. The western half of the land consisted of a series of rocky hills and valleys running in a roughly north-south direction, each valley blessed with a stream emptying southward into one of the waters that bounded the land. One of these, the Bronx River, ran through the center of the territory. The land east of the Bronx River was much less hilly and the soil more sandy as it gently sloped toward Long Island Sound. Here, there were only two major streams, later named Westchester Creek and the Hutchinson River, with some smaller ones meandering eastward. As the temperature warmed, the conifer forest yielded its dominance to deciduous trees that lost their leaves each winter and replaced them with new ones every spring. The streams developed salt marshes along their banks, more extensive for the eastern waterways than the western.

The first evidence of humans in The Bronx seems to date from about 5000 B.C. These people were primarily hunters, depending upon deer, bear, elk, small mammals, birds, fish, and shellfish, as well as nuts, seeds, and other plants. Shellfish formed a large percentage of their protein diet. They did not stay in one place for a long time, but tended to return to a favored site or two from one season to the next. Evidence of these highly migratory people have been found in Throggs Neck and Pelham Bay Park. Aside from some bone awls and needles used to pierce and sew animal hides, the tools these people fashioned were mostly of stone. Their spear points and their dart points had stems or notches. They also used axes and adzes, obviously for cutting and trimming wood. One object which they took a great deal of time in fashioning was the bannerstone. It was a piece of stone with a hollow core which had stone wings projecting out from the hollow core at either end, making it look quite similar to a winged nut one can purchase in a hardware store, only larger. Most likely, it was used as a weight to aid in throwing a spear farther and more accurately.[3]

Sometime between 1100 B.C. and 900 B.C., the roving bands of hunters discovered the secrets of agriculture, no doubt from people living to the south and west of them. The cultivation of corn, beans, and squash had been going on in Mexico for thousands of years by the time the techniques finally reached the far corners of The Bronx. To store the new types of food, they had vessels mostly of steatite or soapstone, obviously the result of trade since neither material is native to The Bronx. An important innovation was the introduction of clay pottery. The ease of fashioning and baking clay pots increased storage capacity greatly. The use of agriculture meant that the roving bands had to spend more time in one place to cultivate the crops, and their agricultural sites were used at least seasonally. Evidence of this activity has been found in Throggs Neck and Pelham Bay Park.[4]

This way of life became more refined from 900 B.C. to 200 B.C. The inhabitant not only hunted game and planted corn and beans, but also harvested shellfish from the nearby seashore. Oysters, clams, and mussels, were favorites. Sturgeon and other fish were caught as well. At this time, the people living in The Bronx used pottery extensively. The vessels, were crudely made, with thick walls and pointed bases. Archaeological evidence for these activities was found in Throggs Neck and Pelham Bay Park.[5]

Between the years 200 B.C. and 700 A.D., the fishing aspect of the economy grew, and the people relied heavily on shellfish for the major portion of their diet. Hunting continued, however, and they fashioned spear and arrow points in a pentagonal shape, or with notches in the corners. Stone hoes were made to till the fields which produced the food to supplement the nourishment obtained through fishing and hunting. In addition, the pottery vessels having pointed bottoms were improved with straight sides decorated with patterns stamped or incised into the clay before firing. Evidence of people living in this manner has been found in Pelham Bay Park, Throggs Neck, and Clason Point.[6]

About 700 to 800 A.D. the roving bands of human beings that had hunted and intermittently farmed in the area began to develop tribal groupings identified by the people who were to arrive centuries later. The basic precondition for the creation of larger groupings began to appear: small settled communities and villages.[7]

In what was to become The Bronx, two, or, perhaps, three tribes appeared. In the western section were the Manhattans (or Rechgawawanks), who also occupied most of the island later named for them. On the eastern shore extending from Hell Gate to Norwalk in Connecticut might have been the Siwanoys. There is some doubt that the tribe actually occupied the area of the eastern Bronx because later arrivals, while using the tribe's name and providing some general information, never identified the names of any individuals. To the north of both of them, with their center in present-day Westchester County, lived the Weckquasgeeks. The territory they all occupied seemed to have definite boundaries. Groups did migrate from place to place to reach the water, however, often through lands occupied by neighboring tribes.[8]

The tribe had grown out of village bands, and it was still the local village that was the most important unit to the people then.[9] In addition, all the tribes in the area shared the same general cultural aspects and had similar ways of doing things. They all spoke variations of the basic Algonquin language, but, of course, that did not mean that a Siwanoy understood a Weckquasgeek. The latter spoke a variation of the Munsee dialect spoken by many tribes living along western Long Island, southeastern New York State, and northern New Jersey. The former spoke in the Quiripi-Unquachog dialect used in southern Connecticut and in the rest of Long Island. Only the root of their languages was the same.[10]

It is believed that the tribes inhabiting the area also shared a common heritage. The Lenape were a family of tribes that included the Manhattans. According to Lenape oral tradition, they had arrived on the east coast from the land of the setting sun. They had lived beside a large body of tidal water, but, for some reason, moved inland. When they had discovered another large body of water similar to the one they had originally left, they decided to remain.[11] Archaeological evidence confirms the slow migration of peoples across the continent from Alaska to the Atlantic coast.[12] In addition, the tribes in the area always addressed the Lenape as "grandfathers," rather than the usual "brothers" used for other tribes, presumably because of their ancient origin. It is supposed that the other tribes evolved by splitting off from the Lenape grouping.[13]

Tribal organization was extremely loose. At times, the group could hardly even be called a tribe. It was governed by a council of sachems, or chiefs, chosen for their age, experience, warlike exploits, or other service. The sachem of the whole tribe presided at the meeting. He was chosen because of his unique abilities. The tribe's sachem had no power to coerce the lesser sachems. He had to try to persuade them that a particular decision was the correct one to make. His own personal power was limited to exercising ceremonial functions, attempting to keep order, settling minor disputes, and taking care of relations with other tribes. Decisions affecting the entire tribe, however, were made by the council, and the decision had to be unanimous in peacetime.[14]

If the council decided on war, another group of leaders had to be consulted. These were the war captains, who were known for their distinction in carrying out military operations. If war did break out, the authority of the tribe's sachem and his council disappeared. The war was conducted solely under the authority of the war captains.

These men could also receive peace terms, but they had to present them to the council for acceptance. If the sachem of the tribe accepted the peace proposals, he then had the authority to appoint people to conclude the negotiations.[15]

Therefore, the authority of the tribe was severely limited, and it was not as close to the average person as was the clan. The clan actually cut across tribal lines, and may have served as a social organization as well as a familial one. Each clan had a symbol to identify it, such as the turtle or wolf. It was forbidden for a member of one clan to marry someone in the same clan; members of the same clan were kinsmen and treated as brothers.[16]

In the daily life of the average inhabitant of the area that would become The Bronx, the village, however, had a far more pervasive influence than either the tribe or clan. The sachem of the village, similar to the tribe's sachem, could not coerce people into following his orders, but had to persuade individuals to follow the course he advocated. It was the right of any individual member of the village to disagree with his sachem, who could not then prevent him from following a different course.

The typical village was a small settlement, usually fairly far removed from its neighboring village. It consisted of a number of wigwams. These structures, made by bending saplings into an arc and covering them with bark, were either round or long in shape with a hole in the roof to allow the smoke of the fire to escape. It appears that more than one family lived in a wigwam.[17]

The purpose of the village was simple: cooperation for survival. Each person in a family had a job to do, and, together, all would cooperate to provide the food and clothing to survive another year.

It was the primary purpose of the men to hunt and to fish. Shellfish, by far, was the favorite dish, and all of the villages in The Bronx area were located near the water, close to the source of supply. Day after day, parties of men would head for the shore to dig clams, oysters, and mussels. Others might wait patiently to spear a stray sturgeon for variety. It is certain, however, that more fish were caught by weighting a net with stone sinkers and stringing it across the mouth of a stream.[18]

Hunting, of course, was never a certain method of obtaining food. Success or failure depended upon the accuracy of the spearthrower or the archer, the alertness of the prey, and the agility of its pursuers. Nevertheless, elk and deer were brought back for a meal on occasion. There were also a variety of birds, frogs, and turtles which could be caught and consumed.

Because hunting and fishing were the main preoccupation of the men of the village, it was they who fashioned the weapons of the hunt. Patiently, they chipped away the fragment of a large rock to form a point for a spear or an arrow, making the edges ever more polished and sharp. These points were triangular. In addition, they worked larger pieces of stone into scrapers for skinning animals, axe heads which they tied to pieces of wood with thongs, and other implements.[19]

Women cultivated the vegetables, most often corn, beans, and squash. They had responsibility for gathering fruit, nuts, and vegetables for the meal. The harvested corn was gathered, the dried kernels removed from the cob, and then the kernels pounded to form a coarse flour. This was then baked to produce a type of corn bread in a cake form that the men took with them on the hunt to sustain them in the chase. Excess corn and beans were dried, placed in pits in the earth, and preserved for use when nature was not so bountiful. For nuts and fruit, women did not have far to go, for the forest usually surrounded the village, and it was easy to shake walnuts and hickory nuts out of trees, and to pick wild berries from bushes.[20]

Children grew up imitating their parents, as children do everywhere. Blunt arrowheads were fashioned for the use of the boys, and doll-shaped pottery pieces were made for the girls. As in every society, their play readied them for the life they had to face as adults.[21]

The elderly also had a place in the economy of the village. Although an old man might not be able to hunt, he could stay at the village and make the arrowheads and spear points others needed. It is generally acknowledged that the wisdom of age was respected. Women also received respect, since heredity was determined through the female line in that society.[22]

The typical family quite often had a dog. The domesticated canines (probably originating with wolf cubs tamed after being captured) were useful animals. Not only did they serve as pets, but as watch dogs as well, since the woods were full of wolves. When one of the dogs died, he was usually buried,[23] although it is possible not all of them were interred.

There was nothing unusual about burying a dog, since other things were buried as well: shells and animal bones from former meals, for instance. Naturally, when a human being died, he was buried also. Practically no objects have ever been discovered interred with a body. Many who were buried were placed in a fetal position,[24] probably to minimize the size of the pit to be laboriously dug with stone tools.

While death was an ever-present reality with these people, all of the inhabitants of any village were probably straight and well-built.[25] The type of life imposed upon them dictated that the only people who would survive would be those strong enough and swift enough to perform the tasks needed for survival in the woodland. Not much was available for protection against the harsh forces of nature.

Clothing, for instance, was at a premium. Men wore a deerskin breechclout as the normal form of dress. In winter, deerskin leggings were added. Nothing much in the way of protection against the biting cold was worn by men. Necklaces made of bear teeth and shoulder garments made of bright bird feathers were worn more for decoration than protection. The only way a man could protect himself from the harsh winter winds was to smear his body with bear grease. He might also carry a skin of a furred animal and wrap himself in it, but this would hamper movement in a hunting chase, and he had to be prepared to discard it. Growing children wore nothing until they reached the age of puberty.[26]

In wintertime, the scarcity of food often dictated that the inhabitants of the village had to break up their communal form of living into family units.[27] Then, a single man, alone, or, perhaps aided by some older children, tracked the game.

In the spring, however, village members would gather and begin again. Land would be divided among the families, probably according to need, for it was on that land that the family grew its crops. It appears that the inhabitants at that time had no notion of private property. All the land was deemed to belong to the village as a unit, and the land parceled out to a family was meant to be used. If the land was not used, the members of the village felt free to award the use of that land to another family.[28]

In the village, everything that could be used was used. A deer or an elk slain for a meal would also have its antlers trimmed into awls and needles to make clothing. The spine of a sting ray also made a good needle or a spearpoint for fishing. A turtle's shell was turned into a container or a bowl. The sinews of animals, if worked properly, made good thread, and some of the iridescent interiors of the shells of clams or oysters were highly prized for making beaded belts known as wampum or seawan.[29]

Wampum was used in trade as a symbol of good faith. It was something given in addition to the trade, not as its price. In negotiations between tribes or villages, wampum was used in the same way to seal the agreement concluded.[30]

In trade or contact between villages and tribes, it was natural that travel would most often be conducted by water because most villages were close to the waterside. For this, the canoe was indispensable. A canoe was made by setting fire to the interior of a log and scraping hollow the charred portion. Using canoes, the inhabitants of The Bronx would travel to nearby villages of other tribes to obtain rare specimens of stones to make tools, and even rare shells to make high quality wampum.[31]

Contact via land routes was likely to be rare. Of course, there were trails that wended their ways through the forest from one village to another, but these were merely footpaths, just the width of a person's foot.[32] Their greatest utility probably was in getting hunting parties into the forest, or to get people from the village to the nearby shore.

Nevertheless, contact was made, and contact could lead to conflict. From time to time, either through accident or design, it was possible for one man to kill another. When this happened involving members from two different tribes or villages, it was not considered an automatic cause for war. What was important was the economic value of the person killed. A fully grown man in the prime of his life added greatly to the capacity of his family to survive. His family felt that it should be compensated, and it fully expected to be approached by the murderer offering sufficient presents to atone for the death. If such presents were not forthcoming, the family expected the other tribe or village to turn the murderer over to it. If neither of these two acts were performed, the members of the family felt fully justified in seeking out the murderer to kill him in return. If the person were not discovered in a sufficient amount of time, they would attempt to kill any member of the other tribe or village as just compensation.[33] After all, that act would equalize things by denying the other tribe or village of the services of an able-bodied individual needed to help it survive.

In this way, the inhabitants of what would become The Bronx lived until 1609 A.D. Their mode of life may have been filled with endlessly recurring and seasonal chores, but there was an ever-present danger in it. Their lives may have been difficult, but they were creative.

Moreover, these early inhabitants left a legacy that is still alive today. One word they used to describe a stream later called Tibbett's Brook survives unchanged: Mosholu.[34] Many of the paths they blazed through the forests are still in use today as modern streets. Portions of today's West 231st Street, Albany Crescent, Bailey Avenue, Van Cortlandt Avenue East, Gun Hill Road, Tilden Street, Sedgwick Avenue, Kingsbridge Road, University Avenue, Jerome Avenue, Third Avenue, Bronxdale Avenue, Unionport Road, Castle Hill Avenue, Tremont Avenue, Barnes Avenue, Bussing Avenue, and Eastchester Road began as such trails.[35]

The life of the inhabitants of The Bronx would be seriously disrupted by the intrusion of a people coming from a distant land on the other side of the huge expanse of water to the east. They would bring with them different ways of survival, and, even more damaging to the inhabitants, different values and goals. The aliens came from the northwestern portion of the continent of Europe, and when they saw people living in the place to which they came, they eventually labeled all the inhabitants Indians. Seeing them half naked in summer, living a life based on hunting and fishing, using mostly stone tools, and abiding in dwellings covered with bark, the inhabitants took on the appearance of wild men and savages in their eyes. It was as wild men and savages that they were to be treated.

CHAPTER II

THE AGE OF EXPLORATION

1609 to 1638

The Europeans who were to change the life of the Indians so drastically did not happen upon the territory that would become The Bronx just by accident. Although they were not necessarily seeking the land they did "discover," they were sailing in the nearby waters by design.

The Europeans were there to uncover a sea route through the great land mass of North America to lead them to the fabled riches of the East Indies. It was the goal of the Indies that had brought Christopher Columbus to the New World four times, and that laid the foundation for a great empire for Spain. More than one hundred years would pass after Columbus's first voyage, however, before anyone would attempt to penetrate the continent near today's Bronx. He would be an Englishman sailing in a Dutch ship.

At the beginning of the seventeenth century, The Netherlands was a loose federation of seven sovereign provinces engaged in a long war of independence from Spain. The conflict had erupted because of the cruel and energetic methods used by their Catholic Spanish rulers to try to eradicate what they saw as the heresy of Calvinist Protestantism then taking root in the Netherlands, and because the Dutch disliked having a foreigner as their king. The Dutch had some very important advantages in fighting this war, not the least of which was their prowess on the high seas. This had been nurtured through several decades of fishing, whaling, and especially sailing trade routes across northern European waters. The Dutch were well prepared to fight on the sea; they were also well-prepared to extend their commerce to unchartered areas of the globe and to deny that trade to any rival.

To achieve those ends The States-General, the governing body of the United Provinces of the Netherlands, chartered The Dutch East India Company to prevent any rivalry among Dutch merchants engaging in the spice trade in the East Indies. The company was given a monopoly on that trade, and, in light of the conflict with Spain, it was also permitted to wage war. The company used its privileges to oust the Portuguese, who had been forcibly united to the Spanish Crown, from a number of locations in the Far East and to lay the foundations of a Dutch empire there.

In 1609, the Dutch and the Spanish agreed to a twelve year truce in the war, and it was in the same year that the Dutch East India Company engaged Henry Hudson to command an expedition. Hudson, an English sea captain temporarily out of a job, was hired to discover a route to the East through the northern waters of Europe, the so-called Northeast Passage.[1]

In early April, 1609, Henry Hudson set sail from Texel, an island at the southern end of the mouth of the Zuyder Zee, in the small ship, *Halve Maen*, with a crew of eighteen or twenty men, some Dutch, some English. In the seas north of Scandinavia, he found the waters a solid sheet of impenetrable ice. The crew, some of them Dutchmen who had been in the tropical East Indies, grew mutinous in the cold weather and demanded that the ship turn back. Instead, Hudson manipulated the crew into favoring a project he had pursued twice before when employed by a London-based company, to discover a passage to the Indies through North America, the so-called Northwest Passage. He presented his men with two propositions. Producing some letters from Captain John Smith, he said there was evidence of a Northwest Passage somewhere north of the Virginia colony, and he proposed sailing there to try to discover it. As an alternative, he presented the possibility of sailing through the Davis Strait west of Greenland. For a crew complaining about the cold, a search just north of Virginia was surely more appealing than one near Greenland. It was then that the ship was set on its new course that would lead to the "discovery" of The Bronx.[2]

Several months later, after exploring the North American coast from Newfoundland to northern Virginia, the little ship, on the second of September, entered what would eventually be called New York Bay. There, the crew encountered representatives of the Indian tribes of the region. They seemed friendly enough, for they were willing to trade tobacco, corn, and currants for knives and beads. On September sixth, however, there was a fight in which John Colman, one of the crewmen, was killed. From that time onward, the seamen became very wary of any party of Indians coming aboard. It was with this attitude that the ship made its way up the great river that would one day be named after its captain. It was on a beautiful, fair, September 14, 1609, that Henry Hudson and his men first set their eyes on the hills of the western part of The Bronx. With the goal of finding the Northwest Passage, however, and having a favorable southwest wind behind them, they were in no frame of mind to stop, and they continued their journey northward.[3]

The captain and his men were bitterly disappointed. In the course of their journey, the river's waters changed from salt to fresh, and they soon reached the head of navigation where they could sail no farther. They had to turn back on September twenty-third.[4]

By October first, the ship returned to the vicinity of the Catskill Mountains. That afternoon, an Indian slipped out of a canoe riding at the stern of the ship, climbed the rudder, entered the cabin, and stole the pillow, two shirts, and two bandoleers belonging to crewman Robert Juet. The ship's mate saw the burglary, shot at the Indian, and then struck him on the breast, killing him. The Indian's companions then fled, followed in hot pursuit by a boat launched from the ship to recover Juet's belongings. One Indian swam toward the boat to try to topple it, but the ship's cook grabbed a sword and cut off one of the Indian's hands, causing him to drown. After the pursuers returned, the ship continued downriver. The next day, a party of Indians filling two canoes shot arrows at the stern of the ship with their bows. In reply, the crewmen discharged six muskets at them, killing two or three. At that moment, about a hundred Indians appeared on a point of land shooting at the ship. Crewman Juet replied by firing a small cannon at them, killing two and frightening the rest into retreating into the woods. The ship weighed anchor, continued downriver and sought shelter across the river in what appeared to be a bay, but what was most likely Spuyten Duyvil Creek, the northernmost and shallowest part of the Harlem River, near where it joins the Hudson River.[5]

That night, a great storm began to blow. The wind and rain

battered the small ship for the rest of the night and all the day following. At one time, the ship went aground in the oozy soil, but was able to float again with a change in the wind. The wind and rain continued through the night of October third, but the ship was able to ride safely at anchor. None of the inhabitants of the region bothered the ship and the crew while they were there. In the few hours before the storm hit them, the crew was able to observe a whitish green cliff, which could have been Marble Hill, bearing trees with discolored autumn leaves. This unusual sight led them to believe that copper or silver deposits could have been the cause of the discoloration.[6]

Fair weather returned on October fourth, and Hudson sailed his ship out of its shelter, onto the river. Once back on the Atlantic Ocean, it was discovered the ship was running low on provisions, causing the crew to become mutinous again. Hudson vetoed an idea of his Dutch mate to winter in Newfoundland and try the Davis Strait route for the Northwest Passage in the spring. He feared his crew would not stand for it. He, therefore, proposed to winter in Ireland. Instead, the ship arrived in Dartmouth, England, in November.[7]

Hudson then wrote of his voyage to the directors of the Dutch East India Company, proposing a new expedition the following year to discover the Northwest Passage. Most importantly, he most likely reported of the trade in various kind of furs available from the Indians along the river he "discovered" in return for such trifles as knives, axes, and beads. Fur was a very important commodity in the cold winters of northern Europe, and a vital item in making fashionable felt hats men wore then. The Dutch, a people making their way in the world through trade and commerce, could see a bargain, and would take advantage of it.[8]

The Dutch East India Company, however, was not interested in Hudson's proposed journey through the Davis Strait. They had hired him to find the Northeast Passage and he had gone elsewhere. Moreover, the directors of the company were not interested in the possible profits from the fur trade in the New World, since they were already earning fabulous sums from their investments in the East Indies spice trade. If Hudson had no desire to find the Northeast Passage, then they had no use for him.

Therefore, it was others who decided to take the entrepreneurial risk. In 1610, after learning of Hudson's discovery, some unknown merchants sent a ship, or several ships, up Hudson's river to trade.

This expedition brought back to the Netherlands the first tangible results of Hudson's voyage, since Hudson had been forbidden by English authorities from leaving England. The charts which the mariners drew of the area to guide their way in the future were very crude. They knew vaguely of the western end of Long Island Sound, and the East River was shown, but they perceived Manhattan as part of The Bronx mainland. The Harlem River had not yet been "discovered" by them.[9]

In the following few years, several Dutch merchants joined the scramble for profits by outfitting ships to sail into the area. It is not recorded if any of them ever set foot in what was to become The Bronx, or if they exchanged goods with any of the tribes living there, but they may have done so. The ships went up the Delaware and Connecticut rivers, as well as the Hudson, and by 1613, the merchants began the practice of leaving a crew member or two behind in wintertime to gather furs to be picked up in the spring.[10]

By 1614, the fur trade in the New World was chaotic. Dutch merchants, each independent of the other, met the same Indians to trade. Some regulation was needed to prevent the merchants from engaging in cutthroat competition that would reduce all their profits. Such a means was a company in which a body of merchants would have a monopoly of the trade. Several petitioned for such a company in the spring of 1614, and the States-General replied that it would give a charter to any group for four voyages to the New World if that group discovered new territories and reported its discoveries to the States-General.[11]

It was then that thirteen merchants, most from Amsterdam, but some from Hoorn on Texel, some partners owning one vessel, others partners owning another, fitted out five ships to search for new lands across the Atlantic. Jan De With commanded the *Little Fox*, Adriaen Block was the skipper of the *Tiger*, Hendrick Corstianssen, hired by the same partners as Block, became the captain of the *Fortune*, Thuys Volckertssen led the crew of the *Nightingale*, while Cornelis Jacobsen May commanded another ship called *Fortune*.[12] It was these five men who were to perform the major feats of exploration along a large portion of the North American coast.

It was left to Adriaen Block, however, to explore the coastline of The Bronx. While anchored at Manhattan Island, Block's ship, *Tiger*, accidentally caught fire and was almost completely burned. Undaunted, the crew cut down several trees in the vicinity to build another ship they named *Onrust* (*Restless*). It was in this ship, the first of European design built in the area, that Block began his explorations. He proceeded up the East River, which he named *Hellegat* (later Hell Gate) after the noisy waters found between the Queens and Bronx shorelines where crosscurrents and eddies made navigation difficult. He probably explored the Harlem River as well. Emerging into the waters of Long Island Sound, he carefully examined the coastline along today's Connecticut and Rhode Island shores. A body of islands he discovered along the western edges of the Sound he called the Archipelago. He must have come ashore at some time, for he knew of the Siwanoy tribe and that they lived as far south as *Hellegat*. He finally rendezvoused with his fellow captain, Hendrick Corstianssen, near Cape Cod, boarded his ship for the return journey to the Netherlands, leaving the *Onrust* and its crew in the Sound for further trading.[13]

It was on the basis of the exploration by Block and his fellow sea captains that the partners who financed the venture received a charter for a company to enjoy exclusive trade in the region now named New Netherland. The charter, however, was to expire in 1618. Nevertheless, the company, called the New Netherland Company, started operations, the most important of which was the fur trade. It is not known if any agent of the New Netherland Company made a special effort to contact the tribes in the Bronx area for trade, but it soon became obvious that the most advantageous place for establishing a trading station was at the head of navigation of Hudson's River. There, near the confluence of the Mohawk River, was a natural gathering point easily reached by water. Therefore, the first settled community of Europeans established by the Dutch was on Castle Island, near today's Albany, and called by them Fort Nassau. It remained until 1617, when a sudden rising in the level of the Hudson River caused by rapidly melting ice swept the fort away. Another was built a short distance from the first site.[14]

When the company's charter expired, the States-General did not renew it, despite several requests to do so.[15] With the monopoly now no longer in effect, several merchants probably took advantage of the situation to gain a quick profit through financing voyages to the hitherto forbidden territory.

By this time, it was not only the Dutch who were sailing the waters in the vicinity of what would become The Bronx. The English, a people also in the process of building a maritime tradition, had several ships in the area. In 1619, one of these ships, commanded by

Captain Thomas Dermer, was exploring the Long Island Sound. He followed the course previously explored by Adriaen Block along the Connecticut shoreline, inching his way along the Sound to its western edge, hugging the coast. Several times, his ship was nearly grounded in the shallow waters, but he was able to get out each time by using oars. As he passed Throggs Neck, Indians on the shoreline shot arrows at the English ship, but he was able to get away. This skirmish indicates that at some time the Europeans had managed to irritate the Siwanoy. It is not known whether Adriaen Block did it, or the crew that he left on the *Onrust*, or any of the agents of the New Netherland Company, or any of the new merchants, or Dermer himself. Dermer managed to escape into the Hell Gate, which he rightly saw as a dangerous cataract having two unequal tides among rocky islands. He probably considered himself lucky to get out of that perilous location suffering only the loss of an anchor.[16]

To the Dutch merchants, the intrusion of an English ship now and then was not as important as the intrusion of other Dutch merchants in what was once an exclusive trading preserve. The situation led to two rival groups requesting exclusive charters from the States-General for trade in New Netherland. At first, the States-General tried to get both groups together,[17] but events would lead to the resurrection of an older idea: the establishment of a Dutch West India Company as a complement to the Dutch East India Company.

The idea of a Dutch West India Company had been broached before the beginning of the twelve year truce in the war with Spain as an attempt to disrupt Spanish commerce with her colonies. With the onset of the truce, however, the States-General did not want to do anything to violate the terms of that agreement.[18] That is why the charter of the New Netherland Company was limited in time, to a certain place, and only for trading purposes. By 1621, with the end of the truce period approaching, the idea of a West India Company again was seen to have merit. In addition, the States-General hoped it might also prove to be a vehicle to unite the different groups of merchants seeking charters to trade in New Netherland.

Therefore, when the Dutch West India Company was chartered in 1621, it was given the exclusive right to trade in the Americas and on the west coast of Africa. This, of course, would bring it into direct competition with the Spanish, and, like the East India Company, it was given the right to wage war.[19] The principal purpose of the merchants who invested in the company, however, was trade, and several trading expeditions were sent out to New Netherland in the following years.

The Dutch claim in the center of the North American coastline, however, ran counter to a recent English charter given to the Plymouth Company. The directors of the Dutch West India Company realized that they had to secure New Netherland from both the English and their fellow Dutch merchants by settling people there. In addition, such settlements would prove valuable, since the settlers could raise food to feed the garrison and the officials in the forts that had to be established for defense.[20]

The Bronx probably was not considered as a place for a fort or a settlement. The head of navigation of the Hudson River, where Fort Nassau once stood, was far more important for the fur trade, and the company built Fort Orange (modern Albany) near that site. Of equal importance was the mouth of the river, at the tip of Manhattan Island, which controlled the gateway to the upriver trading post. Therefore, a new fort, called Fort Amsterdam, was built at the end of the island, and, in 1624, a ship filled with French speaking Walloons (Protestants from today's Belgium) became the first settlers there.[21]

By terms of West India Company's charter, New Netherland was not its only interest, and military expeditions against the Spanish treasure fleet and in Brazil were costing it money. This meant that the lucrative fur trade of New Netherland had to be encouraged more than the less immediately valuable settlements. A number of the company's directors, however, saw the possibility of long term profits in settling families on the land, and they pressured the company into granting a Charter of Freedoms and Exemptions.[22]

This Charter, granted in 1629, established the patroon system. It stipulated that if anyone could create a settlement of fifty people over the age of fifteen within four years, he could own the land as a patroon. This would entitle him to have the rights to all agricultural products, minerals, fishing, and grinding grain on that land. All goods coming into, or going out of, New Netherland had to stop at Manhattan first, since the company reserved that site to itself for settlement. The patroon, however, could also engage in the fur trade, normally a preserve of the company alone, if the company had no agent in his vicinity.[23]

It is not surprising that a number of the directors of the company took advantage of these terms to have themselves made patroons, but it would not be for seventeen years after the passage of the Freedoms and Exemptions that the first and only patroonship would be established in The Bronx. Most of the patroons selected sites near Manhattan Island, close to its settlement, or on the Delaware River, which was then part of New Netherland, or, as director Kiliaen Van Rensselaer did, near Fort Orange. These sites were usually located along the fur trade routes, or, in the case of the Delaware River, near the whaling routes.[24]

It would be difficult to believe that the lives of the Indian inhabitants of The Bronx had not been affected by the incursion of European values, technology, and people, despite the fact that no European would settle there for thirty years after Henry Hudson first saw the place. Within a few years of first hearing a musket fired, the Indians' attitude changed from one of awe and terror of the unknown to one of accepting the weapon's firing as normal.[25] The Siwanoys continued to make the trip to Long Island to obtain shells to make high quality wampum, but wampum now became the price of a transaction, rather than a token of faith. As a result of the insatiable desire of the Dutch for furs, the Indians found themselves spending a good deal of time going into the forest to trap beaver, otter, mink, and other animals. They received some high quality goods in return. Not only were metal knives and axes given, as in Hudson's voyage, but also metal mattocks that made digging up and cutting roots and loosening soil easier, and duffel (a coarse woolen cloth with a thick nap) that was used as a warm blanket at night and a warm cloak during the day.[26] The Dutch West India Company was careful not to trade muskets and gun powder for furs, since the directors did not want these implements in the hands of the Indians.

Whatever the Europeans thought of the Indian tribes living on the mainland north of Manhattan, for thirty years none of them entertained a thought of settling there. Ships going up and down Hudson's River from Manhattan to Fort Orange, or Rensselaerswyck, the patroonship of Kiliaen Van Rensselaer, hardly noticed the place. Every once in a while, a ship's captain might note Spuyten Duyvil Creek as a landmark, but nothing more would be stated in his log.[27] The first man to consider such a place as a home was Jonas Bronck.

CHAPTER III

THE FIRST EUROPEAN SETTLERS

1639 to 1648

For a man who has given his name to the Bronx River and the borough of The Bronx, Jonas Bronck remains very much a man of mystery. The Danish government claims that he was born on one of the Faroe Islands before 1590; that he was the son of Mortan Bronck, a Lutheran minister; that he attended the University of Copenhagen, where he studied theology, medicine, and law; and that from there, he went to the Netherlands to become a businessman. This story is enshrined in the *Danish Biographical Dictionary*, some Danish journals, an English language pamphlet issued by the Danish government in honor of the American bicentennial, and a Faroese language elementary school reader.[1] Unfortunately, this story is not supported by documentary evidence.

In reality, Jonas Bronck was born in 1600 in the village of Komstad in the province of Smaland in Sweden. The nearest city was Jönköping. Bronck's father, also called Jonas,[2] was almost certainly a farmer, since Smaland was overwhelmingly rural. Even a century and a half after Bronck's birth, almost 85% of the people in the vicinity of Jönköping would be engaged in agriculture, while only half a percent would be involved with trade.[3] In the seventeenth century, the land, well wooded, fertile, and dominated by a single family which owned much of it, was used to raise cattle. Most of the inhabitants lived on tenant smallholdings.[4]

Very little is known of Bronck's early life. He did learn to read, for it is known that, by the time he died, he had amassed a library of books in Danish, Dutch, and Latin.[5] Exactly when he learned to read and who taught him is a matter for speculation. He did have a child's book in his library, however. Most likely, it was the parish clergyman who was his teacher. Certainly, members of the clergy would be the most likely to have been educated among all those in a rural parish, and, indeed, some of Bronck's books were concerned with Lutheran theology.

In any event, at some time, Bronck decided to uproot himself, leaving the province of Smaland for life as a merchant seaman.[6] This is most unusual. In Smaland, it is far more common for children to follow their parents and to become farmers. Bronck's personal reasons for this change in the direction of his life are not known, but some clues may be gleaned from the history of the province during his formative years.

When Bronck was eleven years old, the same year Gustavus Adolphus ascended the Swedish throne, the War of Kalmar between Denmark and Sweden began. Smaland became the battleground, with the Danes attacking the coasts and besieging Jönköping.[7] With the conflict raging in his home province, it is difficult to believe that the growing boy had not been affected in some way. It is possible he may have left Smaland at this time just to achieve a safe haven at sea, a possibility supported by the fact that men in those days began their sea careers at an early age. It is even more likely, however, that the riots which upset the province in the following decade were the cause of Bronck's departure.

In 1622, when Jonas Bronck had already attained maturity, the farmers of Smaland rose up in violent protest against a tax on their cattle, and even slaughtered the beasts to escape paying the impost. Two years later, there were more riots in opposition to such taxation.[8] Here was a direct threat to a farmer's livelihood. If the taxes were paid, it would mean a reduction in income, and the cattle slaughter would certainly have led to a virtual elimination of the province's major marketable item. Moreover, it would have taken a significant length of time for each herd to be restored. A young man, willing to be bold enough to leave his familiar surroundings and risk his future on the unknown, might conclude that this was the time to depart.

It is not known where Jonas Bronck went once he left his

birthplace. It is possible he went to Denmark. There were close ties between Smaland and Skane, which was then a Danish province on the southern tip of the Scandinavian peninsula,[9] and Bronck did eventually own several Danish language books. He also could have gone directly to the Netherlands. Dutch influence was considerable in the area of the Baltic Sea in the seventeenth century, and many Dutch merchants traded with, and settled in, Sweden. In addition, Dutch military tactics had influenced the Swedish army during the War of Kalmar and afterward.[10]

It is known that Jonas Bronck did settle in the Netherlands, becoming a merchant seaman and a captain. His knowledge of navigation was probably self-taught. One of the books he purchased was the century-old *Cosmographia*, a navigational primer by Petrus Apianus, which also dealt with some basic principles of geography. Another purchase was Willem Jansz Bleau's *Zeespiegel*, a three-volume atlas first printed in 1623. This book also contained some principles of navigation, such as how to use the astrolabe and how to find the North Star. The bulk of Bleau's writing, however, is devoted to descriptions of coastlines, landmarks, and water depths along the sea lanes from Amsterdam to the Scandinavian countries. Proportionately less is devoted to the coasts of Atlantic Europe, England, Scotland, and Ireland. This indicates that Bronck, as a sea captain, most probably plied the Scandinavian routes. He probably called at such busy ports as Copenhagen in Denmark, Rostock in Germany, and Stockholm in Sweden. Undoubtedly, it was Bronck's trading activities that made him a fairly wealthy man.

In Amsterdam, he lived in a house on the Brouwersgracht,[11] a small canal in the northern section of the bustling commercial city, a short walk from the anchorage where myriad seagoing ships were constantly loading and unloading cargo from the far corners of the earth. The canal was not only flanked by rows of narrow brick townhouses, but was also the site of a brewery which gave the waterway its name. It was not the place where the wealthiest Amsterdam residents lived; that was the Heerengracht, a canal whose northern end terminates at the Brouwersgracht.

In 1638, Bronck decided to marry Teuntie Jeuriaens, daughter of Jeuriaen Reynderss, who lived on the Korte Boomdwarstraat,[12] a simple narrow street in the city. The family was not a prominent one in Amsterdam, and may have been immigrants from Denmark since, a year later, Maritje Piters of Copenhagen would make Teuntie Jeuriaens her primary residual heir.[13] In any event, the couple published their intention to marry on June 18th, and had the ceremony performed in the Nieuw Kirk near the Dam Square on the 6th of July.

It was in Amsterdam that the newly married Bronck made the decision to move to the New World. Again, we are not certain why he chose to do so. There are certain clues, however. Andreas Hudde, a man who had served on the Council in New Netherland, returned to his homeland in 1638. There, he borrowed two hundred guilders from Jonas Bronck.[14] Hudde owned several tracts of land in the Dutch colony, and there is a strong possibility that the two men had discussed the prospects for an enterprising person who would move there.

In addition, the Dutch West India Company became alarmed at the sparseness of population in the new territory, especially since the growing English settlements in Connecticut were beginning to push westward into the area claimed by the Dutch. People were needed to settle on the lands not only to validate the Dutch claim, but also to provide fighting men if that claim had to be defended. Moreover, there was a crying need for farmers to provide food for the fur traders, ships' crews, and company officers who carried on the main business of the colony.[15]

The company's directors soon realized that people did not emigrate to New Netherland because the conditions of settlement there were too strict. The single greatest motivation for any Dutchman to make the dangerous crossing of the Atlantic, to sever ties with family and friends, and to settle in a wilderness lacking the amenities of civilized life as he knew it, was the chance to get rich quickly. Up to that time, the only way of making a profit in New Netherland was by engaging in the fur trade. The company itself, however, cut off the possibility of great profits for outsiders by requiring trappers to sell solely to the company's agents, thus keeping all the profits in the company's coffers.[16] Nevertheless, this system lost the company profits on the fur trade because of these requirements. Therefore, in 1638, the company decided to open the fur trade to all those who would settle on the land.[17] The maneuver worked, and the population of New Netherland began to increase appreciably in the following years.[18]

It is possible that Jonas Bronck, too, saw the making of his fortune in the fur trade, for he became one of the first to journey to New Netherland under the new regulations. There is no evidence, however, that he did engage in the fur trade after he arrived.

The company had also been disappointed with the results of its policy of establishing patroonships. Each patroon was granted possession of a large tract of land with certain feudal rights in return for settling a certain number of families on it.[19] Since many Dutchmen had no desire to live under a feudal lord in the guise of a patroon, the policy seemed to retard settlement. It was clear that smaller plots of land had to be offered to attract farmers to New Netherland.

The company decided that anyone could own land in proportion to the size of his family and the number of his dependents if the land were actually cultivated. In addition, taxes to the company would be forgiven for the first four years. The company also hoped to profit from controlling the sale of excess food raised in New Netherland to the company's other colonies in Brazil and the Caribbean.[20]

It is even more likely Jonas Bronck was attracted to New Netherland by the prospect of farming. His youth, after all, had been spent in a rural area of Sweden, and it is possible that Hudde's description of the well-wooded land suitable for cattle raising had reminded him of home. We do know that Bronck did establish a working farm.[21]

No matter what the reason, Jonas Bronck and several other men chartered the ship, *De Brant Van Troyen* (*The Fire of Troy*), to transport themselves, their cattle, and other commodities to New Netherland. On April 30, 1639, Bronck agreed to pay a fourth part of the cost of the freight and the ship (1,270 guilders, 10 stuyvers, out of a total cost of 4,830 Carolus guilders), to the West India Company within forty days of the ship's return. He was able to get Amsterdam merchant Jacob Lievenssen to guarantee payment if he should default.[22]

By that time, he had made sure that the number of dependents that he could claim when applying for land in New Netherland would extend beyond his immediate family. In Amsterdam, he hired three Germans, Jochem Kaller, Carsten Pieter, and Jacob Gever, as indentured servants. He would pay their passage to the New World, and they, in turn, would work for him for four years. Bronck also promised to pay them thirty two rix dollars a year minus whatever it cost him to clothe them. They also had to be satisfied with whatever he chose to feed them during those four years, and they had to promise not to marry without his permission.[23] Also in Amsterdam, Jonas Bronck made sure that his wife would remain comfortable in the wilderness by providing a servant for her. Clara

Matthijs was hired for this purpose to serve in the house and fields for five years at forty guilders a year, part of which was to pay for her first year's wardrobe purchased in Amsterdam. Similarly, Clara Matthijs had to promise not to marry.[24]

These agreements were concluded near the end of April, 1639, and we can assume that, in early May, Jonas Bronck and his wife set aboard the ship, *De Brant Van Troyen*, which anchored at Hoorn in Texel, the island at the southern end of the mouth of the Zuyder Zee from which most Dutch ships sailed across the Atlantic. At Texel, they were joined by their indentured servants.

The ship anchored at New Amsterdam in the East River probably in early June.[25] By July, Jonas Bronck had already purchased land for his farm and was making preparations for settling there.[26] For a man who had done more than a usual amount of reading, and who had clear evidence of wealth, his choice of land seems strange. He chose 250 morgens (about 652 acres, or almost 264 hectares) located on the southwesternmost part of the mainland on the banks of the Harlem River where no one had settled before.[27] It was a piece of highly wooded property located at the very edge of the frontier. Why would such a man settle there?

As with so many other aspects of Jonas Bronck, there is no direct evidence which can enlighten us as to his motives. Again, however, there are clues. Almost as soon as he landed, Bronck sought out Andreas Hudde, to whom he had lent money in Amsterdam the previous year, and had Hudde reaffirm the existence of the debt in court.[28] Hudde had obtained land in northern Manhattan in 1638,[29] and he may have tried to interest Bronck in that area as well. In addition, the cattle aboard *De Brant Van Troyen* were consigned to Jochem Pietersen Kuyter. In July, 1639, Kuyter was to purchase a rather large plot of land in northern Manhattan corresponding today to about 125th to 148th Streets along the Harlem River.[30] Kuyter had probably sailed on the same ship with Jonas Bronck, and may have conversed with him about the remote reaches of Manhattan Island as a place for settlement. The fact that Bronck finally chose the mainland location is not proof that he had rejected these probable offers, since he was separated from Kuyter's and Hudde's lands only by the Harlem River, and, in an age when water transportation was quicker and cheaper than land transportation, the river can be viewed as a connecting factor, rather than as a boundary. Moreover, if Jonas Bronck had been considering entering the fur trade, a location on the mainland with a seemingly unending forest would be closer to the source of supply than one on Manhattan Island.

Several important problems had to be dealt with, however, before Jonas Bronck and his wife could begin to work on the land. One involved their maidservant, Clara Matthijs. As soon as she landed on the dock at New Amsterdam, she was probably met by Gerrit Jansen, a native of Oldenberg in Germany, who had been in New Netherland for some time. Bronck suddenly discovered Jansen had been engaged to Clara before she had left the Netherlands, and that she had obviously duped him into paying her passage across the Atlantic, despite the fact that her contract with him stipulated that she could not marry. Bronck demanded restitution according to the terms of her contract, and Jansen agreed to pay him one hundred guilders in two installments and one young sow, which would be useful to a new farmer.[31]

A more pressing concern was the hiring of farmhands to clear away the trees and work the land. Bronck had paid the board of two men, Pieter Andriessen and Laurens Duyts, sailing on *De Brant Van Troyen*, and he used the debt, amounting to 121 guilders and sixteen stuyvers, to persuade them to work his property. On July 21, 1639, Andriessen and Duyts agreed to clear land and plant maize and tobacco on a different portion of Bronck's property each year. Each cleared field would be turned over for Bronck's use at the end of the year, and the two men were to pay back their passage money in tobacco or "by the first ready means." They also had the right to demand two cows and two horses from Bronck within a year if Bronck could spare them.[32]

For livestock, Bronck apparently arranged with Jochem Pietersen Kuyter to use at least two horses and a cow from among those consigned to Kuyter aboard the ship, *De Brant Van Troyen*. To care for these, and to further clear and plant on his land, Bronck came to an agreement with Cornelis Jacobsen Stille and his brother, Jan Jacobsen. Beginning with the first of September, 1639, Bronck was to provide them with livestock, a house, and land to cultivate for six years. The brothers were to pay him fifteen schepels (almost 11 1/2 bushels, or just under 404 liters) of grain for each horse and twenty-five pounds (just over 11 kilograms) of fresh butter for each cow. As was usual in such agreements, at the end of six years, Bronck was to reclaim his original livestock and take half of the remaining stock which may have been bred through those years.[33]

Jan Jacobsen, an immigrant from Vreedlandt in the Netherlands, had been in the colony since at least the previous year and, on similar terms, had worked farmland belonging to others.[34] On the same day he agreed to work the Bronck farm, he also agreed to marry Maritje Piters from Copenhagen. His Danish bride may have been the means by which he first met Jonas Bronck and his wife, since she declared Teuntie Jeuriaens or her husband her residual heirs in case of her death.[35] Maritje Piters joined Jan Jacobsen and his brother, Cornelis, in settling on the Bronck farm. Cornelis Jacobsen Stille may have owned some land on Long Island before he joined his brother in signing the six-year contract with Jonas Bronck, for he sold that farm in 1641.[36]

Another person may have joined the small group who first began to clear the land and to plant in the wilderness on the mainland. Jochem Kaller, one of the German indentured servants hired by Jonas Bronck, married sometime before August, 1640, no doubt with Bronck's permission.[37] It is not certain, however, whether Kaller's wife joined him when he first came to the Bronck farm or shortly thereafter.

Even more uncertainty surrounds Peter Bronck. His name first appears in the records of the Bronck farm on the mainland in 1643.[38] We cannot be sure that he came in 1639 with Jonas Bronck and his wife. Even his relationship to Jonas Bronck is unclear. For many years, genealogists had considered him the son of Jonas, since Peter had indicated that Jonas was his father's name.[39] Since Jonas Bronck's father, however, was also named Jonas, there is enough evidence to indicate that the assumption of the genealogists might have been wrong, and that Peter was, perhaps, the younger brother of the mainland farmer.[40]

It was this small group of Danes, Dutch, and Germans who cast their lot with the Swedish Jonas Bronck to begin the first European settlement on the mainland near Manhattan Island. The land had to be cleared, and much of the lumber hewn from the trees on the Bronck farm was first used to construct the buildings to house the people and the livestock. Pieter Andriessen had built his own house some distance east of Bronck's homestead.[41] Bronck's main house, given the Biblical name Emmaus, had exterior walls of fieldstone and a roof of tiles, probably imported from the Netherlands. Nearby rose a barn, a tobacco house, and two hay barracks.[42] Some of the lumber was fashioned into fence posts to mark the boundaries of the property, and some of it was cut by Jan Jacobsen and sold elsewhere for his own profit.[43]

Into his house, Jonas Bronck moved his precious library, the largest in New Netherland, with its books in Dutch, Danish, and Latin covering theology, history, and navigation. He decorated his home with the objects reflecting his status and wealth accumulated through the years. Eleven pictures enlivened the rooms, and two mirrors, one with an ebony and one with a gilt frame, added a touch of elegance to the frontier home. A Japanese cutlass, and a rapier and a dagger, both with silver mountings, were probably used more for decoration than for practical purposes. Three guns and a musket were handy for defense in case of emergencies. A silver salt cellar decorated the extension table, and, at times, seven silver spoons, a silver cup, a silver tray, and the silver chains attached to his four tankards might impress guests. Otherwise, the more numerous pewter plates were probably used.

When dressed for important occasions, Jonas Bronck probably wore his black satin suit and his slashed satin doublet, and perhaps completed his outfit with a pair of black gloves, one of his two hats, and, in cooler weather, a black cloth mantle. In this somber outfit, the gold signet ring he wore could stand out. On ordinary occasions, he could wear any of his three other suits.

From his window, he could see the land cleared by his farmhands in which his crops grew. Besides tobacco, which was a good export crop, wheat, rye, barley, and peas were grown. Some of the grain would be turned into malt and small quantities of beer.

In time, the livestock on his farm increased. The horses and cattle were housed in the barn and fed in winter with hay stored in the hay barracks. As was the custom at the time, the hogs were left running wild in the woods that still surrounded the settlement, and no one bothered to count their number. Five milk cows provided milk and some was churned into butter.[44]

Despite the presence of amenities from home, which were considerable in that wilderness setting, life was hard. In addition to the normal difficulties of operating a farm and trying to make ends meet, there was always the possibility of danger from the nearby, and what must have seemed to these early settlers, inscrutable Indians.

In 1641, that fear turned to reality in the Dutch colony. A young Weckquasgeek killed an aged wheelwright, Claes Corneliesen Swits, because the Indian's uncle, who had been killed by some Dutchman in 1626, had not had his murder avenged. According to the customary rules as he knew them, it was his duty to kill the old man, whether or not it was Swits who had killed his uncle, simply because the aged wheelwright belonged to the "tribe" which had committed the original murder.

The Dutch authorities did not see it that way, however. To them, the two murders had no connection, and the young Indian had to be turned over to them for trial and execution. The only questions were when, and if it could be done without war. Director-general Willem Kieft assembled twelve men to advise him. They counseled him to wait, to repeatedly request the tribe to turn over the murderer, and to prepare his forces. Clearly, the twelve men wished to avoid any confrontation with the Indians if they could.

Unfortunately, by the beginning of 1642, the Weckquasgeeks had not peaceably turned the murderer over to Kieft. In March, the director-general ordered Hendrick Van Dyck and a force of eighty men to march to the tribe's village on the east bank of the Hudson River, to set fire to it, and to kill anyone they could get their hands on. Fortunately for the Indians, the guide lost his way, and Van Dyck was forced to return to New Amsterdam.

The Indians, however, soon discovered their close call, and, frightened, asked the Dutch for peace. A conference was arranged to take place at the home of Jonas Bronck.[45]

Signing of the peace treaty with the Indians at the home of Jonas Bronck.

From a painting by James Ward Dunsmore, 1908.
The Bronx County Historical Society Research Library

It is doubtful that Bronck was one of the negotiators at the conference in his own home, because he was never high in the counsels or affairs of the Dutch colony. Cornelis Van Tienhoven, secretary of New Netherland, did attend, as did Bronck's neighbor across the Harlem River, Jochem Pietersen Kuyter, and another prominent New Netherlander, Jan Jansen Dam. The negotiations were long. At one point, Kuyter showed his exasperation by muttering something under his breath. However, agreement was finally reached.[46] The threat of war was over, at least for the time being.

It was at this time, when all difficulty between the Dutch and the surrounding Indians appeared to be solved, that another group of Europeans arrived to settle in the area that would become The Bronx. These were Englishmen migrating from New England seeking a home in the Dutch colony.

New Englanders had already begun to settle in various locations along Long Island Sound, not only in Rhode Island and Connecticut, but in towns established on Long Island itself. A settlement at the western end of the Sound was no more than a logical extension of this migration.

The Dutch, of course, were wary about the movements of the English, since they feared that English settlement would lead to an assertion that the Dutch claim to that land was no longer valid because no Dutch people lived there. The Dutch authorities, however, well aware of the sparseness of their own settlements, decided in June, 1641, to allow respectable Englishmen led by their clergymen to settle in their own towns provided they swore allegiance to the States-General and to the West India Company, used Dutch weights and measures, and did not erect fortifications. In return, the English were guaranteed free exercise of their religion, the right to trade according to company regulations, to nominate their own magistrates, and to hold the land free of taxes for ten years.[47]

In conformity to these conditions, John Throckmorton and thirty-five families requested permission to settle on the mainland of New Netherland. Throckmorton had come to the New World aboard the ship, *Lyon*, that arrived at the Puritan colony of Massachusetts Bay in 1630. Influenced by the arguments of his fellow passenger, Roger Williams, he left for Rhode Island in 1636 after the Puritan clergy expelled Williams from the Bay Colony for expressing religious thoughts opposed to their own. He became one of the initial fifty-four landowners in the town of Providence. When Williams established the Baptist Church in 1638, Throckmorton and his wife, Rebecca,

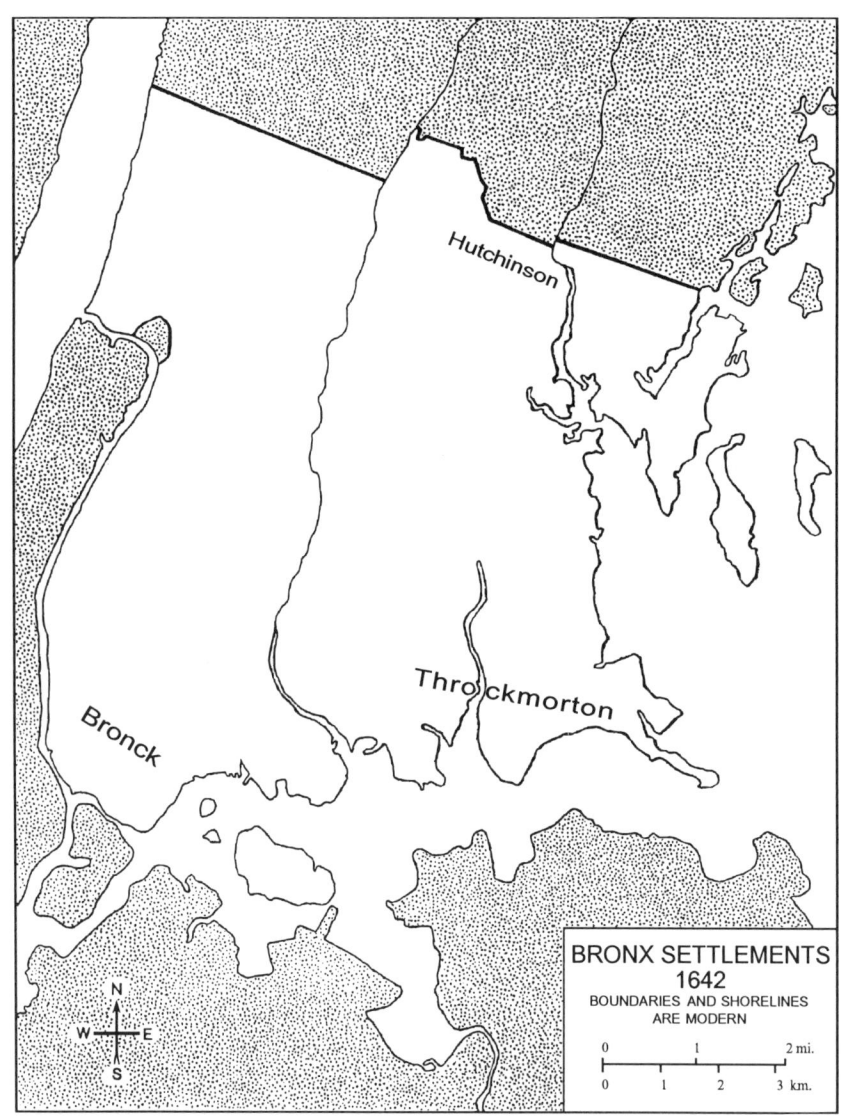

were among the first converts. By 1642, however, it became apparent that Massachusetts authorities sought control over the tiny settlement, and Roger Williams set out for England by way of New Amsterdam (he was forbidden to use the port of Boston) to obtain a charter for Rhode Island.[48] With Rhode Island threatened, New Netherland seemed a safe haven.

On October 2, 1642, Throckmorton received permission from the Dutch to settle on a neck of land thrusting into Long Island Sound. This site was part of a larger area called Vreedlant, which the Dutch had purchased from the Indians in 1640.[49] Soon, the families involved began building their frame houses, using the wood that was abundant everywhere, and grazing their cattle on the nutritious salt marsh grasses characteristic of the site.

Nearby, a woman, named Anne Hutchinson, aided by her son-in-law, also began to erect a house. She had earned a notorious reputation among several of her fellow New Englanders.

Anne Hutchinson had arrived in the New World in 1634, following the Reverend John Cotton from England to Massachusetts. In time, she began to interpret Puritan teachings to mean that once the Holy Ghost entered a person's soul, thus remitting his sins, it was irrelevant whether his conduct was good or bad, since he was following an inner voice that expressed the Divine Will. This idea went counter to orthodox Puritanism, which stressed that the entrance of the Holy Ghost into a person's soul would lead that person to a life of merit and good works. Anne Hutchinson's ideas not only threatened the orthodox Puritan religion with a competing theology dangerous to the religious purity of the commonwealth the leaders were attempting to establish in Massachusetts, but they threatened the authority of the Puritan ministry and the magistrates of the commonwealth. After all, if a person is to follow only the dictates of the Divine Will inside him, what need has he for ministers to teach him the Word of the Lord, or for magistrates to enforce the laws of mortal men?

It was for these reasons that Anne Hutchinson was tried, convicted of the heresy of Antinomianism, and sentenced to exile in March, 1638. She went to Rhode Island with her husband and numerous children, but even there she felt the wrath of the Massachusetts magistrates who were attempting to take control of the colony. After the death of her husband, the defenseless widow decided to move far enough away from the jurisdiction of the Puritan clergy for safety. New Netherland was the closest area not under Puritan influence, and, with the assurance that the voice of the

Divine Will within her provided, in 1642, she settled in Vreedlant on the west bank of a river that was eventually named for her.⁵⁰

Anne Hutchinson's son-in-law, Captain James Sands, began to cut down some trees on the new site, to fashion logs with his axe, and to build a frame house for the widow, her children, and her servant. In the midst of this activity, a group of Indians traveling along a nearby path leading to the water confronted Captain Sands, and, in a friendly manner, made gestures indicating that he should cease his work. They placed an axe over his shoulder, gathered his tools in his hands, and indicated that he should leave. The Indians then continued their journey to the river to spend the day digging for clams and oysters. Captain Sands returned to his work building the house. By the end of the day, the Indian party returned, and, seeing Captain Sands had not stopped work on the house, they repeated the same gestures they had made earlier, clearly indicating he should leave. After the Indians went on their way, Captain Sands left the site and did not return. His mother-in-law, however, sure in following the Word of the Lord, obtained some hands, probably from the nearby Throckmorton settlement, to finish the house.⁵¹

The Indians, most likely Siwanoys, were concerned about the land being used by both Anne Hutchinson and John Throckmorton and his settlers. In their view, the fact that the Dutch had paid for the land two years earlier made no difference. If the Dutch had purchased the land from the leaders of a village who had no authority over the sites, the Siwanoy would view the purchase as not binding on the Indians who actually occupied the area. Most certainly, the Dutch had made no use of the land during those two years, and that, too, was important to the Indians. According to their custom, if no one used the land, it reverted to the village for redistribution. Even if the Dutch had come in 1640, immediately after the Vreedlant purchase, it is likely the Indians would have demanded payment anew for the changes that would have been made to the land. John Throckmorton, however, seeing things in European terms, felt the land was his, since it was given to him by the previous owners, the Dutch West India Company. Mrs. Hutchinson, of course, secure in her knowledge that she was following the word of the Divine Will inside her, could not have cared less about the details of land ownership.⁵²

Consequently, in the summer of 1643, a band of Siwanoy Indians descended upon the hapless English settlers. When they came to Anne Hutchinson's house, they pretended to be friendly, and asked that her dogs be tied up on the pretext that the animals frightened them. When this was done, they killed the widow and all who lived with her, except the youngest daughter, who was carried off to live with them. They then set fire to the house.[53] The band also descended upon the unsuspecting Throckmorton settlement. Fortunately, a passing vessel noticed the plight of the settlers and was able to evacuate the people who lived on the neck of the land, with only two sailors who rowed a boat recorded as casualties. As the survivors sailed away to safety, they saw their houses set afire, their fields ablaze, and their cattle slaughtered.[54] The only permanent thing they left behind was the name of their leader attached to the land they had occupied. From that time forward, it was referred to as Throckmorton's Neck, eventually shortened to Throggs Neck.

Although John Throckmorton had received a patent for his land from Director-general Willem Kieft on July 6, 1643, and, although he continued to hold title to the land for more than a decade, he never returned. He went back to Rhode Island, became a Quaker in 1672, and died in 1684 on a visit to his children who had settled on some land he had purchased in New Jersey.[55]

The incidents at Hutchinson River and Throggs Neck, of course, did not affect affairs at the Bronck farm, but other matters involving the neighboring Indians did so. Indian matters became the foremost concern of the Dutch colony in the spring of 1643. Things had been simmering for about a year. In 1642, a Dutchman killed a Hackensack Indian to steal his beaver skins. Two Dutchmen were then murdered by the Indians in revenge. In the meantime, a war waged by the Mohawks on the Weckquasgeeks forced the latter tribe to seek the protection of the Dutch at Fort Amsterdam, but soon the Weckquasgeeks became uneasy in the shelter of the fort and, after fourteen days, some crossed the Hudson for protection, and others retreated to Corlear's Hook in Manhattan. Director-general Kieft decided he had to avenge the deaths of the two Dutchmen, and, on February 26, 1643, sent a force across the river to slaughter the men, women, and children who had recently fled there. Another Dutch force performed the same task at Corlear's Hook. A separate attack by some settlers on Long Island on a tribe there was enough to engulf the entire colony in a wave of Indian wars which had the character of a general war between most of the neighboring tribes and the Dutch.[56]

It was at this juncture that Jonas Bronck died. As with the details of his birth, there is no precise record of the cause of his death. He may have been caught up in the violence of the Indian wars that were developing, but it is certain that his home and his farm were in no way threatened. The fieldstone house was to stand for many years. The wooden outbuildings, the livestock, and the grain in the fields were left undisturbed in 1643.

The most pressing problem for Bronck's widow, Teuntie Jeuriaens, was protection. Living at the edge of the wilderness with no husband to protect her from the legal depredations of a male-dominated social system, or from the physical depredations which might be visited upon her because of the increasingly restless situation involving the Indians, she needed a new husband quickly. She found him in the person of Arent van Curler.

In many ways, van Curler was a remarkable young man. At the tender age of eighteen, in 1638, he was recruited by his cousin, Kiliaen Van Rensselaer, the patroon of Rensselaerswyck, located at the head of navigation of the Hudson River, to manage the business affairs of the patroonship. Van Rensselaer never left Amsterdam, and sent copious instructions to his young cousin on the site. In general, the patroon was satisfied with van Curler's work, but he would admonish him from time to time on one point or another.[57] In the spring of 1643, van Curler, now twenty-three, was in New Amsterdam on the patroon's business, and there he probably met Bronck's widow, who most likely had to be there to deal with the innumerable things which have to be done when a relative dies. Van Curler was impressed by the widow's housekeeping, especially in that nothing had been damaged. By mid-June, 1643, he was able to announce to Van Rensselaer that he was engaged to be married to her, and that he hoped their future could be spent on a farm at Rensselaerswyck leased from the patroon.[58] Sometime between the 16th and 25th of June, they were married.[59]

It was about that time that the small band of Danish, Dutch, and German pioneers who had come with Jonas Bronck to establish his farm on the mainland dispersed. Arent van Curler took his new bride back with him to Rensselaerswyck.[60] The mysterious Peter Bronck also went there and in time opened a tavern.[61] Carsten Pieter and Jacob Gever, two of the German indentured servants, also apparently moved to the patroonship, Pieter dying sometime before 1646. Gever seems to have worked there as a farmhand.[62] Their fellow German, Jochem Kaller, purchased a farm on Long Island, and evidently lived there with his wife.[63] Pieter Andriessen is difficult to trace, since there were a handful who shared that name residing in New Netherland at the time. He has been identified with the Andriessen called Schoorteenveger (chimney sweep), and, it was this man who then moved to a farm of his own on Long Island.[64] Laurens

Duyts eventually married Ytie Jans, established a farm on what is today called Roosevelt Island, and so mismanaged his personal affairs that he was caught selling his wife into adultery with John Parcell and, in turn, living in adultery with Geesje Jansen. For this, he was not only flogged, had his right ear cut off, and banished for fifty years, but had to suffer the added humiliation of witnessing his wife request permission of the authorities to marry Parcell. The request was denied.[65] Cornelis Jacobsen Stille leased a farm on Manhattan Island, while his brother, Jan Jacobsen, purchased one there.[66] In short, all of the original settlers left the area that would one day become The Bronx. For decades thereafter, however, the farm upon which they all lived would be referred to as Broncksland, and the stream which flowed near the property would be called Bronck's (or Bronx) river from that time onward.

As for the farm itself, Arent van Curler leased it to an Englishman, Thomas Spicer, on June 25, 1643. The lease was to run for five years, and the house, outbuildings, livestock, farm implements, and grain in the field were all included in the lease. At the expiration of the lease, van Curler was to reclaim his cattle, and any that might have been born over the years were to be equally divided between Spicer and him. Similarly, any deaths among the livestock were to be equally borne, except if Spicer proved that the deaths occurred because of Indian attack, in which case van Curler would bear the entire loss. Van Curler was to pay Spicer for any improvements he made in the property, and Spicer was to keep the buildings in repair. At the time the lease was to expire, Spicer was to leave the fields with the same amount of grain he originally found there. For this, Spicer had to pay 25 pounds (just over eleven kilograms) of butter per year for every milk cow, and 105 schepels (just over two bushels, or almost 2,827 liters) of barley or rye annually.[67]

Thomas Spicer could not have started farming at a more inauspicious time. In 1643, the series of wars between the Dutch and various Indian tribes had only just begun, and, at some points, it reached a state of great fury. On March 5, 1644, the house and fields of Jochem Pietersen Kuyter were set ablaze by the Indians,[68] and, although the Bronck farm apparently escaped such destruction, the nearness of an attack just across the Harlem River from his leased home might have had some effect on Spicer. The Indian tribes along the Hudson River remained in a hostile state until an expedition led by Captain John Underhill descended upon a village near today's Greenwich, Connecticut, in February 1644, killing 500 to 700 men, women, and children and setting fire to their wigwams.⁶⁹ The various Hudson River tribes then sued for peace, signing a treaty with the Dutch on August 30, 1645.⁷⁰

Spicer also ran into some personal trouble. In July, 1646, Henry Grady, a sixty-year old Englishman from Devonshire, managed to convince John Jones, Spicer's eighteen-year old nephew, to steal his uncle's grain and lead, and anything else he could get his hands on. Jones then brought the loot to Grady, who used some of it for himself and sold the rest. Grady was caught, flogged with rods, and banished from New Netherland.⁷¹ For Spicer, however, the loss of grain was a considerable hardship.

Also in 1646, Thomas Spicer had an altercation with Thomas Sandersen, a blacksmith at New Amsterdam who had been in and out of court for years because of his tendency to curse and to solve his disputes with his fists and other violent means.⁷² Sandersen, for some unknown reason, kept Spicer off his land, characteristically called him a rogue and a rascal, assaulted him, shot one of his goats, and damaged his cabbage crop. Spicer was not able to obtain legal satisfaction from the burly Sandersen until December of that year,⁷³ but to be kept off his land for any length of time was bound to be financially damaging to him.

By November, 1648, the lease had already expired and Arent van Curler had reclaimed his farm from Thomas Spicer, although there is no record that he ever lived there or leased it to anyone else. It was then that Peter Stuyvesant, who had succeeded Kieft as the director-general of New Netherland, ordered that Fort Orange, which had been damaged by water, be repaired, and that Jonas Bronck's horses be used to pull a wagon built for the reconstruction process. It seems that van Curler was indebted to the West India Company, and that this was enough for Stuyvesant to draft Bronck's horses into the company's service.⁷⁴

In addition, Arent van Curler soon discovered that Thomas Spicer had no intention of paying the rent called for in his lease. On June 14, 1651, he hired David Provoost of New Amsterdam as his attorney to prosecute Spicer for non-payment of rent. Provoost, however, made no progress for three years, and, on October 6, 1654, van Curler hired the newly arrived notary, Dirck van Schelluyne, instead.⁷⁵ This maneuver seemed to bring quick results. Nine days later, the matter came before the Council sitting as a court. Van Curler, through his attorney, asked Spicer for the enormous sum of 3,000 guilders in damages plus interest. The Council ordered Spicer receive a copy of the charges against him, and that both parties post bonds to continue the suit.[76] Both men posted their bonds the same day.[77] On October 25th, however, when the case against Spicer came before the Council again, Spicer requested a fourteen day delay, which was granted.[78] The case never came up again. It is quite probable that the two men came to an amicable agreement out of court, since the Dutch preferred to settle legal disputes that way.

In any event, by the time the case came to court, Arent van Curler no longer had any real interest in the old Bronck farm. On July 10, 1651, he sold it to Jacob Jansen Stoll, a resident of Rensselaerswyck.[79] It is doubtful Stoll ever moved into the fieldstone house on Bronck's land. Just a few years after his purchase, he was living with a group of Dutch pioneers at Esopus on the west bank of the Hudson, and was deeply involved in the progress of the Esopus Wars against the Indians of that region. It was during an Indian assault on the Dutch fortifications that Jan Jansen Stoll was mortally wounded and captured by the Indians.[80]

Stoll's widow sold the Bronck property to Geertrien Hendrucks, a widow who had remarried. The sale was consummated on December 19, 1662, but, with the permission of her husband, Geertrien Hendrucks resold the land on the same day to Harman Smeeman.[81]

It is difficult to believe that Harman Smeeman ever lived on Bronck's land, either. At the time he owned the land, he served as a magistrate in the town of Bergen on the west side of the Hudson opposite New Amsterdam. Undoubtedly, Bergen was his major concern, and, only two years after his purchase, he sold the Bronck farm to Samuel Edsall.[82]

Samuel Edsall, who purchased Bronck's land for 2,000 guilders in beaver skins on October 22, 1664, had been a prominent figure in New Netherland and a major personality in the establishment of Bergen and other settlements on the west bank of the Hudson.[83] Therefore, it is difficult to believe that he ever lived in the stone house built for Jonas Bronck, either.

We can only conclude that, for many years after the departure of Thomas Spicer in 1648, the landowners of Bronck's farm had no real interest in it. There is no evidence that they leased it to anyone, or bothered to take care of it. With their attention focused elsewhere, it was an afterthought to be considered at some future date. The house still stood, isolated and alone. If any further effort was to be made to settle the future borough of The Bronx with Europeans, a new attempt would have to be made.

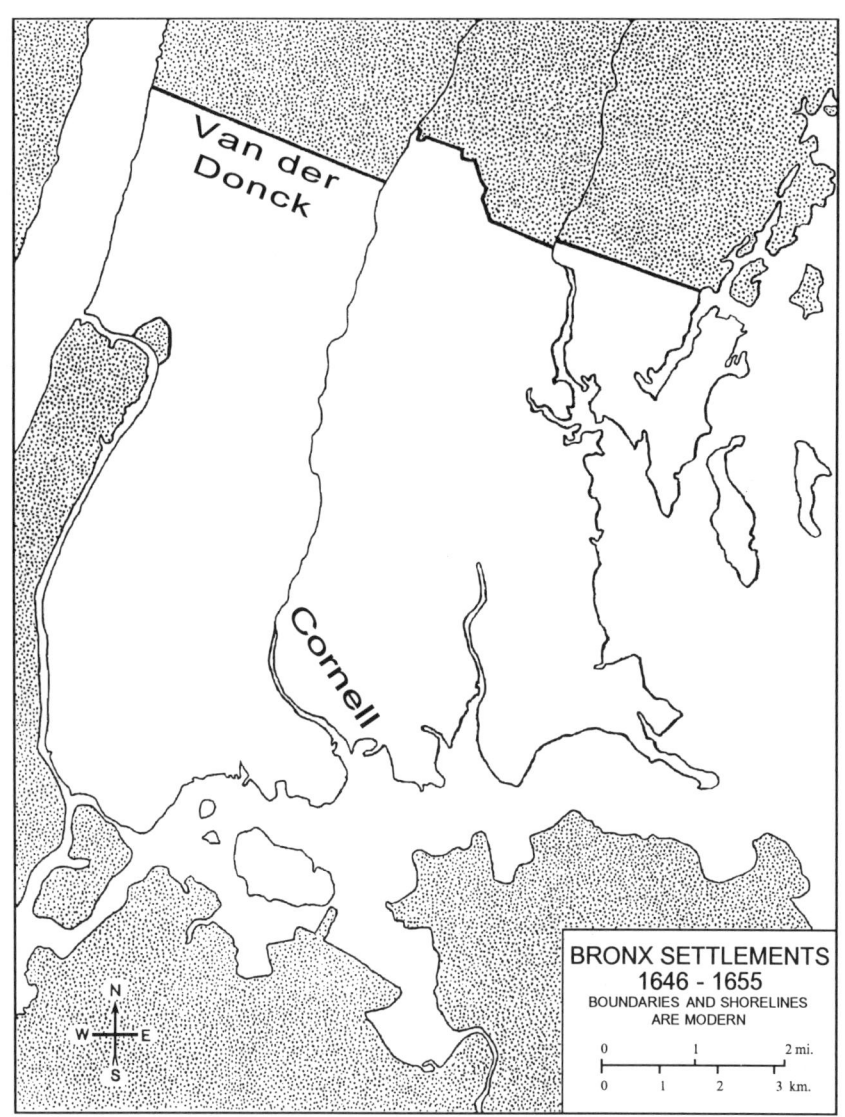

CHAPTER IV

THE ENGLISH FARMER AND THE DUTCH PATROON

1646 to 1655

It was not until 1646, three years after Jonas Bronck's death and with two years still remaining on Thomas Spicer's lease with Arent van Curler, that two simultaneous second attempts were made to settle the land that would one day become The Bronx. They were made at two sites far removed from each other by two different men of disparate backgrounds. One was an Englishman; the other was a Dutchman.

The Englishman, Thomas Cornell, had been in The Bronx previously. He was the head of one of the thirty-five families John Throckmorton brought with him in 1642. Born in Essex in England, Cornell came to the New World about 1638 with his wife and most, if not all, of his nine children. He settled in Boston, where the town meeting permitted him to buy a house. He was also given a temporary license, which was not renewed the following year, to operate a tavern. Although there is no record that he was involved in any of the religious controversies that wracked Massachusetts at the time, his brother-in-law, John Briggs, was an Antinomian, and this may have been the reason why he finally moved to Portsmouth, Rhode Island, near Anne Hutchinson's home. With his family deeply in danger because of the attempt by the Massachusetts magistrates to absorb Rhode Island, he joined Throckmorton to found a settlement in Dutch territory.[1]

After the sudden Indian attack that disastrously ended the Throckmorton settlement, Thomas Cornell and his family returned to Portsmouth.[2] It is obvious, however, that Cornell never forgot the lush salt marsh grasses growing in the area he was forced to leave. These were perfect for feeding cattle. Moreover, it seemed obvious that he could obtain a large landgrant from the Dutch and live like an English lord, much more than he could ever do under the town meeting system in use in New England. The fact that his friend Throckmorton obtained a patent for his land from Director-general Willem Kieft of New Netherland and still retained all the rights to it as an individual was an example he could follow.

On July 25, 1646, Thomas Cornell received a patent of land from the director-general. The location was on the mainland off Long Island Sound along Bronck's river to the south and west of the neck of land which Throckmorton still owned.[3] Today, that property is called Soundview and Clason Point, but, for many years thereafter, it was referred to as Cornell's Neck.

Cornell may have moved to his land sometime in 1646, but no record exists to indicate exactly when he did occupy it. It is certain, however, that when he was already past fifty years of age, he did begin to work his large tract of land. As he did previously when he came with Throckmorton, he erected a frame house using the lumber obtained from the nearby woods. His cattle grazed on the marsh grass, and the manure they produced was spread by him over the soil to enrich it. Then, he began to plant his crops.[4]

Unfortunately, Thomas Cornell made the same mistake Anne Hutchinson and John Throckmorton did. He assumed that he owned the land since he had received a patent for it from the Dutch director-general. The Siwanoy Indians living in the area once again saw a European settling on the land, using it, and changing it. Naturally, they expected compensation for the use of the land, which, it appears, Cornell did not give.[5]

Of course, the inevitable happened. Once more, the Indians rose up, burned Thomas Cornell's house and goods, and destroyed his cattle. Driven from the land, the family again returned to Portsmouth, but, like John Throckmorton, Cornell continued to hold his Dutch patent and considered himself the rightful owner of the property even though he had settled in Portsmouth for the rest of his life. He was a member of the coroner's jury there in 1653, and served on a commission in 1654 to unite the four towns of Providence

Plantations. He appears to have died in 1655.[6]

Once more an attempt was made to establish a settlement on Long Island Sound, and once again it ended in fire and pillage during an Indian uprising. While Thomas Cornell was establishing himself in those reaches of what would one day be The Bronx, however, a distinguished Dutchman began his own settlement in another location. His name was Adriaen van der Donck.

Adriaen Cornelisen van der Donck came from Breda in the Netherlands. He studied law at Leyden, and it was in 1641 as an attorney for some settlers leaving for Rensselaerswyck that he first met Patroon Kiliaen Van Rensselaer in Amsterdam. Apparently, van der Donck planned to move to New Netherland himself and inquired about leasing a farm in the patroonship of Achter Col across from Manhattan on the west bank of the Hudson River. Van Rensselaer, with a keen eye for good character, inquired into the young man's background and persuaded him to take the post of schout, or chief legal officer, of Rensselaerswyck.[7]

After arriving in New Amsterdam, van der Donck presented Director-general Willem Kieft with a letter of introduction, and then continued upriver to present a similar letter to Arent van Curler, the patroon's business agent. Van Rensselaer desired that both van Curler and van der Donck work together to see that the patroonship's affairs ran smoothly and that a profit was produced.[8]

Van der Donck, however, had no desire to remain subservient to Van Rensselaer. The New World had opened up new opportunities to him, and his goal was to take advantage of the West India Company's Freedoms and Exemptions to become a patroon in his own right. Therefore, in 1643, a mere two years after his arrival, he went to Katskill with several prospective settlers to buy land from the Indians there as the first step toward establishing himself as a patroon. However, this attempt was thwarted by Van Rensselaer, who used a clause in the company's Freedoms and Exemptions to deny van der Donck his prize. No one had the right to obtain land deliberately within seven or eight Dutch miles (just over 32.25 or just under 40 English miles, or just under 51 or just over 59 kilometers) of a patroonship, and Van Rensselaer was determined to exercise his right. Moreover, since van der Donck was his agent, he would consider that purchase of land was done on his behalf. He even insisted that van der Donck remain on the farm he had leased in Rensselaerswyck until the lease ran out. Van der Donck was forced to back down.[9]

On his first attempt to obtain a patroonship, van der Donck probably never considered a Bronx location. At that time, the whole area surrounding New Amsterdam was in the midst of a series of wars with the Indians of the vicinity. In contrast, the upper reaches of the Hudson River were comparatively safe. It was natural, then, for van der Donck to think first of establishing himself along the Hudson, the main commercial highway of the Dutch colony, and in an area far removed from the fighting.

Meanwhile, the prospective patroon remained at his job in Rensselaerswyck, and there he performed a service that would lead him directly toward his goal. With an Indian war raging to the south, the Mohawks, who lived in the vicinity of Rensselaerswyck, demanded guns and gunpowder in trade for furs. Director-general Kieft, faced with the prospect of the Mohawks seeking European arms from the French in Canada and extending hostilities to the northern Hudson, desired some agreement with the powerful tribe. In this he had the aid of Adriaen van der Donck, who not only helped him conclude a treaty with the Mohawks in 1645, but also advanced him the funds enabling the director-general to purchase the necessary presents for the Indians to seal the bargain.[10]

It was in that same year that Adriaen van der Donck married Mary Doughty, daughter of the Reverend Francis Doughty, a maverick Calvinist minister who had fled from the Pilgrim colony of Plymouth to Flushing on Long Island. The young man brought his new wife back to Rensselaerswyck and bided his time.[11]

In 1646, his time came. Van Rensselaer died, thus breaking the tie van der Donck had with him. The lawyer from Breda then moved to claim the reward for aiding Director-general Kieft in his agreement with the Mohawks and in providing him with the funds he needed on that occasion. The reward was to be a landgrant, a large portion of which lies in the northwest part of today's Bronx, upon which he could erect his cherished patroonship.[12]

No one really knows why van der Donck chose this piece of property in 1646, especially when he previously had his eye on Katskill. Just about the same time as he received his grant, however, someone else had received the Katskill location from Kieft.[13] One clue for van der Donck's preference for the Bronx location might lie in the way the land looked at the time. Standing on the banks of Spuyten Duyvil Creek looking northward over a broad, flat expanse of meadowland with a meandering stream (later to be called Tibbett's Brook) to one side stretching back to the infinite distance, the landscape, despite the hills to the east and west, looked remarkably like Breda, his homeland in the Netherlands. Later, he did express a desire to build his home in that vicinity.[14]

With his experience on the northern Hudson, and with his previous contact with the Indians there, van der Donck did not make the same mistake in securing his land that Thomas Cornell, occupying Cornell's Neck at about the same time, did. Van der Donck's land had been purchased by the West India Company in 1639, and was called Keskiskeck. Obtaining a grant eleven years later from the company's director-general was no license to use the land to the Indians' way of thinking. Therefore, van der Donck sought out the Indians of the vicinity and not only purchased from them the land covered in his grant, but also some additional meadowland. The entire estate, which he called Colen Donck, extended from the Hudson to the Bronx rivers and from Spuyten Duyvil Creek to the Saw Mill River. From the moment he became a landowner, van der Donck was able to use the title of *Jongheer*, or Young Gentleman. Since the word is pronounced "Yonkheer," his settlement was often called by the English settlers in the Dutch colony the Yonker's land, which later was shortened simply to Yonkers.[15] Yonkers straddled the modern boundary between The Bronx and Westchester County, and it was to do so for more than two and a quarter centuries.

On the swift-running stream at the northern end of his property, the new patroon built a saw mill, and soon it was busy fashioning, among other things, masts for ships. Also, a field was laid out for planting.[16] Thus, work on the new settlement was begun.

Until such time as a dwelling could be completed and his patroonship pay for itself, van der Donck spent a good deal of time in New Amsterdam. Because of his legal training several people there hired him to act as their attorney.[17] His stay in New Amsterdam, however, would lead to events that would thrust him into the center of one of the major political controversies of the Dutch colony, and that would cause him to suspend active day-to-day involvement in the improvement of his property.

In 1647, Willem Kieft was replaced as the director-general by Peter Stuyvesant because of his mishandling of the general Indian war. Stuyvesant, a war hero who had lost a leg in action, was an intelligent, able, and strong-willed man. He was to clash with the equally intelligent, able, and strong-willed Adriaen van der Donck.

The details of the struggle between the two men need not concern us, but the foundation of it went far deeper than their personalities. At the root was the question of how the colony was to be governed. Stuyvesant was the agent of a commercial company, and many of the more prominent colonists believed that, in light of the recent Indian wars, the company was not governing the colony in their interests. They demanded a voice in the colony's affairs. Stuyvesant saw this as a threat to his authority, and he opposed the colonists' demand at every turn. Van der Donck was to be pushed into championing the colonists' cause.

It should be understood in this context that under the Dutch system, government rested upon the shoulders of wealthy patricians who had the time to devote to the art of governing. They saw their duty as caring for the interests and welfare of all the inhabitants of the community. Clearly Stuyvesant saw himself in that role. On the other hand, Dutch history is replete with examples of townsmen wresting liberties and privileges from their overlords.[18] Obviously van der Donck and his backers saw themselves in that role. This does much to explain the attitudes of the two men in the contest between them.

Stuyvesant had instituted a board of nine men, whom he chose, to give him advice on matters submitted to them. In 1649, Adriaen van der Donck became a member of the Nine Men, and was immediately chosen its president. The issue simmering between the new director-general and the Nine Men came to a boil in March of that year. Van der Donck kept a private journal of the meetings of the Nine Men in which he wrote explicit criticisms of Stuyvesant's behavior. One night, Stuyvesant's agents broke into the house of Michael Jansen, where van der Donck had been lodging, and seized the journal. Upon reading it, Stuyvesant arrested van der Donck and threw him in jail on the charge of slander. Then, after due consultation with his Council and the remaining eight of the Nine Men, he deprived van der Donck of his office.[19]

In an act of defiance, the remaining eight men on the board met on July 26, 1649, and chose van der Donck, Jacob van Couwenhoven, and Jan Evertsen Bout as delegates and agents to the States-General in the Netherlands to argue the case of the inhabitants against Stuyvesant and the company. A petition was drawn up, with additional observations, and a long *Remonstrance of New Netherland*, all of which detailed their case and explained their grievances. There is no doubt that, with his legal training, these documents were written by Adriaen van der Donck. They were penned in such a way not only to affect the thinking of the States-General, but also to affect the sentiments of the public to arouse it against the West India

Company.[20]

Their grievances were simple. They contended that the government was ruining the country and was thus unsuitable. They said that a lack of privileges and exemptions for most of the populace was a major cause of a decrease in population. They stated that the duties charged by the company for services performed were much too high, and that the recent Indian wars, which need not have occurred except for the actions of the company's agents, had caused the settlers to lose almost everything they had hoped to gain. They said that the company had encouraged petty traders to come to the colony to make a profit, but not industrious farmers, thus causing a neglect of agriculture.[21]

Armed with these arguments, van der Donck and his fellow agents set forth on their journey to the Netherlands. There, the West India Company was already under attack as being unprofitable and no longer necessary because the war with Spain had ended. It was then, in 1650, that van der Donck published in the Netherlands the *Remonstrance of New Netherland* showing his interpretation of the history of the company's neglect. This prompted the States-General to grant the inhabitants of New Netherland several liberties in a preliminary measure. Elated, the three emissaries contracted with the company to send 200 farmers to the colony. Van Couwenhoven and Bout sailed home with them.[22] Van der Donck remained behind to carry the fight to a complete victory.

Secretary Cornelis Van Tienhoven, however, long prominent in the affairs of the Dutch colony, came to The Hague to argue on behalf of Stuyvesant and the company, and the battle was joined. It was to take two years before Adriaen van der Donck could savor triumph. In April, 1652, the States-General ordered Peter Stuyvesant recalled.[23]

Van der Donck then turned his full attention to his own affairs in New Netherland, including his property in what would become The Bronx. He received from the States-General the right to bequeath his patroonship to anyone he wished. He then gathered his wife, his mother, other members of his family, prospective colonists to settle on his land, and some goods, and loaded them all on a ship sailing for New Netherland. When van der Donck arrived at Texel, however, officers of the West India Company refused to permit him to board, and he was left on the pier,[24] while his wife and family sailed for his wilderness estate.

Obviously, things had changed. War had broken out with England, which attempted to exclude Dutch commerce from her colonies and own shore through the passage of a Navigation Act the previous year. The States-General now had second thoughts in allowing such a disruptive person as Adriaen van der Donck back in New Netherland, especially when the martial arts of old soldier Peter Stuyvesant were of greater value in wartime.[25]

Van der Donck's repeated petitions to return home were ignored. He had word that the neglect of his estate in New Netherland was leading it to ruin. Some guns needed for trading with the Indians he had shipped to Colen Donck in 1651 were sequestered by Stuyvesant, and he received word that hungry land speculators were seeking to grab parts of his patroonship. Luckily, he got the directors of the West India Company to force Stuyvesant to release the guns and to admonish the director-general to make sure that no one trespassed on his land.[26]

Forced to remain in the Netherlands, van der Donck decided to write a book, *A Description of the New Netherlands*. In it, he described the natural resources of the colony, the opportunity that awaited those who settled there, and the life and habits of the Indians he knew in the upper Hudson valley. His purpose, of course, was to promote the colony, and even to attract settlers to his own Colen Donck. For instance, he stated that one of the major creeks or brooks found in the Dutch colony was the Saw Kill, or Colendonck's Kill. He was also the first European to really describe the life of the Indians with any sort of sympathy. He wanted to say so much more, however. He wanted to write a complete history of New Netherland, but the company refused him permission to examine its records. Nevertheless, the book was copyrighted in 1653, first published in 1655, and seemed popular enough to come out in a second edition the following year.[27]

Van der Donck finally pleaded with the company to allow him to return and to permit him to practice his profession as an attorney. This request was denied on the grounds that, since he was the only attorney in the entire colony with legal training, no one was fit to oppose him in court. He was granted the right to give advice to anyone who sought it, however. He was at last permitted to return to New Netherland in 1653 provided he maintained his good behavior.[28]

These terms meant that Adriaen van der Donck, patroon of Colen Donck, could never again take a leading part in the political life of New Netherland. It is unlikely that he would want to lead a political life anyway. After being absent for four long years, he would necessarily devote a major portion of his energies to building up his neglected patroonship.

It is pretty certain that van der Donck's home was completed about this time, and that it was erected near the southern end of his property where the landscape reminded him so much of his native Breda. A corn field was planted in what is today Van Cortlandt Park, a friendly Weckquasgeek Indian was hired to tend the grazing cattle, and the land was divided into several farms.[29] This modest beginning, however, was doomed to failure in the momentous events of September, 1655.

It all started in New Amsterdam when Hendrick Van Dyck killed an Indian woman reaching to take a peach from one of the trees on his land. Soon afterward, a large group of Indians landed their canoes at the city at the tip of Manhattan Island and broke into many houses pretending to look for other Indians, but really hunting Van Dyck, whom they finally shot with an arrow. The Indians then fled across to the west bank of the Hudson, set a settlement there on fire, and took the women and children prisoner.

The colonists, with vivid memories of the Indian wars of the previous decade, panicked, and the entire countryside as far north as the middle Hudson valley fled to the fort in New Amsterdam. These included all the people living on van der Donck's settlement.[30]

It was about this time that Adriaen van der Donck died. The exact date of his death is uncertain, and he died in obscurity.[31] He may have been one of those killed in the events of 1655, or he may have died a natural death. Nevertheless it is a coincidence that the Dutch patroon and the English farmer, who both started their settlements about 1646, both died about 1655. Similarly, both van der Donck's and Cornell's attempts at settlement ended in failure, and both because of Indian action.

Mary Doughty, van der Donck's widow, remarried. Her new husband, Hugh O'Neale, took her to Maryland. Just as Thomas Cornell never renounced his ownership of Cornell's Neck when he left, so Mary O'Neale never renounced ownership of the Yonker's land when she departed.[32]

In spite of these continuing claims, the second attempt to settle The Bronx with Europeans ended in failure. The third attempt finally produced a continuous, permanent, settlement. Yet, of all the early attempts to settle The Bronx, that one had the most tumultuous beginning and the most unpromising start.

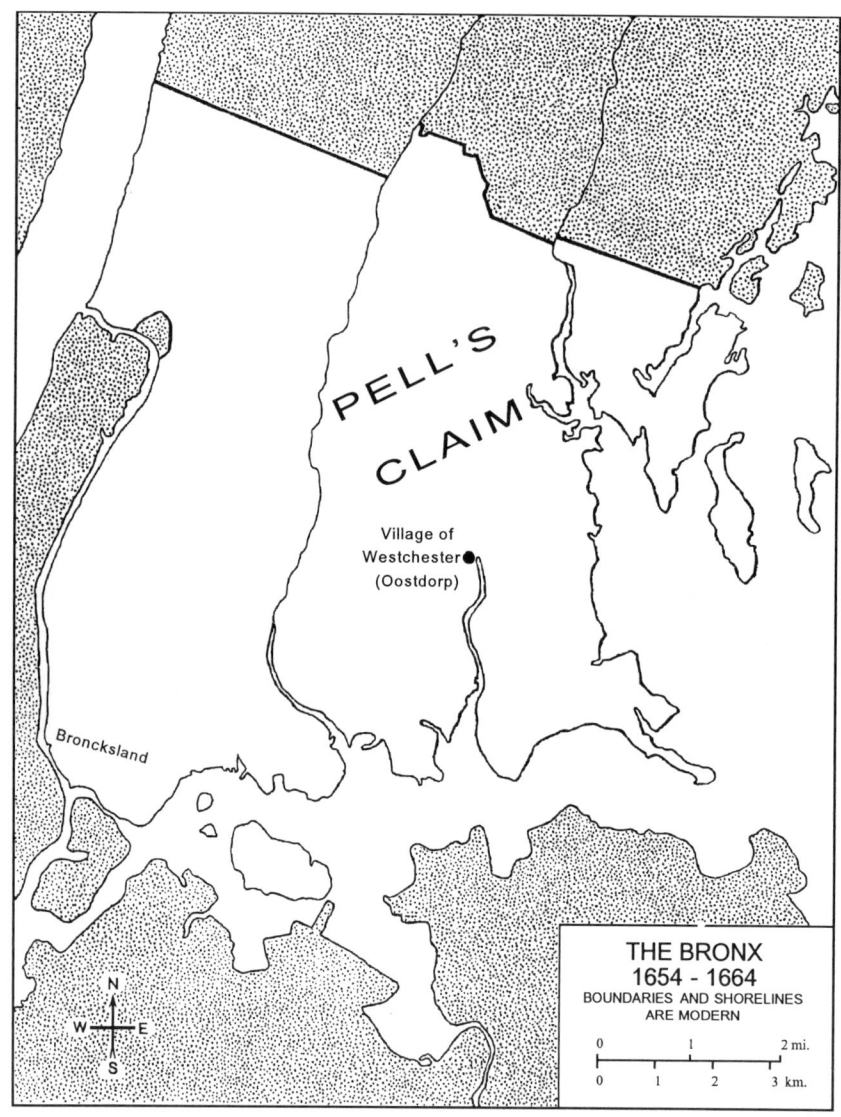

CHAPTER V

THE RISE OF THE FIRST VILLAGE

1654 to 1664

Sometime about the end of October or the beginning of November, 1654, a group of fifteen men from the English colony of Connecticut made their way to a parcel of land that had hitherto been considered part of the Dutch colony of New Netherland, and there began a town they called Westchester. In many ways, it was an ideal location. Situated at the head of navigation of a stream that would ultimately be called Westchester Creek, it had an outlet to the sea by which they could receive goods in exchange for the products of their farms. Above that spot, the creek fanned out into several smaller streams, creating marshes bearing the lush grass good for grazing cattle.

When the presence of these men became known to Peter Stuyvesant, however, the Dutch West India Company's director-general and his Council issued a sharp order. The settlers were to desist from further proceedings and to remove themselves from the territory.[1]

This ultimatum seems out of character for the Dutch. After all, they had officially allowed English settlers into their colony, and both John Thockmorton and Thomas Cornell had lived not too far from where these Englishmen were building their new village.

These new English settlers, however, did not ask the company's prior permission to occupy the land. In fact, they denied that their settlement was on Dutch territory at all.

To Stuyvesant, this was one more example of what the English had been doing to the Dutch for decades. Ever since Hudson's voyage in 1609, Dutch mariners had explored much of the territory along North America's Atlantic coast, including Long Island Sound. Records and charts they had filed in the Netherlands gave the Dutch a valid claim to the entire Sound as far as Cape Cod. With the Dutch West India Company's difficulty in attracting settlers, however, they were forced to sit idly while the Pilgrims from England occupied Cape Cod, Roger Williams and his fellow Massachusetts exiles settled Rhode Island, and Puritan colonists expanded into Connecticut. The Dutch tried to hold the line at the Connecticut River by building a fort there, but this only increased tension as the small Dutch garrison was outflanked by ever larger numbers of English settlers, leaving it a Dutch island in an English sea.

Stuyvesant thought he had settled the whole question in 1650. Ordered by the company to establish a boundary with the English colonies, he journeyed to Hartford, the English town that grew up around the small Dutch fort. Stuyvesant and the governors of the New England colonies appointed a set of arbiters who drew a line through Long Island and a point just west of Greenwich, Connecticut. The English would settle east of that line, and the Dutch, west of it. With this Treaty of Hartford conflict between the English and the Dutch could be avoided.[2]

Now, four years after the agreement was reached, the treaty was being violated. There were several reasons why the small group of men settled in Westchester, but the most important was the gray eminence in the whole affair: Thomas Pell.

Thomas Pell was born in Southwyck, Sussex, England, in 1613, the younger son of a schoolmaster. Orphaned at an early age, he was raised by his stepmother and some guardians connected with the nobility. He studied at Cambridge, and through his family connections, was appointed gentleman of the bedchamber to King Charles I. Facing limited prospects as a second son in a society favoring the first-born, and living in a court that was increasingly under attack by English Puritans, Pell volunteered for service in the Netherlands during the second phase of that country's war of independence against Spain. He rose to the rank of lieutenant, and, in the process, managed to master enough of the crude medical practices of the day to be considered a surgeon. Probably through family connections again, he, and a number of his fellow officers, volunteered to go to the New World to live in a settlement promoted by two noblemen, Lord Saye and Sele and Lord Brooke. Thomas Pell thus arrived in Saybrook in Connecticut in March, 1636.[3]

Thomas Pell's experiences in the New World were varied. When war raged against the Pequot Indians, he practiced his arts as a surgeon. Once the war was over, he moved to New Haven, where he prospered buying a great deal of property and investing in shipping.

It was as the owner of a ship in 1647 that Thomas Pell had his first brush with Peter Stuyvesant. A vessel sent to the Delaware River, then in New Netherland's jurisdiction, returning to New England through the East River was halted by Dutch authorities who confiscated its cargo of beaver skins for poaching on the company's preserve. Because of this, Pell was forced to renege on a business arrangement, since his purchase would have been made with the confiscated pelts.

Pell also married while living in New Haven. Since his new wife was a widow with debts, he was called upon to pay them. Seeing no logical reason to do so, he was held in contempt of court, causing him to seek a new home further west in what later was called Fairfield.[4]

Pell had come into possession of some land at Fairfield as a reward for his service in the Pequot War, but it was only in 1653 that he actually began to live there and to buy more property in the town. Since Fairfield was at the edge of the wilderness, he came into contact with the Siwanoy Indians.[5]

It was at this point that Thomas Pell gathered fifteen men to enter Dutch territory to begin a new village. There are several reasons why he did so. War had broken out in Europe between the Netherlands and England, spurred by the English Navigation Acts. Pell's effort could be seen as a blow struck for the English in America. On the other hand, while in New Haven, Pell, a former gentleman of the bedchamber, had refused to take an oath of loyalty to Oliver Cromwell's Puritan republic, saying that he had already done so while in England. If he were suspected of being a royalist because of his actions, this venture could dispel their doubt. Nevertheless, his settlement on Dutch territory and his raising of troops to drill in case of a confrontation with the Dutch was interpreted by some Connecticut officials as an attempt to build a refuge for royalists.[6]

Whatever the motive for the maneuver, on June 27, 1654, Thomas Pell met with five Siwanoy sachems to buy all of what is today the eastern half of The Bronx and a portion of eastern Westchester County. To prevent any uprisings of the sort that had killed Anne Hutchinson and had chased away Throckmorton and Cornell, Pell had the Indians agree to send a delegation every spring to mark the bounds of the land. The deed was witnessed by several Englishmen and Indians.[7] Tradition places the site of the agreement at an oak tree that stood for many years in what would become Pelham Bay Park.[8] That oak has since died, and a new tree was planted in its place within a wrought iron fence on the grounds of the Bartow-Pell Mansion.

After securing his land, Pell then gathered fifteen men to settle the village of Westchester. Because the area was so remote from New Amsterdam, and because no one else lived in the immediate vicinity, it was some time before Peter Stuyvesant knew they were there and ordered the new settlers to leave. Oddly enough, the order came after the war between England and the Netherlands had already ended.

The men of Westchester village ignored Stuyvesant's order. In early March, 1655, they met in town meeting, and, as their first collective act, divided the land into lots and determined who would occupy which one.[9] Obviously, further Dutch action was needed to oust them from their settlement.

On April 19, 1655, Cornelis van Tienhoven, now the fiscal, or public prosecutor, of the Dutch colony, dispatched Claes van Elslandt with a message to the inhabitants of Westchester village, and especially to Thomas Pell. The note recounted the history of the territory, showing its purchase under Willem Kieft, and stated that the new settlement was contrary to the terms of the Treaty of Hartford. The inhabitants were warned against proceeding with building, clearing, pasturing cattle, or cutting hay, and were told that if they continued their occupation of Dutch land, they would be prosecuted according to law. They were ordered to leave within fifteen days of receiving the message.[10]

Van Elslandt, accompanied by Albert the Trumpeter, boarded a boat, sailed up Westchester Creek, and sighted the village by April 22nd. Four armed men met the vessel and demanded from the messenger his reasons for coming. Since the boat was in the middle of the creek, van Elslandt inquired where he could land, and suggested a spot near the houses. The men on shore asserted that he would not land, but the messenger, claiming he was cold, jumped ashore, followed by Albert the Trumpeter. Immediately, both men were placed under guard in a hut near the shore while the rest of the small community was summoned. Van Elslandt attempted to see the houses and improvements made by the English, and also the coat-of-arms of the English Parliament the inhabitants asserted they had hung on a tree, but he was not permitted to do so. The village leader, a man whose name van Elslandt did not know, came running with eight or ten armed companions, and pointed a pistol at the messenger's head. Undaunted, van Elslandt carried out his duty, read van Tienhoven's message word for word, and handed it to the man holding the pistol. The village leader slyly replied that he did not understand Dutch, and that if Fiscal van Tienhoven had sent the message in English, he would have given him a written reply. He added that he expected word any day from England or the Netherlands about the final boundary between Connecticut and the Dutch colony, but, in the meantime, the village would live under English rule. Then, with some sarcasm, the leader stated that if they had some wine, they would offer some to the messenger, but they had none. As a final gesture, they permitted van Elslandt and Albert the Trumpeter to depart, but only after the English had discharged their guns to frighten them.[11]

After the messenger returned to New Amsterdam with news of his reception in the village of Westchester, the Dutch authorities penned protests to the New England colonies, requesting them to oppose this violation of the Treaty of Hartford.[12] Stuyvesant thought the plan might work because the war between England and the Netherlands had ended, and because many New Englanders disapproved of Thomas Pell's actions.[13]

Despite this, the Westchester inhabitants not only remained, but seemed to be fomenting trouble elsewhere. Word reached Stuyvesant that Lieutenant Thomas Wheeler, probably the village leader with whom van Elslandt dealt, had told some visitors from the town of Gravesend on Long Island (now part of Brooklyn) that Indians were about to attack and that all English in Dutch territory should separate themselves from their Dutch neighbors for safety. While it is true that there was a sudden, short, devastating Indian incident in September, 1655, that drove the inhabitants of half the Hudson valley into Fort Amsterdam, at first the director-general greeted this bit of information with great skepticism.[14]

Stuyvesant also had informed the directors of the Dutch West India Company about the encroachment of the English. He was then instructed by them to forward a copy of the Treaty of Hartford to the company in the Netherlands for possible ratification, and to prevent the English from further encroaching on the company's territory.[15]

By March, 1656, Stuyvesant was ready to act. Affirming that the village of Westchester harbored fugitives and thieves from Long Island, and that Lieutenant Wheeler had been in communication with the Indians in September, 1655, the director-general ordered Captain Frederick de Coninck, Captain Lieutenant Brian Nuton, and Fiscal Cornelis van Tienhoven to proceed immediately on the night of March 6th with a detachment of soldiers. The troops were to take possession of the houses of the Englishmen and tell them to leave with all of their movable property and livestock. If the inhabitants were to resist, the soldiers were to treat them as enemies. They had orders to demolish all the homes, with the exception of two or three to house the goods and soldiers. The soldiers were permitted to leave some of the less prominent men to guard the villagers' goods, but even then, those men would have to leave within three days. The criminals and fugitives who had purportedly fled to the village were to be sent to New Amsterdam.[16]

The small Dutch force accomplished its mission to the letter. At Westchester, twenty-three armed men who protested that the land belonged to them were easily disarmed. A few men, with the women and children, did stay in the village to guard the remaining possessions. Those English inhabitants of New Netherland who had fled to Westchester to escape prosecution for debt, or for other reasons, were imprisoned aboard the warship *De Waagh*, anchored in New Amsterdam's harbor. Those who had come from New England prompted by Thomas Pell were detained in the New Amsterdam City Hall under civil arrest.[17]

The wives of those detained then petitioned Stuyvesant, probably reminding him of the difficulty of their moving in wintertime. The director-general was willing to be merciful, and resolved to release the English prisoners if they promised under written oath to leave the Dutch colony within six weeks and not to return without his special consent. They were also to pay the costs of the military expedition against them. No similar reprieve was promised to the fugitives or to those who did not sign the oath.[18]

The following day, on March 16, 1656, Thomas Wheeler and fifteen other prisoners petitioned Stuyvesant to remain in Westchester under the authority of the States-General of the Netherlands provided they retained their liberties in choosing their own town magistrates, had the right to decide which people could reside among them, and had their arms returned for their own protection. The director-general was willing to free them and, upon their taking the oath of allegiance, to allow them to live in Westchester. They were not permitted to have the same privileges as the English towns in Dutch territory on Long Island for which the Westchester petitioners asked, however, but only the same privileges as the Dutch towns. The inhabitants could nominate double the number of officers and magistrates from which Stuyvesant would choose.[19] This was the usual Dutch practice. The director-general did show his capacity for conciliation by choosing Thomas Wheeler as the first chief magistrate.[20]

As for the remaining prisoners, on March 25th, Stuyvesant had five of them released and ordered them out of the jurisdiction of New Netherland unless any of the inhabitants of the new village would give bail to ensure their good behavior. One of these five was Captain Richard Ponton.[21] In the following decades, he would become a leading resident of Westchester and a constant troublemaker for the authorities.

The village of Westchester survived, although for the remainder of the existence of the Dutch colony, it was to be called Oostdorp, or Easttown. Why did it survive where the previous attempts at settlement did not? There were several reasons.

Certainly, the most important was that the settlers lived close to each other in a village. Unlike Jonas Bronck, Anne Hutchinson, Thomas Cornell, or Adriaen van der Donck, the inhabitants were near each other and could come to each others' assistance in case of trouble. This could be seen when Claes van Elslandt tried to deliver his message and when the Dutch military force was sent there.

A second reason was good relations with the surrounding Indians. Thomas Pell laid the foundation for this with his purchase from the Siwanoys and the provision that the boundaries of the purchase be reviewed each year. Even without Pell the village's inhabitants retained the confidence of the Indians. They had been able to discover the plans for the short uprising of September, 1655, enough in advance to warn their fellow Englishmen on Long Island. In contrast, the demise of the Throckmorton settlement of thirty-five families, which probably was also organized as a town, occurred because it did not have the prior friendship of the Indians.

A third reason for the village's survival lies in the creation of a village militia. Lieutenant Wheeler and Captain Ponton would certainly make defense a high priority, unlike the former merchant seaman Jonas Bronck, lawyer Adriaen van der Donck, housewife

Anne Hutchinson, farmer Thomas Cornell, or townsman John Throckmorton. The fact that the villagers had arms that Stuyvesant was compelled to confiscate and that the inhabitants petitioned for their return, shows that those who dwelt in Westchester were ready to follow their leaders in defending their lives and property. Their prompt assembly at the arrival of Claes van Elslandt and the Dutch military force indicates that they had undergone some military training.

A fourth reason for the settlement's survival lies in the weakness of the Dutch. Faced with a sparse population in spite of their efforts to increase it, the Dutch were willing to allow the settlers to continue living at the village provided they took an oath of allegiance to the States-General of the Netherlands. Faced with the possibility of hostile Indian action (such as occurred in September, 1655) at almost any time, and feeling the effects of the recently concluded commercial war with the English, the Dutch had to conserve their slender military resources. They could not maintain too militant a posture toward the English for any length of time.

A fifth reason for the village's survival lies in the flexibility of its inhabitants. When faced with the choice of leaving the Dutch colony or taking an oath to support it, most took the oath. By so doing, they preserved their settlement.

The only loser seemed to be Thomas Pell. He had spent about £500 in his attempt at acquiring property in the Dutch colony and in settling Westchester village in what would some day be The Bronx.[22] Throughout the entire controversy, he had remained in Fairfield, and the outcome of the contest seemed to indicate that he would never play a role in the area again. Events, however, were to prove otherwise.

In the meantime, the recently released prisoners returned to their settlement where their wives and children were waiting. Whatever damage had been done to their homes had to be repaired, and their farms had to be placed in good working order again.

In 1657, Brian Nuton, one of the men who had led the recent expedition against them, Cornelis van Ruyven, secretary of the colony, and Carl van Brugge, business manager of the company store, were sent to the newly renamed Oostdorp to survey the needs of the settlement. At the request of the inhabitants and on the visitors' recommendation, Stuyvesant sent to Oostdorp twelve muskets, twelve pounds of lead, twelve pounds of powder, and two bundles of matches for the village's defense, and a writing book for the magistrates to record the proceedings of the court.[23]

The inhabitants of Oostdorp, meanwhile, went about their everyday business, which was mostly agricultural. Herds of cattle roamed in the fields of fenced off marsh grass. Pigs were also kept; there seems to have been few horses. One or another of the settlers kept a swarm of bees from which honey was gathered. Trees were felled to clear the fields, which were planted with grain, tobacco, onions, and peas. Fruit trees were brought into the settlement to create orchards producing apples, peaches, and cherries.

Agriculture, however, was not the only occupation of the inhabitants. We know that they maintained a close relationship with the English settlers in the Long Island towns, and several residents borrowed some funds from the Long Islanders from time to time. Some of this money probably went into developing the farms, but at least once, the residents of Oostdorp used their favorable site at the head of navigation of Westchester Creek to make their settlement a local fur trading station. Some Indians from the central Hudson River valley traveled to Oostdorp with beaver, otter, bear, elk, fox, and raccoon skins. Through the years, because of good agricultural and commercial prospects, Oostdorp, which had begun with only fifteen men, showed a slow, but steady, population growth. A considerable number of the small group of new inhabitants came from the English towns on Long Island.[24]

Even so, Oostdorp remained pitifully poor, especially when compared to the flourishing Long Island towns. In an age when concern for the salvation of the soul placed religion at the center of community life, Oostdorp had no church and no minister. On Sundays, the members of the small settlement gathered in a house, and Nicholas Bailey made a prayer, Robert Bassett read a selection from a book of sermons, and the gathering sang a psalm. Moreover, in common with many other colonial settlements, money was in short supply. Barter was the common means of exchange, and this could be livestock, liquor, grain, wampum, or even a pair of breeches. Life was so difficult in the early days that fewer women than men were attracted to the settlement. It appears that there were about three men for every two women in the village. Naturally, this caused some dissension in the small community, and there were cases of adultery brought to the magistrates.[25]

Although the village was now under the authority of the Dutch, and the inhabitants, for the time being at least, acknowledged that they were living in New Netherland, the villagers were thoroughly

English in their thoughts and manners. As in the New England colonies from which they had all come, each farmer was addressed as goodman and each spouse as goodwife. They spoke English among themselves, and made records of their transactions in English. Quite often, they would count the value of items in terms of the familiar pounds, shillings, and pence as much as in the Dutch guilders and stuyvers. They even referred to their village as East-Town, rather then the Dutch Oostdorp.[26]

This loyalty to English customs was most probably the reason for their reaction when Connecticut renewed its claim to the territory in 1662.[27] Charles II had been restored to the English throne in 1660, and, in time, he granted a charter to the Connecticut colony defining its borders as running from sea to sea. Of course, this meant that the English settlement in New Netherland could now be considered as lying in English territory.

In October, 1662, the Assembly at Hartford informed the people of the village of Westchester (its name when it was originally settled by migrants from Connecticut) that they were now within the bounds of the English colony, and ordered them to send deputies to the Assembly. In addition, any case could be heard at a court at Fairfield. The Assembly then demanded that the Westchester inhabitants declare themselves subjects of the king.[28]

The villagers were caught between their English feelings and the memories of the effectiveness of Dutch arms. By April, 1663, Peter Stuyvesant inquired why the villagers had not nominated magistrates as they had in the past. They communicated their dilemma to him. Tongue in cheek, they insisted that they had not plotted against the Dutch, but they could not retaliate against the people of Connecticut because they were not in the same jurisdiction as the New Englanders. By May, Stuyvesant ordered them to communicate the reasons why no nominations were made and to send the present magistrates to New Amsterdam. It was in response to this command that William Betts and Edward Waters came before the Dutch director-general and told him that they had called the community together to obtain the nominations, but that the people refused to name anyone. The magistrates then gave Stuyvesant the correspondence from Connecticut copied by Richard Mills, a schoolmaster from Long Island. Stuyvesant then ordered the inhabitants of Oostdorp to ignore the letters from Hartford and to choose nominees for magistrates, warning them that the names of those who refused would be recorded and they would be prosecuted.[29]

Faced with this threat, the villagers did make their nominations from which, on May 24th, Stuyvesant chose Robert Huestis, John Barker, and Nicholas Bailey to serve. In addition the director-general, sent for those whom he had grounds to believe were instrumental in fomenting the villagers to act against Dutch authority, and he imprisoned them. The following day, he sent for Richard Mills and had him placed in a dungeon for thirty-five days because he could not produce the original Connecticut documents he had copied. They had been hidden by Richard Ponton, one of those men reluctant to pledge his loyalty to the Dutch authorities in 1656. The confinement did harm to the schoolmaster's health, and he died soon after being released.[30]

These events caused the Connecticut government to act in July. The Council of that colony sent Captain John Tallcot with a force of sixteen or eighteen men to the town of Westchester to settle affairs there, and, if the inhabitants wished, to choose a constable and to administer the oath to the person so chosen.[31]

Thoroughly alarmed, Peter Stuyvesant journeyed to Boston in September, attempting to reach an agreement with the New England colonial governors, but was unsuccessful. On October 18, 1663, Edward Jessup, who had recently arrived in Westchester from Long Island, was invested with the title of commissioner, having the power of a magistrate, by the Connecticut authorities, and several Westchester citizens were declared freemen of the colony, thus attaining full civil rights in Connecticut. In a desperate effort to save something from the rapidly deteriorating situation, the Dutch director-general decided to send three commissioners to Hartford to negotiate a final settlement of the boundary.[32]

On the same day that Connecticut had appointed Jessup to his post in Westchester, the three Dutch commissioners sent by Stuyvesant arrived in Hartford. They were Cornelis van Ruyven, the secretary of the Dutch colony; Oloff Stevenson van Cortlandt, a burgomaster of New Amsterdam; and John Lawrence, a merchant. They had departed from New Amsterdam on October 15th, sailing up the East River and through Hell Gate, staying overnight at Minniwits (now City) Island. By October 17th, they had arrived in Milford, where they procured horses and rode to New Haven. There, they met the gray eminence in the affair, Thomas Pell. Accompanied by Pell and Ensign Alexander Bryan of Milford, the three Dutch commissioners arrived in Hartford, informed the Connecticut Legislature of their arrival, and waited while the Assembly chose three men to negotiate with them.³³

During the negotiations, the Dutch commissioners noted that there were representatives from Westchester conferring with the Connecticut delegation, probably also prompted by Thomas Pell. This observation, combined with the stubborn refusal of the Connecticut commissioners to relinquish any of the land granted under their new charter, convinced the Dutch delegation that schoolmaster Richard Mills had committed his acts at the instigation of the Connecticut authorities, who were fomenting a revolt. In a final attempt to reach an agreement, the Dutch commissioners proposed to turn over the government of Westchester to Connecticut while the English towns on Long Island (which were also being claimed by the English colony) would remain under Dutch jurisdiction. Under the Dutch plan, a commission to meet the following year, or the king of England and the States-General in Europe, would fix the final boundary. The proposition was rejected by the Connecticut delegation on October 23rd, and the conference ended without resolving the issue.[34]

Subsequently, conditions in the Dutch colony deteriorated rapidly. With limited military resources, faced with an Indian war in the central Hudson valley that had been going on for several years, confronted with a revolt among the English towns on Long Island, and unable to count on any cooperation from New England, Stuyvesant wrote to Connecticut governor John Winthrop, Jr., agreeing to the final proposition made by the Connecticut delegates. Under this plan, the Dutch turned control of Westchester over to Connecticut and withdrew their jurisdiction from the Long Island English towns as well.[35]

Neither the Dutch West India Company nor the States-General, however, agreed with Stuyvesant's act. In January, 1664, they resolved to attempt to reach agreement with King Charles II over the boundary, and, in the meanwhile, wrote to Westchester and the Long Island towns reminding them of their allegiance to the Dutch.[36]

Undaunted, the Connecticut authorities, in March, authorized Thomas Pell to purchase all the uninhabited land between Westchester and the Hudson River to make it part of the town. Two days later, the first sale to Englishmen by the Indians of land on the west bank of Bronck's River was made. Edward Jessup and John Richardson purchased the land later to be called the West Farms from nine sachems in the presence of three witnesses from Westchester.[37] This was an added provocation for the Dutch because the English claim to that territory had never been previously acted

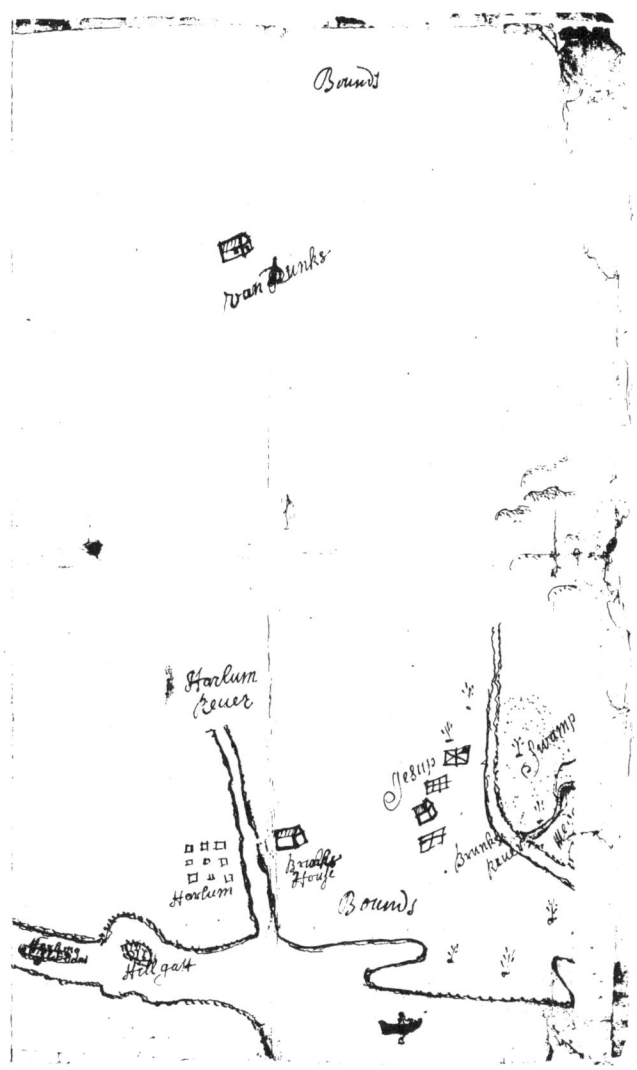

BRONCKSLAND, WEST FARMS, AND YONKERS IN THE 1660s

This map, drawn shortly after the purchase of West Farms by Richardson and Jessup, indicates areas of settlement on the mainland north and east of the Harlem ("Harlem") River. Jonas Bronck's house ("Brunk's House") still stands opposite the village of Harlem on Manhattan Island. Far to the north is the house of Adriaen van der Donk ("van Dunks"). Near the Bronx ("Brunk's") River is the house of Edward Jessup ("Jesup") and three cultivated fields. Across the river is a swamp, The East River ("Hellgatt") is shown out of its true geographical position, here extending westward.

New York State Archives

upon. It seems obvious that the true intention of the Connecticut authorities was to eliminate New Netherland altogether. At the same time, Westchester was also the center of some intrigue whereby the English offered to ally themselves with the central Hudson valley tribes fighting the Dutch.[38] Nothing seems to have come of this attempt.

In April, Edward Jessup, the commissioner appointed by Connecticut, was authorized to administer the oath of allegiance to the king to those who had previously been admitted as freemen in Westchester. Probably to strengthen the English claim to the town, in June, sixteen inhabitants signed a document recognizing Thomas Pell's purchase of the land in 1654, acknowledging that they did not yet pay him the money that was due him for the village land, and surrendering all right and title in the land to him. This must have gratified Pell, who had never reconciled himself to the loss of his £500 investment when the Dutch had enforced their jurisdiction over Westchester in 1656. Having secured his title, Pell then freely gave his permission to the inhabitants to cut their hay and to enjoy the improvements they had made, recognizing that Edward Jessup, the townsmen, and the freemen had the right to lay out the lands according to need.[39]

As the tension over the Connecticut-New Netherland boundary was becoming more acute, events in Europe were evolving that would eventually end the dispute. The commercial rivalry between the Netherlands and England grew so tense that the English authorities began to prepare for another war. A fleet was placed at the disposal of James, duke of York, brother of King Charles II. The king also granted his brother all of what had been considered, up until that time, New Netherland, defining the boundary between his grant and Connecticut to place the entire village of Westchester within the duke's territories. The fleet set sail for the New World even before war was declared.

By early September, 1664, the English fleet was anchored off New Amsterdam. Faced with a superior force, sparse military resources, and rebellious inhabitants on Long Island and the mainland, there was nothing the Dutch could do but surrender. On September 6th, the orange, white, and blue horizontally striped flag of the United Provinces of the Netherlands was lowered from the flagpole at New Amsterdam. The white flag of England bearing the red cross of St. George rose in its place. At that point, the territory first explored by Henry Hudson in 1609, including what would some day become The Bronx, entered a new era.

CHAPTER VI

THE GREAT LAND GRAB

1664 TO 1673

In the wake of the English conquest of the Dutch colony in 1664, more was at stake for the inhabitants than a change of loyalty from the Netherlands to England, or a change of name from New Netherland to New York. The people had been living under Dutch authority, and all they possessed, including the land upon which they lived, had been guaranteed in their possession by Dutch law. Now the law was to be English. To his credit, Richard Nicolls, who was named by the duke of York to govern his colony, recognized the problem of legalizing all valid Dutch land claims.

In the area that would become The Bronx, however, this policy did not end questions about land ownership. As Nicolls himself observed in a report to the duke, the territory was "nothing considerable," the land consisting of "onely empty names and places possesst forty yeares by former graunts...."[1] Obviously, the village of Westchester was not considered substantial enough to count. Nevertheless, with all of the unclaimed property in The Bronx, there were some people who would attempt to grab as much of the land as they could, whether it was secured by a Dutch patent or not.

Naturally, the man who was first in attempting to grab as much land as he could was Thomas Pell. After all, his interests in the territory dated from 1654. Even before the English conquest, he had

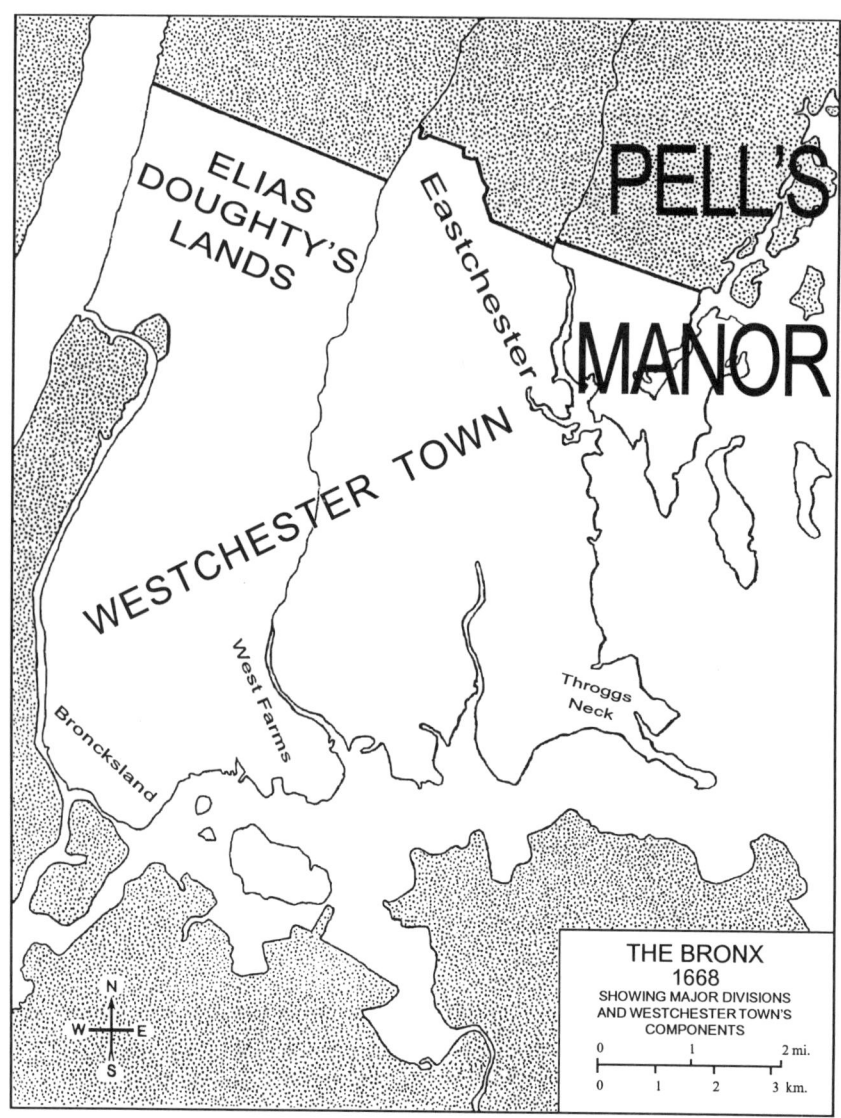

obtained Westchester's recognition of his title to the village's land. Only five days before the Dutch surrender, the Westchester villagers had petitioned the king's commissioners for New England recounting the history of their settlement and pointing out that neither Pell nor the inhabitants had received any recompense for the sufferings and damage they had experienced.[2]

In early June, 1664, Thomas Pell, relying upon his purchase from the Siwanoy Indians in 1654, as guaranteed by Connecticut, granted a portion of his land west of the Hutchinson River to James Eustis and Philip Pinckney, two friends from Fairfield, and their associates. They were to pay Pell the cost of his purchase. The settlement was established there after the English conquest. At first called the ten farms, after the first ten inhabitants, who agreed to be guided by the terms of a covenant among themselves, it was soon to be known as Eastchester.[3] The grant included the land upon which Co-op City now stands and all of today's Bronx northwest of it to the Bronx River. The vast majority of the grant, however, lies in today's Westchester County.

Thomas Pell vigorously attempted to appropriate more land in the area, and his next target was Cornell's Neck. Assuming his 1654 purchase included that territory, Pell tried to sell portions of it. Immediately, this action was protested by Charles and Sarah Bridges in early November, 1664, and the court established under English authority ordered Pell to cease such activity until the case could be tried. Sarah Bridges was the daughter of Thomas Cornell and claimed those lands as her own.[4]

At the trial, which began a year later, the Dutch patent to Thomas Cornell was produced, and it was asserted that Cornell's widow, Rebecca, as sole executrix of his estate, had conveyed the property to her daughter, Sarah. Pell countered with his 1654 purchase, claiming that he had the right to buy lands in the king's dominions, and that Connecticut had given him the authority to do so. In reply, the attorney for the Bridges pointed to the terms of the articles of surrender and the peace treaty whereby all Dutch land grants were confirmed. This argument swayed the jury, and Sarah Bridges won her case.[5]

This case, by confirming Dutch grants, also affected the town of Westchester, which was seeking to establish its authority over the lands in Throggs Neck. John Throckmorton had sold his property there in 1652 to Augustine Hermans, a New Amsterdam merchant. Hermans, in turn, sold a portion of the land to Thomas Hunt. In

1666, the town of Westchester claimed that it always had jurisdiction over Throggs Neck, and Hermans, who never seems to have lived there, opposed the town's claim and took the case to court. In September, 1666, the court decided that Westchester had no claim to Hermans's land. Moreover, in 1669, in response to a complaint by Thomas Hunt, Westchester had to redesign its fences so that Hunt's cattle on Throggs Neck could get to the nearest water supply in the town's jurisdiction.[6]

This raised the question however, as to exactly where the boundaries of the town were located. Since Westchester's settlement was based on Pell's 1654 purchase, with the courts excluding Cornell's and Hermans's lands from the town, and with a new settlement established, called Eastchester, also based on Pell's purchase, there was a real need to define the town's boundaries. The town's inhabitants had previously petitioned Governor Nicolls to send some persons to lay out the bounds of the town, and he had promised to do so, providing the lands were first divided into lots and apportioned among the inhabitants according to the wealth of each individual.[7]

By July, 1666, the governor was ready to grant a patent to the town, but he was stopped by a protest from Thomas Pell. Pell pointed out that he had title to Westchester, as well as other places. Nicolls was willing to listen to Pell's complaint, but stated that the trial concerning Cornell's Neck placed the matter at rest, and that, as governor, he had full authority from the duke of York to dispose of the lands.[8]

Meanwhile, aided by two appointees of the governor, the constable and overseers of Westchester drew up plans to divide the land into lots. They were informed by the governor's secretary that the lands by Rattlesnake Brook (a portion of which survives in today's Seton Falls Park) were to be used by Eastchester, and that some land within Westchester had to remain in common for the use of future settlers. Evidently, the Westchester townsmen were firmly determined to take control of the valuable meadowland between the Hutchinson River and Rattlesnake Brook. In July, 1666, some lots there were laid out and granted to some Westchester men. When the inhabitants of Eastchester arrived at the meadow to cut hay, the Westchester men forbade them to do so. The Eastchester officials then complained to the governor, who issued a stern warning to the constable and overseers of Westchester not to molest the Eastchester men and not to lay out lots in that meadowland.[9]

Establishing title was a widespread problem and the owners of land in the entire Bronx area wanted Governor Nicolls to confirm their possession. The desire was a natural one, if only to clear title so the land could be inherited or sold at some future date. In the atmosphere of the time, however, with boundaries undefined and with possession dependent only upon an Indian sale or a Dutch patent, it became absolutely necessary that the new English authorities acknowledge the ownership of the property. It was needed to prevent anyone, or any organized group, from grabbing it.

The first person to obtain such a patent was John Richardson, who, with Edward Jessup, had purchased land west of Bronck's River from the Indians. He informed the governor of plans to divide the lands between the two men, and, in early May 1666, he received a patent for the use of half of the land that would soon be called West Farms.[10]

Naturally, Thomas Pell would not be left behind. He had already been hurt by the court's decision concerning the disposition of Cornell's Neck and by the attempt of Westchester to obtain a patent of its own. Since he had always insisted that his Indian purchase derived ultimately from the authority of the Connecticut government, it was necessary for him to obtain a patent from New York to secure whatever lands he claimed which still remained in his possession. In October, 1666, Governor Nicolls signed a patent which affirmed Pell's ownership of all the land included in today's Pelham Bay Park, City Island, and smaller islands in Long Island Sound, and a large slice of territory in today's Westchester County, including New Rochelle, Pelham Manor, Pelham Heights, and North Pelham. Not content with the mere confirmation of ownership, Pell had Nicolls declare the land a manor, which meant that Pell and his tenants there had the right to have local cases tried in a local court, and not at a court in any other jurisdiction. For this privilege, Pell was to pay the duke of York one lamb each May first, if the duke demanded it. Oddly enough, this patent creating the manor gives no name to the land.[11]

Two days later, Governor Nicolls confirmed Hugh and Mary O'Neale in the ownership of van der Donck's land, or Yonkers, stipulating that the duke might, at any time, have the use of the timber on the land to build ships, docks, harbors, wharfs, or houses.[12] The stipulation was probably prompted by the presence of a sawmill on the property. The O'Neales, however, needed the patent in order to sell the land. Soon afterward, all the Yonker's land was turned over to Elias Doughty, Mary O'Neale's brother, and the couple returned to Maryland.[13]

In March, 1667, the new settlement of Eastchester received its patent. Philip Pinckney, James Evarts, and William Haiden received the grant on behalf of all the inhabitants. The patent stipulated that the settlement, for the first time called Eastchester, was part of Westchester, and that cases could come before the court at that town, but that the Eastchester inhabitants had the right to choose a deputy constable and to solve all their disputes through arbitration. The boundaries of the settlement were defined, but some meadowland was to be held in common with Westchester.[14] In light of the attempts by Westchester to appropriate meadowland for itself, this provision was to cause some trouble in the future.

About a month later, Governor Nicolls issued a patent for Cornell's Neck. The owner of the land probably thought this act was necessary despite the favorable decision Sarah Bridges received in her court case against Thomas Pell. Sarah Bridges had turned over ownership of her land to her eldest son by a previous marriage, William Willett, and he needed confirmation of his ownership. Governor Nicolls was happy to oblige him. For Willett, the document was potent evidence in 1668 when he had to protest the actions of some Westchester inhabitants who tried to prevent his farmhands from cutting hay on his own land.[15]

Finally, with the claims of Eastchester and Cornell's Neck established by patents, and Thomas Pell presumably mollified by the creation of the remainder of his land into a manor, Governor Nicolls turned to the town of Westchester. In February, 1668, John Quinby, John Ferris, Nicholas Bailey, William Betts, and Edward Waters received the grant on behalf of all the inhabitants of what was now officially designated the town of Westchester. All the privileges of a town were accorded the inhabitants, and the boundaries were defined to include Broncksland (the former farm of Jonas Bronck), West Farms, Cornell's Neck, Throggs Neck, and Eastchester. Moreover, the town was given the right to all parcels of land not disposed of by patent within the bounds of the town.[16]

This last provision must have shocked Samuel Edsall, the current owner of Broncksland. Although he had purchased the land, there is indication that he did not live there, and he had not yet secured a patent for it from the English authorities. By May, 1668, this oversight was rectified by a patent that simply confirmed Edsall's ownership of the property.[17]

Thus, by 1668, almost all of today's Bronx had been claimed by Europeans confirmed in their holdings by a patent from the duke's governor. The only territory that remained without dispute in the hands of the Indians extended from the Harlem River to the Bronx River north of Broncksland and south of the Yonker's land. All it needed was an enterprising European to see the possibilities and to grab it. Such a man was John Archer.

John Archer came to the New World about 1656 from Nieuhof in the Netherlands by way of Amsterdam. He first went to Virginia, where he engaged in the tobacco trade, which must have made him comfortably wealthy. By 1657, he had moved to New Netherland, residing, for some unknown reason, in the new and troubled village of Oostdorp. At the same time, he established his tobacco business in the city of New Amsterdam. As a newly rich person, he began to buy land and goods to a larger than normal extent, and the Dutch named him *Coopall*, or "Buy-all." At Oostdorp, he had sued Richard Ponton, one of the men who had refused to sign the oath of allegiance to the Dutch in 1656, for debt. Ponton, through delay and legal maneuvers, managed to dispose of most of his property, at times with the help of village magistrates, so that Archer would not be able to collect. On the other hand, it was in Oostdorp that Archer met Catherine Carles, the granddaughter of Thomas Newman, who had served as village magistrate in 1657, and he married her at the Dutch church in New Amsterdam in 1659. He accompanied his aged grandfather-in-law to Stamford, where Newman went in order to die under the English flag, and returned to Oostdorp in 1664 just before the English conquest. In the newly renamed town of Westchester, Archer continued to buy as much real estate as he could until August, 1666.[18]

In that year, Elias Doughty of Flushing, who had received the ownership of the Yonker's land from his sister, Mary O'Neale, began the process of selling parcels of the huge grant. He was to sell some to Frederick Philipse and Thomas Lewis, most of which lay in today's Westchester County, as well as some to William Betts of Westchester and his son-in-law, George Tippett, whose property lies in today's Riverdale and Van Cortlandt Park. Doughty, however, appears to have sold the first portion of the Yonker's land to Archer, when, in March, 1667, John Archer purchased from Doughty some upland and meadow. In September, Archer purchased additional meadowland, and a year later, Doughty confirmed the sale of all that Archer had bought from him. The land consisted of a strip along the southernmost portion of the Yonker's land roughly from the Spuyten

Duyvil Creek and the Harlem River to the Bronx River. By 1668, Archer had already sold all his holdings in the town of Westchester, and he committed his destiny to the banks of the Harlem.[19]

Why Archer decided on this move remains a mystery. There are probable reasons why he did so, however. In Westchester, he was a Dutchman in an overwhelmingly English town whose inhabitants had come to blows with Dutch authorities more than once. Despite his English wife and sworn allegiance to England, it seems that Richard Ponton and his friends would do almost anything to thwart him. In addition, Archer had made his money as a merchant, and buying and selling were natural to him, whether the product involved was tobacco or a parcel of land. Moreover, as a businessman, he could see possibilities for profit where farmers, bound to the land with its crops and livestock, might not. It is obvious that he saw possibilities for profit in the vicinity of Spuyten Duyvil Creek.

These possibilities revolved around the use of the Westchester Path, a road that led from Spuyten Duyvil Creek to the town. Since the farmers of Westchester had so much of their property in livestock grazing upon the marsh grass, some of that cattle had to be sold for beef. The easiest way to get the cattle to the largest market in the area, New York City at the tip of Manhattan, was to drive them over the Westchester Path to Spuyten Duyvil Creek. There, at low tide, the crossing was easy and safe. Archer already controlled the mainland approaches to the wading place where people and livestock could ford the stream. If he controlled the Manhattan side as well, he could establish a system whereby all who crossed the creek would pay a toll. The profits would be limited only by the capacity for population growth in the area.

In January, 1667, however, some residents of the town of New Harlem, near the northern end of Manhattan, had plans of their own for Spuyten Duyvil Creek. They resolved to place fences across the creek to stop any traffic there, and to allow Johannes Verveelen to operate a ferry from the town at about today's 125th Street to Broncksland. In addition, they proposed to purchase Broncksland and add it to the town. This is another reason why Samuel Edsall, its owner at the time, sought and received a patent for his land. By July, Verveelen received a lease for his ferry from the mayor and aldermen of New York City, with an acre (less than half a hectare) on the Bronx side. He was to build a house on each side of his ferry, a task he never completed. It was fairly easy for Westchester inhabitants to avoid Verveelen by driving their cattle to Spuyten Duyvil and throwing down the fences erected there, even though it made them liable for prosecution if caught.[20] Clearly, Spuyten Duyvil was the preferred route.

John Archer then moved to obtain control of that route by purchasing the land on the Manhattan side opposite his mainland holdings. Immediately, the town of New Harlem not only challenged his right to that land, but also accused him of allowing four of his cows to trespass on some meadows on the mainland which, it was asserted, belonged to the town. Archer traced his right to the ownership of the Manhattan lands back to a grant made by Dutch director-general William Kieft. New Harlem rested its case on the patent given the town by Governor Nicolls.

In November, 1668, the case concerning the Manhattan lands came before Governor Francis Lovelace, who had succeeded Nicolls, and his Council. The Council decided that the Manhattan property belonged to New Harlem on the grounds that so much time had lapsed between Director-general Kieft's grant and any use made of the land, and that Governor Nicolls's patent to New Harlem, which included the property in question, should prevail over the Dutch grant. Archer, however, was to be compensated in some undefined way for his loss.[21]

The question of ownership of the mainland meadows was delayed for some time because Archer could not produce the patent for his land or a bill of sale. In addition, the town of Westchester asserted its rights, stating to the governor that if the land in question were not included in the O'Neale patent for Yonkers, then it belonged to the town by virtue of the provisions of its own patent.[22] The governor appointed a group of men to survey the property and to report to him. Evidence seems to indicate that by 1669 John Archer sustained his case.[23]

That was not the end of Archer's troubles, however. Nearby was the island of Paparinemin, filled with valuable lush marsh grass. It was a triangular shaped island formed at the junction of Tibbett's Brook and Spuyten Duyvil Creek bounded roughly by today's Irwin Avenue, Broadway, and West 230th Street. In July, 1669, Archer accused Richard Betts and George Tippett of cutting and carrying away more hay from the island than they were entitled to do, thus leaving him and other inhabitants of his place destitute. The governor made several attempts to stop the trespass, but Betts and Tippett not only continued to cut hay as before, but accused Archer of cutting hay on their own property.[24]

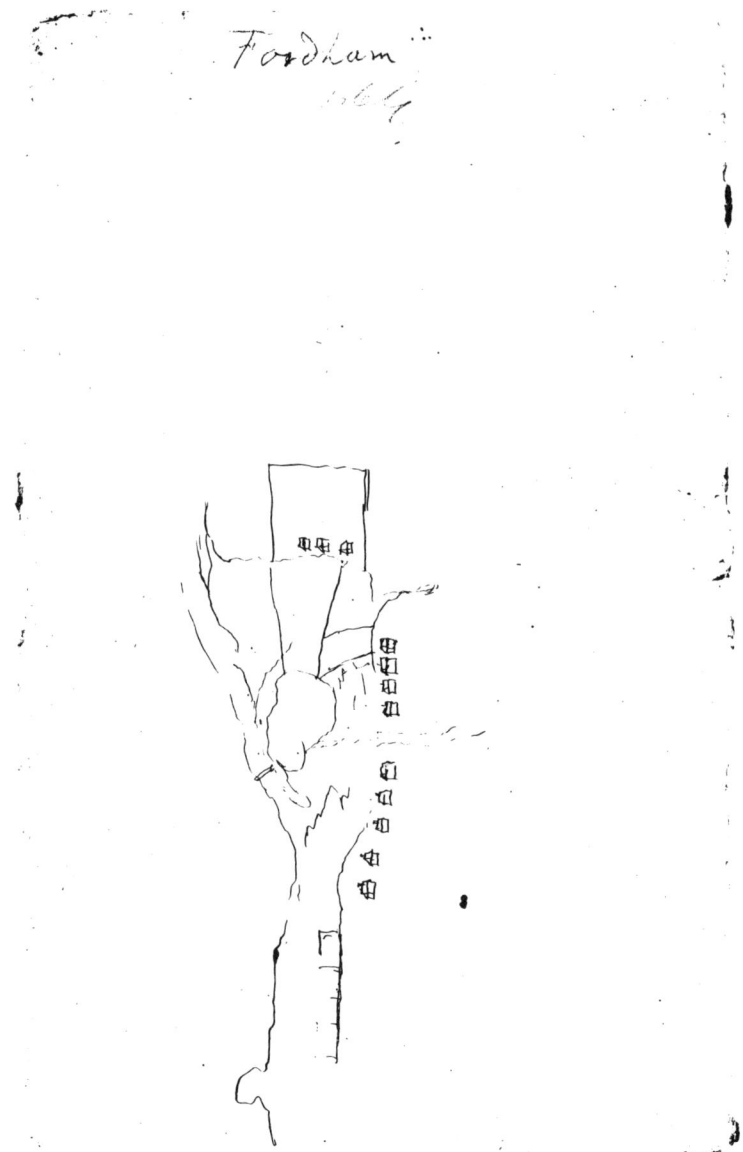

FORDHAM VILLAGE IN THE 1660s

This map, drawn shortly after the founding of the village of Fordham, shows the houses of John Archer's tenants arranged along the east bank of the Harlem River.

New York State Archives

In the meantime, Johannes Verveelen, the ferrymaster at New Harlem, petitioned to move his ferry to Spuyten Duyvil Creek. Obviously, the attempt to divert traffic away from the creek did not succeed, and the only way to save the business was to move it where the traffic continued to pass. Governor Lovelace approved the idea, and, in 1669, granted Verveelen the use of all of Paparinemin for eleven years, on which he was to build his house as well as an accommodation for travelers with four good beds, entertainment for strangers, and provisions for them, their horses, and cattle. Verveelen was also to pay one-third the cost of constructing a bridge between the island and the mainland. Rates for the use of the ferry and accommodations were established, with the stipulation that persons on special warrant from the governor, all magistrates in public service, and soldiers in an emergency were to receive free passage.[25]

John Archer was now in a desperate situation. His scheme to have traffic at Spuyten Duyvil controlled became a reality, but another person was to have the profits. In addition, his title to the lands he claimed was under attack not only by Betts and Tippett, but also by Verveelen's occupation and use of Paparinemin.

The situation was all the more acute because Archer now had several tenants living on his property. He had received permission from Governor Lovelace to settle sixteen families on his land, and, by 1669, eleven families, beside his own, had already agreed to live there. All of them had come from New Harlem, and most of them were Dutch. Archer had leased the land to them, usually 20 to 25 acres (just over 8 to just over 10 hectares) each, for a certain number of years, in return for some slight consideration, such as a fat fowl, per year. The tenants were to clear the land and to plant what they wished, while Archer agreed to supply them each with a house and lots. Together, the settlement on the banks of the Harlem constituted a new village named Fordham.[26]

The danger to Archer consisted in the possibility that later claimants might whittle away his land a little at a time. He had invested just about all he had in Fordham, not only in purchasing the land, but in providing the houses for the villagers and building roads for their use. This possibility was made even more real when Governor Lovelace named ferrymaster Johannes Verveelen the constable of Fordham. Archer could not look upon Verveelen, who had strong associations with New Harlem, and who occupied land he considered his own, as friendly to his interests.[27]

To forestall any such possibility, in September, 1669, Archer met with a group of Indian sachems just before Verveelen was to begin his new ferry service. He purchased from them not only Paparinemin, but almost all the land in today's Bronx then not secured by a patent from the colonial governor. This huge territory included all the property from the north along a line running from today's Broadway and West 238th Street eastward to a point in the Bronx River just above Gun Hill Road to the south along a line from today's High Bridge eastward to the Bronx River.[28]

The southernmost line of Archer's expanded holdings was determined by the land of Daniel Turneur, a prominent resident of New Harlem who had been one of the backers of Verveelen's original ferry route. In June, 1668, Turneur had received a patent from then Governor Nicolls for what was, at that time, a peninsula bounded by the Harlem River and what would one day be called Cromwell's Creek.[29] Today, the land lies south of the High Bridge with the Harlem River to the west and Jerome Avenue to the east. Thus, Archer's purchase in 1669 left the Indians in the area in undisputed possession of only a small strip of land extending from Daniel Turneur's land to the Bronx River, north of Broncksland and south of Archer's newly acquired property.

Archer's Indian purchase, however, did not end the controversy between Archer and Betts and Tippett over the ownership of the meadowland and the cutting of the hay. Again and again, through the years, Betts and Tippett laid claim to the valuable meadow ground, accusing Archer of cutting hay on land belonging to them. Again and again, Archer complained to Governor Lovelace, who had surveys made and who meticulously apportioned the land between the litigants. Finally, in 1672, Governor Lovelace ordered the whole matter to be decided before the Court of Assizes, and the jury decided in Archer's favor.[30]

The question of the meadowland, however, was not the only controversy with which John Archer had to deal. There was also the question of ownership of some hogs. According to the practice of the time, hogs were let loose to run in the woods. The ears were marked in a distinctive manner to indicate ownership. In 1670, John Archer complained that Tippett had unlawfully removed Archer's markings on some hogs he owned, and had slaughtered others. A court called in Fordham to decide the issue apparently came to no conclusion, and, upon complaint to the governor, Archer was ordered to claim all unmarked hogs for the duke of York. In the following winter, Tippett, John Heddy (another of Archer's neighbors on the Yonker's land), Thomas Hunt, Jr., William Smith, and Jan Hendricks were caught eliminating the owners' marks on the hogs and substituting their own. By October, 1672, the case came before the Court of Assizes, which found all the defendants guilty. Except for Jan Hendricks, who confessed and apparently aided the prosecution, all received fines, with the added proviso that if Tippett and Hunt did not pay, the two were to be given thirty-one lashes each at the whipping post in New York City.[31]

Naturally, all of Archer's activities in defense of his interests cost a great deal of money. He needed money to buy the additional land from the Indians, to improve his property, and to fight the innumerable court cases arising out of the questions of the ownership of the meadowlands and the hogs. For these funds, John Archer turned to Cornelis Steenwyck, one of the richest men in the colony of New York at the time. In 1669, he borrowed 1,100 guilders wampum from him in return for a mortgage on the village of Fordham. An additional 1,100 guilders wampum was borrowed on the same terms the following year. Between the two loans, Archer also borrowed an additional 1,000 guilders wampum from Werner Wessells of New York City, which was secured by a mortgage on Archer's own real and personal estate at Fordham.[32]

Heavily in debt and still in need of money, Archer sought out Steenwyck again. Because much of Archer's money problem rose out of his constant litigation, it is probable that Steenwyck advised him to have his lands at Fordham created into a manor. That way, Fordham would have its own courts and not be subject to any other jurisdiction short of the Court of Assizes and the governor and his Council. Therefore, in November, 1671, Governor Lovelace granted John Archer a patent for his land creating it the manor of Fordham in return for a quit-rent of twenty bushels (just under 705 liters) of peas a year, payable on March first, but only if demanded.[33]

Following the granting of the patent, Archer was able to borrow from Steenwyck 7,000 guilders repayable in twelve years. As security, Archer turned over to Steenwyck the deed to Fordham, to be returned once the loan was repaid. A year later, the two men decided that Archer was to pay interest on the loan at the rate of ten percent a year.[34]

This did not mean that John Archer had ended all of his troubles. He continued to have nettlesome problems with his tenants and his neighbors. First, in September, 1671, David Demarest, who claimed an ill-defined lot of meadowland adjoining Fordham near

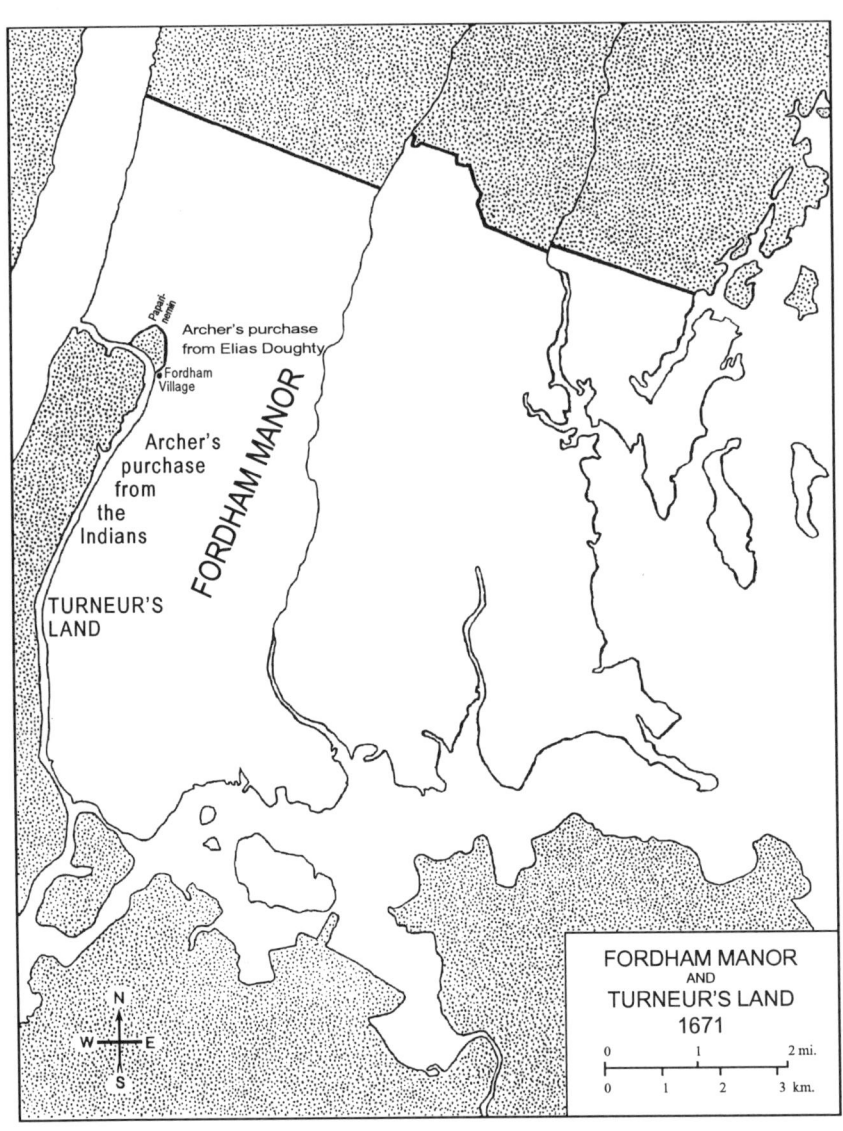

Spuyten Duyvil, accused Archer of cutting his hay. A court in New Harlem appointed surveyors to define the lot to settle the case. At the same court, tenant Martin Hardewyn asserted that Archer had broken his fence and had ruined his grain. Another tenant, Marcus Du Sauchoy, accused Archer of throwing his furniture out of doors, evidently an early attempt at eviction. In general, the inhabitants of Fordham complained that their landlord ruled over them with vigor and with force, and that he was the cause of the troubles between the inhabitants and the town. Since the manor was created one month after all these cases had appeared before the court in New Harlem, the final disposition of the complaints against Archer would be decided in a court that he controlled. Significantly, nothing was heard of these cases again. In April, 1673, Governor Lovelace decreed the establishment of a court at the manor of Fordham consisting of the steward, with the constables and overseers of the town and a few discreet inhabitants as assistants. John Rider was named steward.[35] For the time being, at least, John Archer seemed to have found a way to end his trouble with his tenants.

John Archer's attempts to grab land, however, did not end such attempts in the area that was to become The Bronx. South of Fordham Manor, there was still a slice of territory that was not yet claimed under the authority of an English patent. Governor Lovelace first thought that those lands might be used to settle the endless litigation involving control over the meadowland at Spuyten Duyvil. In 1672, he voiced the idea that, perhaps, the owners of the Spuyten Duyvil meadows might want to exchange their land there for a parcel of Broncksland or part of the adjoining unclaimed territory. Nothing seems to have come of this idea. Daniel Turneur, however, had made moves to secure his small patent near that area. Already, in 1671, he had obtained an Indian deed to the land he had held under English patent since 1668. At that time, he also purchased a small strip east of his holdings from the Indians, which Governor Lovelace confirmed in March, 1672. One month later, Turneur leased a piece of woodland on that property near what would one day be called Cromwell's Creek to a soldier, Jan Dirksen, for three years.[36]

In the West Farms, Edward Jessup, who had played a leading role in the events in Westchester before the English conquest, and who had joined John Richardson in purchasing the land west of the Bronx River, became ill and died in 1666. His wife, Elizabeth, sole executrix of his will, remarried and, in 1668, sold the entire Jessup interest in the West Farms to her son-in-law, Thomas Hunt. Hunt already owned some land on Throggs Neck, and this purchase added to his holdings. His son, Thomas Hunt, Jr., was one of the men caught substituting their own markings for the legal ones on the hogs running wild in the Spuyten Duyvil area in 1671. Thomas Hunt, Jr., was to cause additional trouble in the future. In the meantime, Thomas Hunt, Sr., and John Richardson divided the West Farms between them in 1669, and, about a year later, Richardson's son-in-law, Gabriel Leggett, arrived to live there.[37]

Meanwhile, east of the Bronx River, there was some difficulty between the two settlements of Westchester and Eastchester. As early as November, 1668, Westchester officials noted that the Eastchester inhabitants refused to pay their proportion of taxes to Westchester, despite the patent which stated specifically that Eastchester was within the jurisdiction of their town. They then requested action from Governor Lovelace, who obliged with a letter stating that it was Eastchester's duty to pay its proportion of taxes. The inhabitants of Eastchester, however, protested. They insisted that their patent made them a separate town, that they received no services or other benefits from Westchester, and that they had expended a considerable amount of time and money making and repairing highways without any help from Westchester. The governor, thereupon, reconsidered his position, and, in December, he excused the Eastchester inhabitants from contributing any funds to Westchester for the public works they did for themselves.[38]

There were other troubles from Westchester, however. Probably because the common land between the two towns was not defined nor fenced in, it was not difficult for hogs from Westchester to cross into Eastchester and eat the grain growing there. In February, 1672, the people of Eastchester agreed that any resident could capture such hogs and charge the owners for their keep and any damage they might have done.[39]

Despite this difficulty, both villages were growing. By 1670, the population of Westchester had grown so much that Nicholas Bailey, John Ferris, and Joseph Palmer were appointed by the town to set out new bounds for the lots in the fields inhabited by the first settlers, and to lay out additional lots for newcomers.[40]

One of the newcomers was Katherine Harrison, a widow, who had come from Weathersfield, Connecticut, with her children, seeking refuge in Richard Ponton's house. She had been under suspicion of being a witch there, and this made the Westchester inhabitants uneasy enough to demand her removal. A final examination by the

Court of Assizes in October, 1670, however, indicated that there was no evidence of her being a witch, and it ruled she could live in Westchester or any other part of the colony she wished.[41]

In Eastchester, population growth led to a mill being built to service the farmers who grew grain. Not only a miller, but a smith, a weaver, and a tailor established residence there by early 1673.[42]

There is some evidence of cooperation between the two towns. In 1670, representatives of both met to plan a country road to run from Westchester to Eastchester, and, by the following year, it was already under construction. In addition, both towns cooperated in selecting an appropriate site for the mill. Perhaps most important of all, the two towns agreed on a boundary between them, and, by 1672, Richard Ponton and John Quinby of Westchester joined a larger group of Eastchester men to peruse the bounds.[43]

Of course, with the population growing, there was more commerce in the entire Bronx area, and roads and bridges had to be built to facilitate that commerce. It will be remembered that Johannes Verveelen had to pay one-third the cost of a bridge from the island of Paparinemin to the mainland. The mainlanders had to pay the remainder. At first, William Betts, George Tippett, and John Heddy, who insisted they lived far from Fordham, petitioned Governor Lovelace to excuse them from contributing their time and money for the building of this bridge, and proposed that they build a bridge over the Bronx River to Eastchester instead. The Fordham inhabitants thought that the bridge to Eastchester was a good idea, and proposed that they join the three men in building it, once the bridge from Paparinemin was completed. Governor Lovelace also thought a bridge to Eastchester would be an important improvement, and, in 1670, ordered Betts, Tippett, and Heddy to aid in the building of the Paparinemin bridge, after which, the Fordham inhabitants were to join the three men in building the Eastchester bridge. For this great work of public improvement, they were all granted free passage on Verveelen's ferry to Manhattan for as long as Verveelen operated it.[44]

Despite the population growth, the number of people living in the Bronx area was woefully small. The concentration of inhabitants in Westchester and Eastchester could not offset the handful of families in Fordham, the three families on the Yonker's land, a single tenant on Daniel Turneur's land, and the small number of people settled in the West Farms. In 1673, the entire population probably numbered much less than 300.[45] In fact, so sparse and scattered was the population that the mainland north and east of Manhattan Island was not looked upon as a single unit. When the English first organized the colony, they established judicial districts called towns and ridings, the latter term borrowed from the name of judicial districts in Yorkshire in England. Westchester, with its dependencies in Eastchester, the West Farms, and Broncksland, was grouped with several towns on Long Island into the North Riding and had to pay taxes for building the riding's courthouse at Jamaica.[46] Fordham, until it became a manor, was grouped with New Harlem and New York City, and was dependent upon the New Harlem and New York City Mayor's Courts.

The two territories that probably had the least population in relation to their size were Pell's manor and Broncksland. Thomas Pell did not even live on his manorlands in New York, but preferred to stay in Fairfield, Connecticut, serving in that colony's Assembly as deputy for the town. He leased some of his New York land to others and allowed them to use some of his livestock and farm implements. As far as is known, only three men lived on his manor at this time. Houses and barns were built, however, cattle and oxen grazed in the fields, and a number of horses joined the hogs in running through the forests. Pell did have a residence in which he kept a number of beds, household implements, and a handy medical book. He seems to have begun building a manor house, since he was cutting logs and gathering nails, bolts, and other necessary items to construct one. In the fields, wheat and corn were grown, and flocks of sheep were sheared, their wool weighed and probably sold. Some Indian trade goods remained on hand as well. In all, the worth of Pell's property on the manor and in Westchester totaled £1,294 14s. Although his property in Connecticut was worth less, only £779 5s. 5d., the more valuable and refined pieces of tableware, furniture, and clothing were housed there.[47]

It was in Fairfield that Thomas Pell died in 1669. With a few exceptions, he left all his property to John Pell, the son of his older brother, then living in England. It is interesting to note that, even at the end, Thomas Pell had not paid Charles and Sarah Bridges the cost of the damages they had won in the court case that settled the ownership of Cornell's Neck, and the couple had to demand the £16 10s. 10d. due them from the executors of Pell's will.[48]

John Pell, Thomas Pell's nephew and heir, never met his benefactor. He was the son of Dr. John Pell, a distinguished scholar of the day, known for his contributions to mathematics and for his

John Pell
1643 — 1700

Painting attributed to Sir Godfrey Kneller
Fort Ticonderoga Museum

service as Oliver Cromwell's ambassador to the Protestant Swiss cantons. Because Dr. Pell usually was somewhere lecturing at a university, or on the country's business, young John Pell hardly ever met his own father. Thus, he was raised by his mother on her father's country estate in Suffolk. Because of the family's connections with the nobility, twenty-one year old John Pell was able to secure a minor appointment in 1665 in the court of King Charles II as a server-in-ordinary. As such, it was his duty, at times when the king dined in state, to take the dishes from the servants and hand them to the great lords of the household, who, in turn, served the king.[49]

In 1670, the news arrived in England of John Pell's inheritance. Family tradition states that the king sent for the young man when he heard of the news and knighted him, making him Sir John Pell. There is no record of his being knighted, however. Armed with several letters of introduction to prove he was his uncle's heir, he sailed for the New World.[50]

After a short stay in Boston, where he met both the governor of Massachusetts and the governor of Connecticut, John Pell took a boat to Fairfield. There, he discovered that the executors of his uncle's will had rented the house on a long-term lease and had sold much of the property, including some of the livestock there. Young Pell immediately brought the executors to court, suing them for damages. After a series of legal maneuvers delayed settlement, however, Pell was willing to sell all of the Fairfield property and move to his holdings in New York.[51]

By January, 1671, John Pell had arrived at his manor. Seeing a partially completed manor house, he engaged masons, carpenters, and workmen from New York City to enlarge and complete it.[52]

In the process of putting his affairs in order and in building the house, John Pell met Governor Lovelace and John Pinckney, his uncle's old friend and one of the original settlers of Eastchester. He also met Rachel Pinckney, John's lovely daughter, and, several years later, married her. One additional obligation he had was to assume his share of the burden of completing the post road from New York City to Boston,[53] portions of which were already in place because of the efforts of the men of Eastchester, Fordham, and Yonkers in building roads and bridges.

Therefore, by 1673, Pell's manor finally had a resident proprietor interested in its improvement and welfare. As for Broncksland, developments there would lead to the same result, but this was not evident at the time of the English conquest, when, it appears, no one lived there.

In June, 1668, Samuel Edsall, who had received a patent for Broncksland the previous month, sold it to Richard Morris. Morris had fought on the parliamentary side in the English Civil War, attaining the rank of captain. Upon the restoration of the monarchy, he took up residence on the island of Barbados, where he married a wealthy lady, owned a good deal of land, and, as was common in the West Indies, some slaves to do the work.[54]

Morris was probably attracted to New York because he was a merchant. Barbados, like most of the West Indies, had to import its food from the North American continent, and New York was a major supplier. Why he chose to purchase Broncksland is a mystery. Perhaps, he thought he could make a bigger profit growing grain there and transporting it to Barbados in his own ships. After all, Broncksland may have been the largest farm close to New York available at the time to suit those needs.

In any event, he does not seem to have moved there until 1670. To help him plant the fields, he had several slaves, probably brought with him from Barbados. This is the first definite evidence of the use of slaves anywhere in what is today's Bronx. Indentured servants, however, worked beside them as well.[55]

In 1672, Richard Morris's wife died, and he followed shortly thereafter. No will had been made, and the apparent heir was a young son named Lewis, not yet one year old. Five men were appointed trustees of the estate, and Morris's brother, Colonel Lewis Morris, was informed of what had happened.[56]

Colonel Lewis Morris, elder brother of Richard, had also fought on the parliamentary side in the English Civil War, for which King Charles I had confiscated Tintern, his estate in Monmouthshire. He was indemnified for this by Cromwell's government. Subsequently, he moved to Barbados, where he became a member of the Council and a privateer attempting to capture Spanish ships in the Caribbean. It was in the West Indies that Lewis Morris first came into contact with the ideas of the pacifist Quakers, and he embraced that faith, repudiating his martial past. As a Quaker, he was heavily fined for not contributing to the support of the established Anglican Church. It was then that he heard the news of his brother's death and of his orphaned nephew bearing his name.[57]

Of course, the big question to be settled concerned the guardianship of the little boy and the ownership of Broncksland. Certainly, anything could happen to a large amount of land owned by an infant and administered by trustees who might not look out for his interests.

Colonel Lewis Morris had already been informed that some trouble had occurred on that land. While the infant was brought to Harlem to be nursed there, the indentured servants attempted mutiny, and two or three of the slaves joined in by stealing and receiving stolen goods. Trustee Thomas Gibbs immediately quelled the mutiny and chastised the slaves.[58] This was evidence of what might happen if things continued the same way. It was at this point that Colonel Lewis Morris resolved to leave Barbados for New York to administer his nephew's estate.

By the time he arrived in New York, he was met with a totally unexpected situation. An event occurred that would not only affect the Morris family, but also relations between John Archer and his tenants at Fordham, and the governing of the towns of Westchester and Eastchester. In some ways, the experience of 1664 happened all over again, but this time, in reverse.

CHAPTER VII

THE DUTCH INTERLUDE

1673 TO 1674

The event which shook the entire colony of New York, including the territory that would become The Bronx, grew out of a war that was declared in the spring of 1672. Charles II, always in need of funds, agreed to take money secretly from King Louis XIV of France in return for declaring war on Louis's enemy, the Dutch. English warships then began to interfere with Dutch shipping, and war began.

The conflict eventually spread to the New World, and, in 1673, a Dutch fleet, commanded by Cornelis Evartsen, Jr., began plundering English shipping in the West Indies and off the coast of Virginia. Without warning, it turned northward, caught the English garrison at New York by surprise, and captured the duke of York's colony almost as easily as the duke's forces had conquered New Amsterdam nine years earlier.[1] Captain John Manning, commander of the fort at New York, had sent word to Captain Richard Ponton, militia commander at Westchester, and to other militia commanders at nearby Long Island towns to come with a force to repel any invasion. No one arrived, even when the urgent request was repeated.[2]

The Dutch, suddenly finding themselves in possession of their old colony, proceeded to the task of administering it. Once again, they called the colony New Netherland, but New York City was renamed New Orange, after William, prince of Orange, stadtholder of the Netherlands.

On August 13, 1673, a council of war at the fort ordered several towns, among them "Oostdorp or Westchester and its adjoining hamlet, called Eastchester," to send their deputies to the fort, along with their constables' staves (the symbol of their office) and English flags. In return, they would receive the prince's flag, if enough were available.[3] Eight days later, the deputies arrived, delivered their credentials to the council, and offered to submit themselves to the laws of the States-General and the prince of Orange. The council then ordered the people of the two towns to nominate double the required number of men for magistrates, from which the council would choose. Westchester was to have two magistrates, while Eastchester was allowed only one. These officers could decide all suits in the town up to the value of thirty English shillings. Cases of greater value, however, had to be decided before all three magistrates in the town of Westchester.[4]

The following day, the Westchester deputies surrendered one English flag and one staff, and, along with several deputies from Long Island towns, petitioned the council for certain privileges and rights. Provided they acted loyally and did not take up arms against the government, the council was willing to grant them the full privileges and rights of the Dutch nation.[5]

The deputies then went home to inform the inhabitants of the towns of what had happened and to conduct the nominations for the magistrates according to Dutch law. The inhabitants of Eastchester met on August 24th and nominated William Haiden and John Hoit for magistrates, and proposed John Pell for the post of schout, or law officer. The council agreed to the election of John Hoit, but remained silent about appointing a schout for Eastchester. The council selected Joseph Palmer and Edward Waters from among those nominated for magistrates of Westchester, and they were sworn into office on September 2nd.[6]

By mid-September, 1673, the Dutch fleet had to leave the newly renamed New Orange. This also meant that the council of war, which had been governing the colony up to that time, had to depart. To continue the Dutch administration, the council chose Anthony Colve, a captain of infantry, as governor-general of New Netherland.[7]

In October, newly installed Governor-general Colve issued provisional instructions for the magistrates of Eastchester and for several other towns in New Netherland, informing them of the scope of their authority and of the standard of behavior to which they were to adhere. They were told that they could decide cases up to the value of "sixty guilders beaver." Criminal offenses were to be tried before the governor-general and his Council.[8]

Almost immediately, trouble ensued when Captain William Knyfe and Lieutenant Krynsen asked the Westchester inhabitants to swear allegiance to the States-General and the prince of Orange. Thomas Hunt, Jr., refused to comply, and he was ordered out of the jurisdiction of the government within fourteen days, with the right of taking his movable property with him, provided he had paid all his debts. Nevertheless, one month later, his father, Thomas Hunt, Sr., petitioned the governor-general and his Council to allow his banished son to reside in New Netherland. It was agreed that the brash young man would be allowed to return on taking the oath of allegiance and on giving security for his good behavior.[9] The younger Hunt did return, but he was to attempt his revenge on the Dutch after a year had passed.

There was a minor problem with the eight men who were Quakers living in Westchester. Since Quakers do not take oaths, they signed a declaration of allegiance promising to be faithful to the States-General and the prince.[10]

Meanwhile, the tenants of John Archer at Fordham saw the Dutch reconquest as an opportunity to change their relationship with their landlord. Under English law, Fordham had been made into a manor, having its own local court controlled by Archer. On October 4, 1673, the inhabitants of Fordham appeared before the governor-general and his Council at New Harlem complaining about the ill-government they had received from their landlord. They requested the same privileges of nominating their own magistrates as Westchester and the other towns had. This would, of course, take the local courts out of Archer's control. Governor-general Colve then summoned John Archer and told him about the complaint. The single member of the Council present was Cornelis Steenwyck, the man to whom Archer was deeply in debt. Probably because of his prompting, Archer volunteered to give up his right to rule Fordham, but reserved his rights to his own property, land, and houses there. Hearing this, the governor-general and his Council authorized the Fordham inhabitants to nominate for magistrates six men exclusively of the Reformed Christian religion, from which the governor-general would choose three. The people of the town, however, were cautioned to be sure that half of their nominees were Dutchmen.[11] By October 18th, Governor-general Colve made his choices and named Johannes Verveelen, the ferryman at Spuyten Duyvil, Michael Bastiensen, and Valentine Claessen, who was to be the founder of the Valentine family in The Bronx.[12]

This situation left John Archer in desperate straits. He was no longer able to keep creditors away, and two of them, Thomas Gibbs and John Curtis, accused him of trying to defraud them by disposing of his effects. It will be remembered that Richard Ponton did the same thing to Archer when they were both residents of Westchester. Unlike Ponton, Archer could expect no help from the magistrates of the area where he now resided. In May, 1674, his creditors, Gibbs and Curtis, complained to the governor-general, who ordered the Fordham magistrates to stop any sale of Archer's estate and effects. At one point, Johannes Verveelen grabbed Archer's books concerning the town of Fordham, and he had to be ordered by Governor-general Colve and his Council to return them.[13]

John Archer's troubles paled in comparison to those of Colonel Lewis Morris's at the time. Morris arrived at about the same time the Dutch had reconquered their colony in an attempt to salvage the estate of his orphaned nephew. In October, 1673, he petitioned the governor-general for the guardianship of his nephew and his estate. He insisted he wanted to manage it for the orphan's good. In addition, he requested to have the same privileges enjoyed in the neighboring English colonies of Virginia or New England. Colve decided that Lewis Morris would have the guardianship of the infant, with the power to take into his keeping all goods, effects, slaves, and indentured servants of his late brother, provided he paid Richard Morris's funeral expenses. Lewis Morris, however, first had to deliver a correct inventory of the property left by his late brother. He was also allowed to import items necessary to administer the properties, provided they were carried in ships already in New Orange, or which would anchor there, and the normal customs duties were paid. As a resident of Barbados, however, he was denied the privileges of Virginia or New England. On the other hand, he was given the right to show where the property belonging to his deceased brother's estate was located, and an order would be given for its restitution.[14]

While the New Netherland government could issue orders, it was difficult under the circumstances for Morris to carry out all of the provisions. Several items belonging to the Morris farm on Broncksland had been removed by the colonel's brother-in-law,

Walter Webley, and Webley was one of those who had refused to take the oath of allegiance and was being expelled from the colony. On an urgent request from Lewis Morris, Governor-general Colve allowed him to remain if he took the oath, which, evidently, he did do.[15]

Moreover, there were always those who would try to claim the land, especially when it was owned by an infant. Nelis Mattysen and Christiana Lourens, for instance, claimed Stony Island, the land today called Port Morris, and petitioned the governor-general and his Council for a grant for it. Luckily for Morris, the petition was denied and postponed, it appears indefinitely, on the grounds that Colve did not have any information about the property.[16] Morris's struggle to control Stony Island, however, was to continue for several years in the future.

On November 1, 1673, Lewis Morris received a serious blow. The authorities discovered that, as a partner in the purchase of Broncksland, two-thirds of Richard Morris's estate really belonged to him, a resident of Barbados at the time of the Dutch reconquest. Therefore, under a proclamation previously issued, Lewis Morris's interest in the estate was confiscated by the government and Balthazar Bayard was named to administer it. In addition, John Lawrence, Stephanus van Cortlandt, and Walter Webley were named to administer the remaining one-third interest as guardians for the orphaned infant with the authority to settle all debts and to sell the remaining personal property. Lawrence and van Cortlandt resigned their positions in February, 1674, and Dirck van Clyff and Balthazar Bayard were appointed to replace them.[17]

Undaunted, Colonel Lewis Morris continued to trace parts of his orphaned nephew's missing estate. Armed with a special pass from Colve, he journeyed to Oyster Bay and to English-held New Haven, where he did discover part of the infant's legacy. In November, he requested from the governor-general permission to return in a sloop belonging to the Broncksland estate. Colve tersely gave his consent.[18]

Even Walter Webley, Morris's kinsman, had to go to New England on a pass. He was hauled before the governor-general and his Council, however, for going into the enemy's country and for bringing letters there. The fact that he had a pass to do so, and that the letters had been shown previously to the colony's secretary, did not prevent him from being fined eight beaver skins.[19]

The government of New Netherland was particularly sensitive about contact with New Englanders. After all, it was wartime, and the English were the enemy. Although the New England colonies were divided about the wisdom of invading the Dutch colony,[20] an invasion always remained a possibility. In addition, a large resident English population in New Netherland was suspect of harboring traitorous ideas. The Dutch remembered the events of 1664 quite well.

As early as November, 1673, John Hoit, the magistrate of Eastchester, was given specific instructions from the governor-general to stop anyone passing through his town to New England. In addition, he was to halt the progress of anyone passing through Eastchester coming from the English colonies. The only exception was those persons who could produce a special pass or license.[21]

The following April, both Francis Rombouts and Gelyn Verplanck of New Orange were hauled before Governor-general Colve and his Council on the charge of leaving the city and conferring with Nathaniel Davenport of New England at the home of John Pell. Rombouts held that Davenport had come to Pell's manor accidentally, and that he did not know that Davenport would be there. While he was there, however, they did have a conversation concerning Rombout's private estate in New England. Verplanck admitted frankly that he had gone to Pell's manor to speak with Davenport about his own New England estate. The Council found both men guilty of defying the proclamation against having any conversation with men from New England, but in light of the circumstances outlined in their defense, Rombouts was fined twenty-five guilders in beaver and Verplanck, fifty guilders in beaver.[22]

No doubt the fears of Governor-general Colve and his Council were heightened by the strange incidents involving Francis Beado. In September, 1673, about a month after the Dutch reconquest, Francis Beado came to William Smith at Fordham telling him that he had a commission to burn, kill, and ruin the Dutch because they were his enemies. He also stated that his commission consisted of his sword or his half pike. He was also afraid that Michael Bastiensen's wife would betray his intention to burn the homes of Bastiensen and Werner Wessells because she had seen his half pike, and he requested Smith to warn Thomas Gibbs, who had been living at the Bastiensen house, of his intentions.

At about the same time, Beado also talked to George Tippett when Tippett was about to journey to the mill. Beado questioned him about the defenses of the fort, and later requested the loan of two or three guns. Tippett deferred discussing the matter until after he would return. When he came back, Beado had gone. Tippett's wife informed her husband that the visitor had threatened to burn the Dutch houses there. Alarmed, Tippett immediately warned Johannes Verveelen, the ferrymaster at Spuyten Duyvil.

Francis Beado also contacted James Pinnet, another Fordham resident, to request his assistance in robbing William Lawrence of Flushing and carrying his slaves to Virginia, and in robbing a Dutch house on Long Island where there were some arms and rum to be had. He also disclosed the names of some confederates who were supposedly aiding him.

Beado made similar statements to people on Long Island, saying that he was going to proclaim the king, and that he had a commission to raise troops there. In an expansive mood, he also stated that he had spent £32 to obtain information from the captains of Dutch ships in the harbor of New Orange, and that the Dutch had plans to capture Rhode Island, to fortify it, and command all of New England. He insisted that he was sent from New England as a spy.[23]

The twenty-seven year old Beado, a native of London, was either a very inept spy or highly deranged. He was captured and imprisoned. On December 8, 1673, his trial before the governor-general and his Council took place. Not only was the evidence overwhelmingly against him, but he confessed. For coming into New Netherland without permission, for threatening to destroy people and property with fire and sword, and for thus disturbing the peace, Francis Beado was branded on the back with a red hot iron and banished from New Netherland for twenty-five years on pain of death if he should return before that time.[24]

Perhaps with the Beado incident in mind, Governor-general Colve warned the inhabitants of New Harlem and Fordham to keep a watchful eye on all designs against the colony, and against their settlements in particular. The residents were to be ready to transport themselves and their families to New Orange on the enemy's approach, or upon special command from him. He also appointed Resolved Waldron of New Harlem as the chief militia officer of the two towns.[25]

By March 14, 1674, the defenses of New Orange were almost completed, and Governor-general Colve sent a message to the people in all the Long Island towns where Dutchmen were in the majority, and to New Harlem and Fordham, to rush to the city with proper side arms in the event of any attack. If any Dutchman were to refuse, he would be declared a traitor and an enemy, and would forfeit his life and property.²⁶

By May, 1674, another incident occurred, but this time in Westchester. There, John Sharp, who had been previously banished by the Dutch, suddenly appeared. He was caught with a letter from New England in his possession, which was against the regulations recently proclaimed. In addition, he made statements in Westchester and elsewhere that appeared to foment mutiny and disturbance. After his capture, he was tried and sentenced to banishment for ten years on pain of death if he should return before that time.²⁷

All the preparations, watchfulness, and suspicions of the Dutch authorities proved futile.— not because any revolt among the English inhabitants of New Netherland actually broke out. None did. Nor was there a serious threat of invasion from the New England colonies. The preparations proved futile because of conditions in Europe.

The English war against the Netherlands, started to fulfill a pledge Charles II made to Louis XIV in return for the payment of secret funds, was not popular with Parliament. Therefore, Parliament refused to vote any money necessary to prosecute the war. By 1674, the king recognized that he could no longer carry on the struggle, and signed the treaty of Westminster ending the conflict between the two countries. The Dutch, anxious to have England out of the war so that they could concentrate on their French enemy, were in no mood to exact any penalty from the English. Therefore, by terms of the peace treaty, New Netherland was returned to English rule.

It took some time before the actual transfer of power took place, however. It was in this transition period that Thomas Hunt, Jr., who had been banished shortly after the Dutch reconquest and allowed back only at the insistence of his father, attempted his revenge. On November 5, 1674, he and five or six others rode into the town of New Harlem, bothering several of the Dutch inhabitants. They demanded drink for themselves and oats for their horses, and, if the inhabitants did not have oats, they declared they would take wheat and peas. They identified themselves as the king's soldiers. Each person who they approached in this threatening manner, however, refused to be extorted, and Hunt and his companions finally had to leave empty-handed. The residents complained to Governor-general Colve, who held an inquiry on November 7th, but no action could be taken at that time. On November 10, 1674, Anthony Colve turned control of the province over to Edmund Andros, who had been appointed governor by the duke of York.²⁸ The Dutch tricolor was lowered at the fort for the second and last time, and the problems of those living in the Bronx area would have to be solved again under English rule.

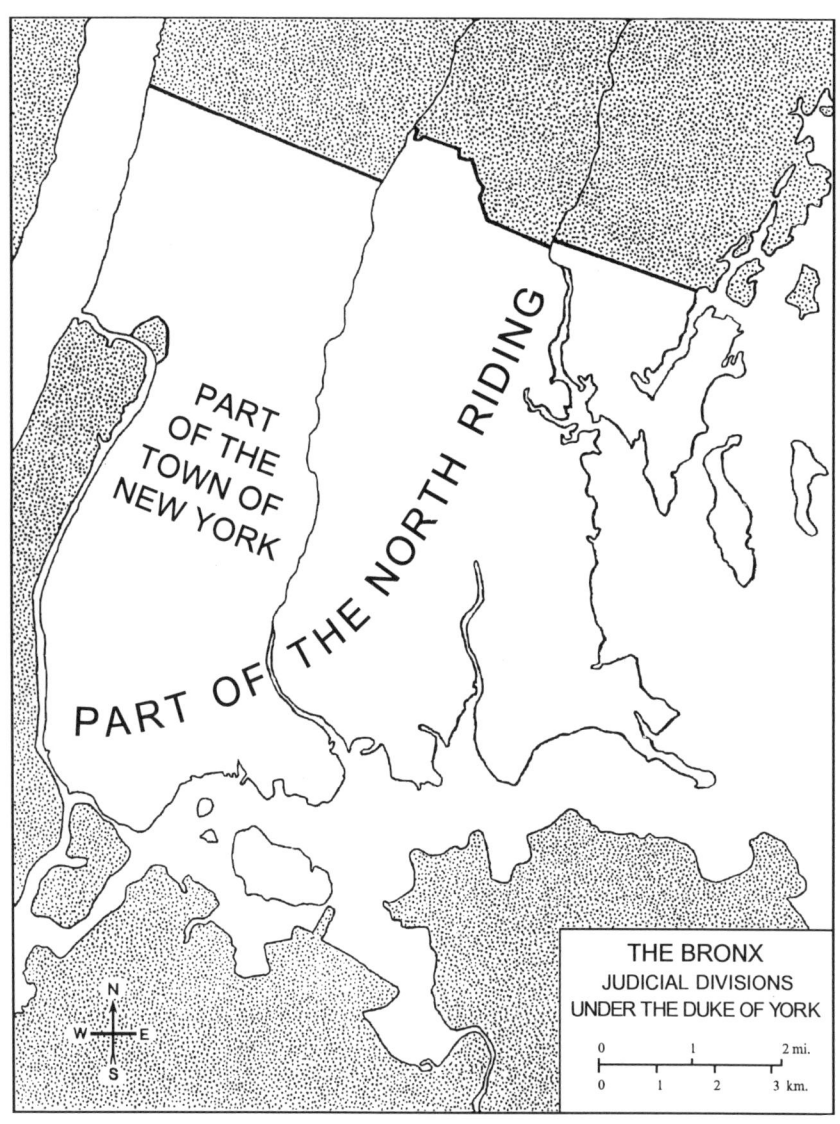

CHAPTER VIII

FROM RIDING TO COUNTY

1675 TO 1683

With the resumption of power by the duke of York, conditions in the colony returned to where they had been before the Dutch interlude. In fact, Edmund Andros, who the duke appointed governor, confirmed all the owners in possession of their property as one of his first acts.[1] The return of English authority also meant the return of English methods of administration, and once again the area that would one day become The Bronx was divided, with John Archer's manor of Fordham placed under the general jurisdiction of the city of New York, while the remainder of the territory became connected to Long Island in the North Riding of Yorkshire centered at Jamaica.

The two mainland towns in the riding, Westchester and Eastchester, began to grow and develop slowly in the years following the return of the English. In Westchester, this growth manifested itself in a decision taken in 1677 to erect a bridge and wooden causeway from the center of the village across Westchester Creek and over the marshlands to Throggs Neck. While the bridge over the creek was to be maintained by an assessment on all those who paid the country rate in the town, the causeway was to be maintained by those who owned fields in Throggs Neck.[2] The causeway quickly became a main artery of commerce within the town. Brush and timber derived from clearing the fields were taken to the center of the village, either for use there or for transshipment to the city of New York. Unfortunately, a number of inhabitants simply tied the timber or brush to a horse or ox and dragged the bundle across the causeway. Since it was made of wood, the constant abrasion caused heavy damage. To halt this practice, in July, 1679, the town court, with John Pell presiding and the town's constable and overseers in attendance, decreed that anyone who brought brush or timber over the causeway without using a sled or a cart was liable to a fine of five shillings.[3]

Westchester also made a step toward taming the wilderness that surrounded it by trying to exterminate the wolf population. Early in 1680, following an order of the colony's Court of Assizes in October, 1676, the town meeting ordered William Barnes, John Hunt, and Samuel Well to build and maintain wolf pits for three years. In return, they would receive twenty shillings for building the pits and ten shillings for each wolf caught and presented to the town constable.[4]

The inhabitants also took a step toward reconstructing civilized life as they knew it by establishing a tavern. At a town meeting held in July, 1681, with John Pell presiding, the inhabitants chose John Hunt to operate the tavern, requesting the justices of the riding to license him for one year. The town also decreed that Hunt could sell beer at two pence per quart (just under one liter) and rum at three pence per gill (slightly above one-tenth of a liter). No one else would have the right to sell rum without Hunt's permission, but in return, Hunt would have to take grain from the farmers in the town at the current price,[5] since cash was so scarce. The tavern, of course, would provide the people with a place to congregate after a long day's work, to relax, and to discuss the issues of the day. In time, it would also provide them with a building open to the public where meetings and other events could be held in the absence of a town hall.

The growing town even attracted the attention of members of the clergy. Ever since Westchester was founded in 1654, it lacked a resident clergyman. Marriages could not be solemnized nor baptisms recorded without the presence of a clergyman. Since most of the inhabitants of Westchester came from New England, or from the towns on Long Island established by New Englanders, it would be expected that they would seek a Puritan minister to officiate at religious functions. A handful of the inhabitants had become Quakers,[6] who did not depend upon a minister, but the others hoped that one would take up residence and stay. None did so, but at least

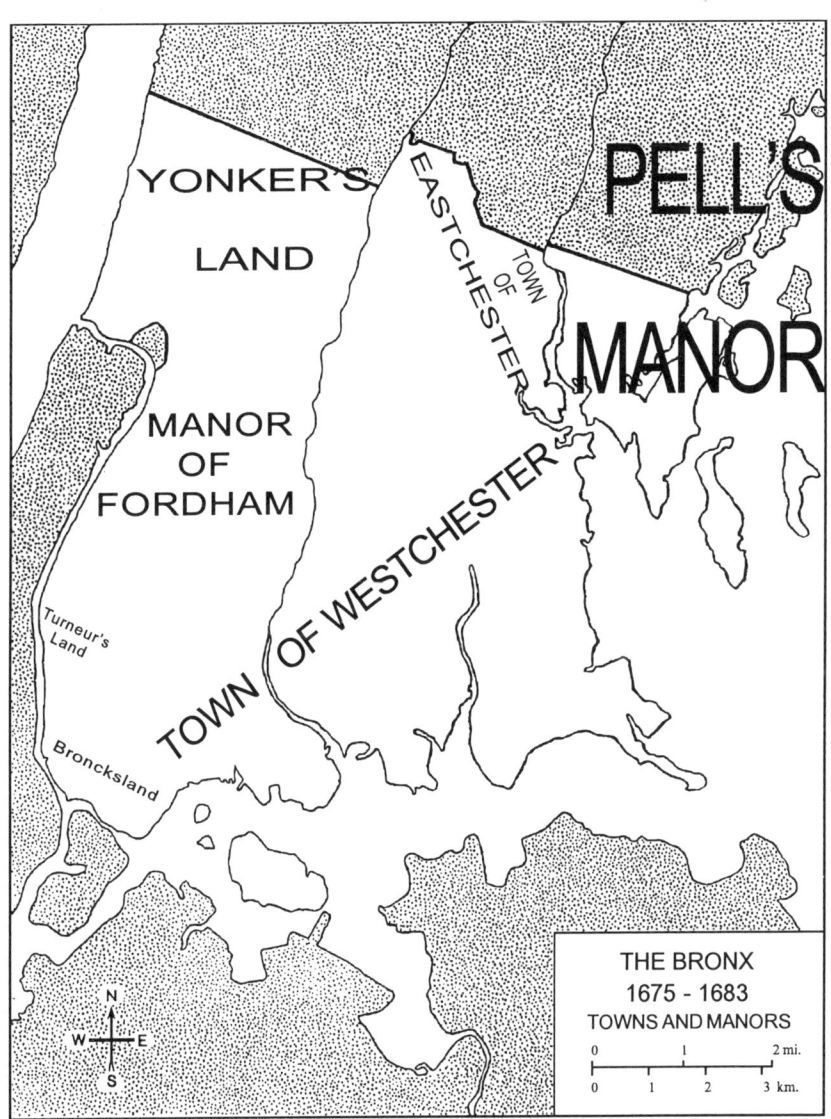

two did come to visit.

In the summer of 1674, four months before the English resumed control of New York, the Reverend Ezekiel Fogg was noted as being in Westchester, and he was there again in the summer of 1676.[7] It was not until October, 1680, however, that another minister, Morgan Jones of Newtown on Long Island, visited the village by Westchester Creek. Several of the town's inhabitants turned out to have marriages and baptisms performed. Some of those baptized had already passed their young childhood. For instance, Ann Wood, the daughter of Consider Wood, was sixteen years old when the Reverend Jones baptized her, and Miles Oakley's eldest son, who was also baptized during Jones's visit, was eleven.[8] Morgan Jones remained in Westchester through the winter, but he never did take up a permanent residence on the mainland.

This fact did not deter the residents of neighboring Eastchester from trying to entice each of these ministers into establishing his permanent home in their town. In early August, 1676, word reached Eastchester that the Reverend Ezekiel Fogg had expressed a desire to live in that town, and the people voted to send a delegation to Westchester to invite him formally. At the same time, Richard Shute was chosen by the town to go to Governor Andros to confirm Fogg as Eastchester's minister and to request permission to build a chapel. Shute was also to request the governor to free his town from making any payment toward building a church in Westchester.[9] This effort came to nothing. The Eastchester inhabitants changed tactics and attempted to join with the people of Westchester in September, 1677, to attract another minister. Eastchester was willing to offer £40 a year, a house and some land,[10] but nothing came of this effort either. Despite this attempt at cooperation, when Morgan Jones appeared in Eastchester in December, 1680, two months after he had first arrived in Westchester, the townsmen tried to entice him to stay among them as a permanent minister by making him an offer of £40 a year and a good living.[11] It did not work. Neither did the maneuver of October, 1683, inviting him to the town to be a schoolmaster.[12]

The inhabitants of Eastchester were also busy trying to expand the activities of their town in areas other than religion, and, in many cases, meeting the same difficulties. As far back as 1671, the town permitted John Jackson to build a grist mill and to operate it under an agreement.[13] In March, 1678, however, by a majority vote in the town meeting, the people chose to abrogate this agreement.[14] Somebody else had to be found to run the mill, and, in early July,

1679, they believed they had found a man willing to perform not only that function, but also to be the town blacksmith. (John Embree, who had borrowed £22 raised among the townsmen to take the position of blacksmith in 1676, evidently had departed from Eastchester.) Will Haiden, Philip Pinckney, Samuel Drake, and Richard Shute were chosen to write to John Taylor, an established smith, inviting him to come to Eastchester to practice his trade.[15] In March, 1680, the town granted him three acres (1.2 hectares) of upland for his home lot,[16] and he placed his mark on an agreement to also operate the mill. Taylor agreed to grind grain on a first come-first served basis, except in periods of drought, when there would be insufficient water for the mill to operate. In that case, only the inhabitants of Eastchester would be served. In return, Taylor would receive a sixteenth of the wheat he ground, and a twelfth of the corn. He also agreed to pay John Jackson £28, which Will Haiden, on behalf of the town, promised him in compensation for the abrogation of the earlier agreement.[17] Nevertheless, John Taylor had second thoughts about the venture, for, in November, 1680, the Eastchester inhabitants chose John Tomkins to go to his smithy to see him and to get from him in writing a statement whether or not he would carry out his part of the agreement.[18] Taylor refused to give such a statement, and, in early December, Samuel Goding was given permission to buy the mill.[19]

Although Eastchester had difficulty in obtaining someone to operate its mill, others with occupations useful to the town arrived with little fanfare and were welcomed by the community. In November, 1680, Thomas Sigmund, a tailor, was granted three acres (1.2 hectares) of land on condition that he build a home and live there for three years, or else he had to return the land to the town. The terms were no different from those afforded others who were granted land by the town meeting the same day,[20] but the community could now count a tailor among its inhabitants.

An inducement was still needed to attract a blacksmith. In April, 1682, Gabriel Lynch was offered a piece of upland if he practiced as a blacksmith. He may not have done so, for, in early December, 1682, the town voted to grant the usual three acres (1.2 hectares) to encourage Thomas Smith to carry on the same trade on condition that the land would revert to the town if he should leave. Otherwise, it would belong to his heirs forever.[21] On the same day, land was also granted to James Wright if he would carry on his trade as a boatman.[22]

Although Eastchester seems to have been more advanced than Westchester in thinking of ways to attract people to the community to fill specific needs, in one way, the people of that town were behind. It was only in March, 1683, that the inhabitants at a town meeting went on record establishing a tavern, and that was two years after their neighbors in Westchester had done so. Moses Hoit was chosen as tavernkeeper.[23]

This slow, peaceful development was interrupted by an event that struck terror in the hearts of the settlers of the area. In neighboring New England, the spread of towns and cultivated farms encroached on the hunting grounds of the Indians there and eventually sparked an Indian uprising led by a chief whom the English called King Philip. This nearly year-long war broke out in the summer of 1675, reached a peak of fury in the fall of that year, and finally ended before the summer of 1676 with the death of King Philip. For New England, it proved to be the most highly destructive war of the colonial era.

Because the mainland of the North Riding was so close to the scene of war, and since the manor of Fordham abutted the North Riding, the inhabitants of the area were justifiably alarmed. After all, there was no assurance that the war would not spread into the colony of New York. There was also no guarantee that the Indians living in the midst of the settlers would not suddenly rise up and massacre everyone in sight as other tribes were doing in the Massachusetts, Connecticut, and Plymouth colonies.

The alarm was first heard in Westchester in the summer of 1675, when Captain Richard Osborne, commander of the town's militia, ordered his men to assemble at his house because of the danger of a possible Indian attack. Thomas Seabrooke, one of the men who answered the call, loaded himself up with ammunition, opened the door of his farmhouse on Castle Hill, and said to his wife, "Wife I am going out. I know not but I may be knocked on the head. If I never come again I give all I have to thee. . . ." Seabrooke then turned to John Clarke, who was a guest in his house and who had witnessed the scene, and said to him, "Pray take notice of what I say." Luckily for Seabrooke, his wife, and everyone else, the alarm turned out to be groundless,[24] but the threat of an Indian attack on any settlement remained very real.

Indian depredations in New England were beginning to mount to the point where most of the towns of western Massachusetts and Plymouth would soon be laid waste, devoid of people. In the area that would one day become The Bronx, measures for defense seemed imperative, and protection was stepped up. Fortifications were begun by order of Governor Andros. In Eastchester, the inhabitants voted at a public meeting that Will Haiden's house be fitted out as a fort, and John Jackson, Richard Headley, and Samuel Drake, Jr., were chosen to stake out the place for the fortification. Under the supervision of John Jackson and Richard Shute, the men who built it were paid 2s. 6d. per day. Those who provided three cattle to do the carting were paid 6s. per day, and those who provided two oxen got 5s. per day.[25]

John Archer, who took control of his manor of Fordham once again, was similarly busy erecting fortifications there, and demanded that the four families living on the Yonker's land contribute their labor to the cause. This, they found both obnoxious and dangerous. They lived more than a mile (over one and a half kilometers) from the village of Fordham, and felt that, in case of an Indian attack, if they relied on the fortifications there, the long journey would unnecessarily expose them to danger. Instead, they petitioned the governor to be allowed to stay in their area and to build their own defenses around a wooden blockhouse that was already there. Governor Andros, noting that they were vigilant and kept watch on all occasions, excused them from participation in building the fort at Fordham.[26]

Perhaps for a similar reason, Governor Andros appointed Will Haiden of Eastchester a lieutenant in the militia and informed Captain Richard Osborne of Westchester that, because the two towns were so far apart, for the time being, the men would be able to train within the confines of their own towns. Both units, however, were still to be part of Osborne's company, and were to support each other if war should break out.[27]

Fortunately, that contingency did not have to be faced because of the prudence and good sense of Governor Andros in his dealings with the Indians, the responsibility for which was partly derived from the excellent advice of John Pell. In the debate in the Court of Assizes over selling powder and shot to the Indians, Pell, who, as a justice of the riding was a member of the Court, counseled a moderate approach,[28] and the governor was careful not to provoke the neighboring tribes as the Dutch director-general, William Kieft, did thirty-two years earlier. In accord with this policy, the Court urged all magistrates in the colony to do justice to the Indians on an equal basis with the Christians.[29]

In the summer of 1675, when the war first broke out, the governor and his Council were, understandably, concerned about the Indians, members of the Weckquasgeek tribe, on Pell's manor. The members of the Council thought that the holding of Indian hostages would be the best course[30] and unless they agreed to send hostages to New York City, John Pell was ordered to make a daily account of those living at the manor.

By early September, 1675, as a precaution, the inhabitants of Eastchester agreed that two of their number would act as watchmen every night, walking to all the houses of the town.[31] That month, at the height of the war in New England, Andros sent an armed sloop out into Long Island Sound to intercept any hostile Indians who might wish to cross that body of water. At the same time, he set out in his pinnace to see, firsthand, the Indians at Pell's manor. He saw no danger coming from them, and ordered that their guns be returned to them because of their good behavior and their need to hunt for meat.[32]

Yet, by harvest time, mid-October, 1675, the Court of Assizes, reflecting the general concern, issued an order to all of the Weckquasgeek Indians living in Pell's manor to move, earlier than they expected, to their usual winter quarters on Manhattan Island near Hell Gate, probably to isolate them from contact with New England. This evacuation order, however, did not apply to the part of the tribe which lived in Yonkers on the property of Frederick Philipse. They were permitted to load their canoes and peaceably pass along the shore, but they were not permitted to leave the jurisdiction of the New York colony. All their other canoes on Long Island Sound were to be brought to the nearest towns to be laid up and secured by the constables. Those that were not, were to be destroyed when found.[33] Ten days later, the order was put into effect by a directive from the governor's Council.[34] In their haste to evacuate the area, the Weckquasgeeks left behind on Pell's land about half of all their grain.

By November, the Court of Assizes also ordered a halt to all trading with the Indians in their villages to forestall any incident that could lead to war. Obviously the exchange of Indian goods for liquor was uppermost in the Court's mind, since its sale to Indians "in Yorkshire upon Long Island and Dependencies" was specifically prohibited. As an additional precaution, no powder or lead was allowed to be sold to them except by consent of the town's constable. If all efforts to prevent war failed, the Court also ordered that additional rates be levied according to the occasion to finance a conflict if it did occur.[35]

By February, 1676, members of the colonial government began to distrust the part of the tribe which lived in Yonkers on the property of Frederick Philipse, thinking that they might be willing to join King Philip. Therefore, in early March, the Council, in the absence of the governor, who was in Albany, in polite language, allowed those Weckquasgeeks to move to the northern part of Manhattan near Spuyten Duyvil Creek, admonishing them to behave well in order to be assured of the government's protection.[36]

In early April, two of the tribe's sachems met with the Council, expressing indignation that anyone could believe that they would want to join King Philip when all they wanted to do was some oystering in Spuyten Duyvil Creek. They promised to give the governor any notice of a disturbance in return for receiving notice from the government of any intention it might uncover to harm them. The two sachems then requested permission to send some young men in canoes to John Pell's land to retrieve the grain they left there, and to go to Greenwich in Connecticut to fetch six members — old men, women, and boys, who had been left behind. This matter was left in abeyance until Governor Andros returned from Albany.[37] Upon his return, he offered the tribe a permanent residence on a neck of land of their choosing on either Manhattan or Long Island, which they rejected.[38]

By May, 1676, King Philip was dead and the war in New England was over. The Indians returned to Pell's manor, but the order forbidding them to use their canoes remained in effect. They complained to John Pell, noting that it was unfair to deny them their canoes when they had always been at peace, while the Indians living near Stamford in Connecticut had been permitted to keep theirs despite the fact that they were in a war zone. Their concern was communicated to the governor and his Council, which, in turn, ordered Pell to inquire about the truth of the Indians' allegations. Meanwhile, they were permitted to use three canoes, and if Pell found that what the Indians alleged was true, they could have all their canoes back.[39] With the reduction of tension at the end of the war, the Indians probably would have received them.

The coming of peace, welcome though it was, also focused the attention of the colonial authorities on the state of defense of New York City. It was thought prudent to strengthen the fort there by building a wooden stockade, with the material to be supplied from the nearby towns. The trees were to be fashioned within each town to a uniform shape of sixteen feet (about 4.75 meters) high and seven inches (just under 18 centimeters) thick. The men of Eastchester agreed to hire a wagon to carry down their share, but Westchester was promised boats from the city to transport its stockades. Unfortunately, all the boats and sloops around New York City were engaged, and the men of Westchester were advised to place the stockades on rafts and float them down to New York. This task of providing material for the city's fortifications was not completed soon, for as late as 1678 Westchester was charged with providing 500 of the 3,000 stockades needed that year.[40]

Lumbering, however, was not the main preoccupation of the two towns. The raising of livestock was, and cattle was the major concern. In Westchester, in 1675, a total of 340 head of cattle were counted, while there were only 63 oxen (which, obviously, were not considered by the inhabitants to be in the same class as the other bovines, even though they were castrated bulls), 88 pigs, and 64 sheep. Of the land in the town, only 238 acres (about 95 hectares) were devoted to the cultivation of crops, while 494 acres (over 197 hectares) were set aside for grazing. Although the cattle herds were increasing generally each year (there were nine more one-year old cows than two-year olds), none of the people of the town could be considered wealthy. Robert Manning owned 26 cows, the largest number among the townspeople, grazing them on his 60 acres (about 24 hectares) of meadowland, the largest grazing pasture in Westchester. There were not as many horses. Most families owned only one, and some had none at all.

In many ways, Eastchester was not as well off as Westchester. Although it had about half the population of its neighbor, Eastchester held only 40% of the number of cattle (135 as opposed to 340), which were grazed on land only about 30% the size of Westchester's meadowland. The Eastchester inhabitants, however, had more than their share of pigs (about 69% that of Westchester) and oxen (about 58%). There were no sheep grazing in Eastchester, but this was not as worrisome as the steady decline in the cattle population. Each year for the previous three years fewer cows gave birth, declining from 27 births in 1672 to 19 in 1674.[41]

Obviously, the people of Eastchester had to make a special effort to insure the survival of their herds. In early May, 1675, Will Haiden and Moses Hoit agreed to maintain a sufficient number of bulls to service the town's cows for a period of seven years, receiving in return sixpence for every calf born. This arrangement, however, must have led to disagreements, for, almost one year later, it was declared void. Instead, the town agreed to keep one three-year old and one four-year old bull to be paid by an assessment on the owners of the cows and two-year old heifers.[42]

Although Eastchester had problems, Westchester experienced steady growth. In the eight years from 1675 to 1683, the population of the town had grown only slightly. Yet, there was an appreciable increase in the amount of livestock. In those eight years, there was a 14% increase in cattle (388 in 1683 as opposed to 340 in 1675), a 12% increase in oxen (71 as opposed to 63) and a whopping 84% increase in the number of pigs (162 as opposed to 88). To accommodate this, 10% more of the land was devoted to grazing (543.5 acres, or just over 217 hectares). The most significant portent of the future, however, was the extremely rapid increase in the number of sheep, a tremendous 120%, or 141 in 1683 as opposed to only 64 in 1675. Moreover, four inhabitants, William Richardson, Edward Waters, John Palmer, and Richard Osborne, had prospered to the point where they each used an extra man in order to operate their farms.[43]

Yet, all was not merely peaceful growth in the territory that would one day become The Bronx. Throughout the years after the Dutch interlude, there were many instances of the proprietors of great landed estates trying to add to their holdings at the expense of their neighbors. The court records of the period are filled with complaints and countersuits concerning proper boundaries, and a number of cases involved a resumption of old grievances.

Such, certainly, was the case with John Archer. It will be recalled that Governor Edmund Andros had confirmed all the owners in possession of their property, and Archer, who had lost so much under the Dutch, was eager to resume his proprietorship of the manor of Fordham. Of course, this included the resurrection of the court at the manor that would preclude anyone from suing him in another court, except the Court of Assizes. By the end of 1675, Matthias Nicolls, the governor's secretary, wrote to Richard Cage, the constable of Fordham, giving permission to hold the court at Archer's house.[44]

As could be expected, the running feud between John Archer and Johannes Verveelen, the ferryman at Spuyten Duyvil, was resumed. Verveelen, who insisted that his property was not subject to the jurisdiction of Fordham and its court, complained to the

Mayor's Court in New York City in August, 1675, that John Archer was cutting hay on his land. The Court appointed arbitrators, who decided in favor of Verveelen. Archer, of course, did not recognize the jurisdiction of the Mayor's Court, and simply carried off four loads of his rival's hay. Undeterred, Verveelen appealed to the Court of Assizes, which heard the case in October, 1675. After the Court read Archer's patent to Fordham, and agreed that Paparinemin was his, it then read Verveelen's complaint and decided that Archer had stolen Verveelen's hay. It ruled that the order of the Mayor's Court should stand until any "inconvenience" appeared.[45]

Archer's jurisdiction over Paparinemin was, therefore, affirmed by the Court of Assizes, but the proprietor of Fordham refused to follow the orders of that court in satisfying Verveelen. In fact, in January, 1676, Archer and some confederates went once again to the ferryman's house, and, by force of arms, took 980 guilder's worth of wheat, merchandise, and household goods. Verveelen took the matter to the court at the manor, but lost his case there. He then tried to appeal once again to the Court of Assizes, but he was permitted to do so only upon giving security, which he probably could not do. Therefore, he decided to appeal to the Mayor's Court, complaining of Archer's complete disregard for Governor Lovelace's grant of Paparinemin to him, of the orders of the Court of Assizes, and of the award of the arbitrators in the original case. Since Fordham was now firmly out of the jurisdiction of that court, Verveelen's appeal was hopeless.[46]

Johannes Verveelen was not John Archer's only problem. In 1675, the Fordham proprietor accused David Demarest of occupying a piece of meadow near Spuyten Duyvil belonging to his manor. The case came before the Court of Assizes in October, each party represented by counsel. Archer's attorney submitted a declaration by which Demarest was ordered off the land. The defendant's attorney countered by denying that the declaration had any force, whereupon Archer's Indian deed, a certificate from the Indians certifying that the property belonged to Archer, and the patent to Fordham were produced. After other papers and documents were read, the case was submitted to a jury, which delivered its verdict the following day. The jury decided in Archer's favor, with Demarest charged with paying the court costs. The attorney for the defendant immediately announced his intention to appeal the judgment. When the appeal came before the Court of Assizes, now sitting as a court of equity rather than as a court of common law, it was decided that

Demarest's case had enough merit to have the previous judgment overruled.⁴⁷ David Demarest thus remained in occupation of the meadow claimed by John Archer.

The lack of ready funds also plagued Fordham's proprietor. In March, 1676, Archer hired John West as his steward at Fordham, promising to pay him £3 for each court session held there. West did hold one session and, in addition, represented Archer in cases held at the Court of Sessions of both the North Riding and the West Riding, for which he was to be paid £1 9s. 6d. Thus, West was entitled to a total of £4 9s. 6d. What he received was 50 sticks of firewood worth only 3s. 6d. He demanded the balance from Archer, who refused to pay. West, therefore, brought suit against him in the Mayor's Court in September, 1678, a gesture that was destined to be futile.⁴⁸

A similar fate met the suit by Hartman Wessells, a physician in New York City. In February, 1677, Archer apprenticed his son, John Archer, Jr., to Wessells for six years. Wessells treated the boy cruelly and, before a year had passed, Archer took his son back. Since this was a violation of the contract, the physician sued the Fordham proprietor in New York City's Mayor's Court, insisting that the damage done amounted to £40. Archer, in response, complained to the governor about Wessells's behavior toward his son, insisting that the Mayor's Court had no jurisdiction over him. Consequently, the judgment of the Mayor's Court was never carried out.⁴⁹

Despite these victories, the incidental costs involving his numerous court cases and appeals, the costs of building the defenses of Fordham during the scare caused by King Philip's War, and the general costs of operating the manor impelled John Archer to seek out Cornelis Steenwyck once again to mortgage his property. In early December, 1676, Steenwyck agreed to lend Archer 24,000 guilders seawan at six percent interest payable each year for seven years. Thus, by December, 1683, the entire principal sum had to be returned, the interest having been paid yearly. Steenwyck, knowing Archer's financial plight and his ability in avoiding prosecution, probably insisted that the mortgage take the form of a sale of Fordham to himself and his heirs, returnable to Archer once the debt had been fully paid. In fact, Archer had to deliver to Steenwyck the deed to Fordham before the mortgage document would be signed.⁵⁰

John Archer was now burdened with the additional imperative of finding 1,400 guilders (or its equivalent) each year for the following seven years to pay off the interest payments, and of amassing 24,000 guilders (or its equivalent) by 1683. No doubt this was one of the main reasons he took the post of sheriff of New York in 1679. As sheriff, he would receive fees for a variety of services, and these funds could go toward paying his debts. He was recommended for appointment to the post by Thomas Ashton, his predecessor. Ashton, however, had several actions in progress when he stepped down, and he came to an agreement with Archer about collecting the fees that were still due him.[51]

The need for large sums caused Archer to change his policy in regard to the occupation of land on his manor. Previously, he had been interested solely in renting sections of the land to tenants, retaining title to the property at all times. Starting in 1678, however, he began selling farms. With the consent of Cornelis Steenwyck, seven people purchased land in Fordham. Typically, the farms were not compact pieces of property, but scattered sites of upland, meadow, and marshland. Thomas Statham bought 103 acres (a bit more than 41 hectares) of land near the Bronx River that already had a house and other buildings, an orchard, and fenced fields, as well as a small parcel of salt meadow near Spuyten Duyvil, and a small portion of the fresh meadow near the village of Fordham. Similarly, Roger Barton purchased 102 acres (almost 41 hectares) near Statham's property by the Bronx River, as well as pieces of salt and fresh meadows. On the other hand, Jonathan Hudson took six acres (almost 2.5 hectares) of upland in the planting field that was formerly the farm rented by Richard Cage, once Archer's constable, together with ten acres (about four hectares) near a swamp, a share of the salt meadow and of the fresh meadow, and two home lots, each of which had a house. Similar land divisions were made for John Concklin, Jeremiah Cannife, William Jones, and Nathaniel Stevens.[52]

In January, 1679, Archer finally dealt a major blow to his old nemesis, Johannes Verveelen. He sold Paparinemin to the government of the colony of New York. Archer specified in the deed that it was still to be considered part of his manor of Fordham, and the colony was to pay him one fat capon every New Year's Day. All the title, right, and interest in the island, however, was now in the hands of the colonial government.[53]

Verveelen, having lost the title to the island to John Archer, and then seeing that title transferred to the colony, was now faced with the loss of his ferry. One year after the purchase, the governor's Council voted to view Spuyten Duyvil to see if a bridge could be erected there. The ferryman's license would run out in November,

1680, and a bridge would be a more useful aid to travel and commerce than a ferry. Indeed, when the license expired, it was not renewed. Verveelen probably continued to operate his ferry anyway, and, in January, 1681, he got Governor Andros to officially extend his ferry privileges for another seven years.[54]

To the north, the families living in Yonkers experienced only one incident in which their land titles were contested, and this came at the hands of the Weckquasgeek Indians. In early August, 1676, a few Weckquasgeeks appeared before Governor Andros saying that they had not been paid for the Yonker's land. According to the Indian reckoning, this may have been so, but it was not so according to the English view. The patent to Hugh O'Neale and the deed from Elias Doughty were produced. After viewing these two documents, the Indians agreed that they had been paid for the land.[55] Their readiness to see things the English way was surely influenced by their dependency on the colonial government for protection.

While the dispute over the Yonker's land was easily settled the threat to the town of Eastchester was not. In the years following the Dutch interlude, its boundaries were threatened not only by the larger town of Westchester, as in the past, but also by John Pell. The dispute with Pell concerned the placement of fences that marked the boundary line between Pell's manor and Eastchester. In June, 1675, the Court of Sessions of the North Riding attempted to settle the dispute by ordering three people to view the boundary and to make a judgment of the best way to secure both sides of the line. Eight days after this decision was made, the Eastchester inhabitants chose Philip Pinckney and Samuel Drake to negotiate with the three men chosen by the Court to view the Hutchinson River, the boundary between Pell's land and the town. Evidently, the fence that Pell erected did not please the Eastchester inhabitants, and they chose Samuel Drake, Sr., to appear on behalf of the town at the Court of Sessions in December. An amicable agreement was reached by early December, 1676, however. This agreement specified the place where the people of the town would join their fence with Pell's. It also stipulated that if any cattle or pigs from Eastchester jumped the fence, the animals would be placed in a pound, and the owners would pay the cost of poundage and any damage done to the inhabitants of Pell's lands. Similar arrangements were made if a cow or pig jumped the fence into Eastchester.[56]

This agreement did not signal the end to the bickering between the town and Pell, however. By February, 1677, Pell accused

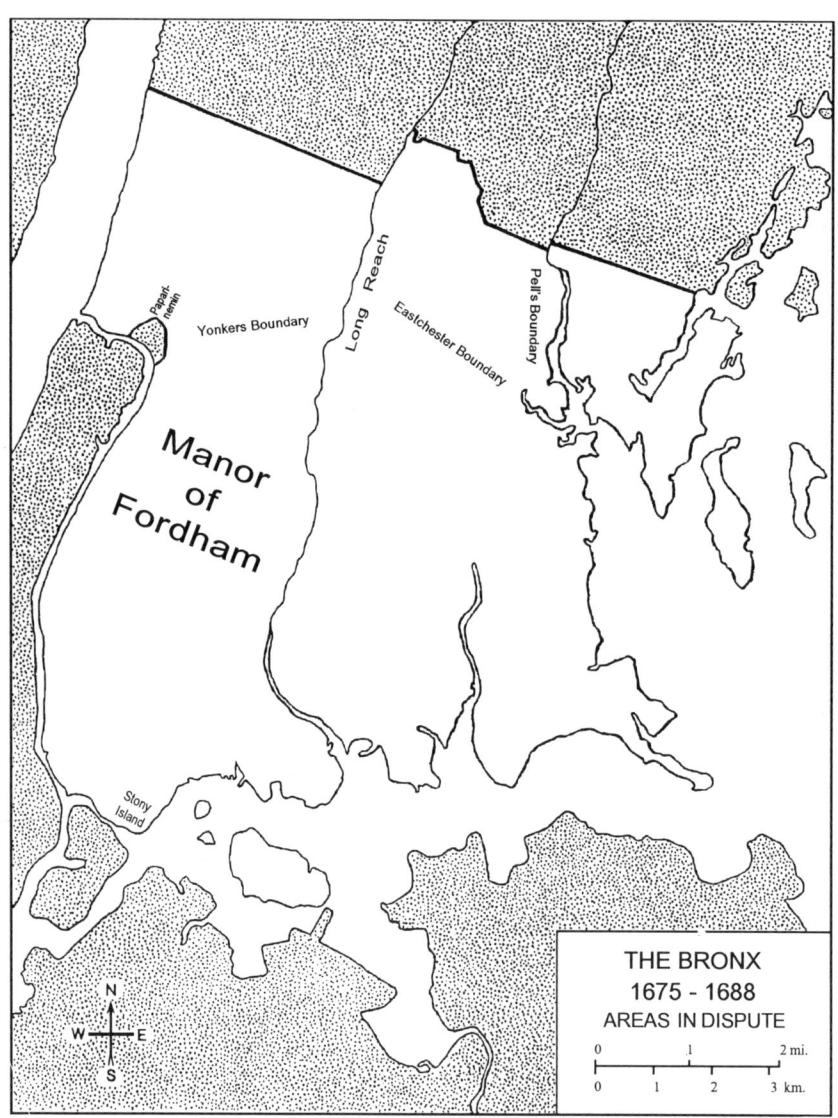

THE BRONX
1675 - 1688
AREAS IN DISPUTE

Eastchester of encroaching on his land, and he wrote a letter to the inhabitants of the town to that end. The people, on reading the letter in early March, were insulted enough to appoint Will Haiden and Richard Shute to sail to Pell's home and have the communication burned before his eyes. By early November, a meeting was arranged with both Pell and Governor Andros. Philip Pinckney was chosen to represent the town. The governor was to decide any differences over the boundary between the two patents.[57] The governor's award was considered final.

The encroachments of the people of Westchester on what the Eastchester inhabitants considered their own land continued, however. A dispute arose with Thomas Mullineux of Westchester over the ownership of a strip of land at the boundary between the two towns. In September, 1680, Mullineux began to fence in some of that land, and the Eastchester inhabitants voted to send Nathaniel Tomkins, the town's constable that year, and Philip Pinckney to Governor Andros to have him settle the matter. Eastchester received the governor's support, and, in the following month, the constable was sent to Mullineux to warn him to desist from erecting his fence. At the same time, Will Haiden and Richard Headley went with him to stake out the property into sections on behalf of the town of Eastchester.[58] The town's residents probably believed their occupation of the disputed territory would prevent any future incident. Indeed, in April of the following year, they agreed that if John Pell and the Westchester men came to run a boundary line or to molest them in the enjoyment of their land, they would all go to warn them to desist.[59] Two weeks later, arrangements were made to meet with Pell at Moses Hoit's house to determine the boundaries of the Eastchester patent, with Will Haiden and Philip Pinckney representing the interests of their fellow Eastchester townsmen.[60] The tactic seems to have worked.

If Eastchester was constantly harassed in validating its title to its land, the same might be also be said of Colonel Lewis Morris, who, at the time the Dutch interlude ended, was busy trying to gather the scattered inheritance of his nephew, also called Lewis, and to secure title to Broncksland. Morris's most difficult task was to retake possession of the slaves who had been sold under the authority of the Dutch government.

One instance was the case of Bess, who, Morris claimed, he had given to his brother's wife when they all had been in Barbados. While all of Colonel Morris's property was forfeit by decree of the Dutch governor-general, the orphan nephew of Colonel Morris had the right to inherit one-third of his parent's estate over and above the household goods, clothing, plate, and other property. If Colonel Morris's contention were correct, then Bess was the property of his nephew. Bess, however, was included in the number of slaves sold under Dutch authority as being part of Lewis Morris's confiscated estate, and she became the property of Peter Aldrich. Walter Webley, the colonel's brother-in-law and the trustee of the orphan's father's estate, sued Aldrich in the Mayor's Court in New York City in 1675 for the return of the slave. The facts of the case were clear, and the jury found for Webley, ordering Aldrich to pay the court costs. Aldrich immediately appealed to the Court of Assizes, but it did him no good there, since that court unanimously decided that Bess had to be returned.[61]

A case involving Anthony and Susannah, two other slaves, was more difficult to resolve. As with Bess, Anthony and Susannah were among the slaves at Broncksland sold when Lewis Morris's estate was confiscated by the Dutch. They wound up in Esopus, the property of Louis DuBois, who purchased them at public auction conducted by the sheriff there. In the spring, just after the English regained control of the colony, both slaves were with DuBois when they escaped to the woods. They managed to cross to the east side of the Hudson River, where they asked some Indians for the direction to take to return to Colonel Morris's residence. As soon as DuBois learned where they were, he hired Gabriel Minville, a leading attorney in New York City, to ask Morris for their return. When Morris refused, DuBois instituted suit in the Mayor's Court in New York City, saying that Lewis Morris was detaining his slaves contrary to law, and that, since he had lost their services during the harvest, he was entitled to £30 in damages. The Court found in DuBois's favor.

Since Broncksland was not in the jurisdiction of New York City, however, but within the North Riding, Morris continued to hold both Anthony and Susannah. Thirteen months after their escape, DuBois finally had a hearing before the Court of Sessions of the North Riding, which, to Morris's dismay, confirmed the judgment of the Mayor's Court. Morris then appealed to the Court of Assizes. When it met in October, however, it ruled that the case was not to be judged because so much time had elapsed. In defiance of this ruling, Morris still refused to return the two slaves.

In January, 1680, the case was brought before the Mayor's Court once again, and, as in the first instance, Morris was ordered to deliver the two slaves to Louis DuBois and to pay the damages. Undeterred, Morris appealed to the governor and his Council, requesting permission to take the case to the Court of Assizes once again, but this time as a case in equity, rather than one of common law. The Council hesitated. Its members wanted to hear the case for themselves, and wanted to hear both parties to the dispute and the two slaves before allowing the appeal. Obviously, the councilors did find some merits in Morris's case because an appeal was allowed, and, in October, 1680, the Court of Assizes reversed the decision of the Mayor's Court, saying that Morris could keep both Susannah and Anthony, and that DuBois was to pay the court costs.[62]

Lewis Morris, however, was not only interested in recovering the property of his nephew, but also in restoring his own confiscated portion of the estate, especially the land. Soon after the English regained control of New York, Walter Webley, on Morris's behalf, petitioned the governor to add some land to the Morris holdings, specifically the neck of land at the northwestern edge of Broncksland and some land lying between John Archer's house and Spuyten Duyvil Creek. The ostensible reason for this request was that fourteen hands were already working the land, and that, since Colonel Morris was scouring the countryside to discover the scattered slaves, more would be added. Therefore, additional land would be needed to put such large numbers of servants and slaves to work. Moreover, if this land would fall into the possession of others, it could provide shelter for any of those toilers who should run off the Morris estate.[63]

The petition remained unanswered for some time, but, by early April, 1676, Governor Andros was willing to give Lewis Morris some satisfaction. Andros issued a patent to Lewis Morris for all of Broncksland, in which it alleged that the colonel from Barbados was in possession of all of that property originally granted to Jonas Bronck. This assertion placed all of the land in Morris's hands, thus effectively eliminating any title to the property that might have been claimed by his infant orphaned nephew, whose interests he had supposedly been pursuing. Moreover, Andros's patent extended the Morris holdings to include all the adjacent land not included in any other grant. The bounds of the property thus ran up the Harlem River to Daniel Turneur's land, then northward to John Archer's line, eastward to the property of John Richardson and Thomas Hunt of the West Farms of the town of Westchester, then to what was then considered Long Island Sound through the Bronx Kill to the point of beginning. The whole encompassed 1,920 acres (about 768 hectares), for which Morris was to pay to the duke five bushels (a little more than 176 liters) of good winter wheat every year as quit-rent.[64]

In May, 1676, Morris's neighbors at the northwest corner of his property assembled six Indians to sign a deed for the land originally purchased by Daniel Turneur in 1671. The primary reason for this was Turneur's death. His widow, Jacqueline Turneur, and his son, Daniel, Jr., along with the Indians, went to New York City to acknowledge the sale before Governor Andros. The governor was absent, however, and the Indians could not wait for his return, so they made their acknowledgment of sale before four other witnesses. Interestingly, the northern line of the property was stated as running eastward to the Bronx River,[65] which would have interfered with Morris's grant.

Oddly, the clash between the young Daniel Turneur and Colonel Lewis Morris came not over this territory, but over Stony Island, just off the mainland coast near the eastern end of the Bronx Kill. In the summer of 1679, Morris sent at least three of his slaves to the island to cut hay there and to return with the load to his house by canoes. Turneur and Cornelis Laurens Jensen of Harlem, whose cows had been grazing on the island, soon discovered that there was not enough hay left there for the cattle to eat. Turneur and Jensen claimed to have owned the island for sixteen years, carrying the title back to its purchase by Turneur's father and two others in 1663. They demanded £40 in damages. Morris, however, claimed that the island had always been part of Broncksland, and that he had a right to cut hay on his own property. Turneur and Jensen complained to the Mayor's Court at New York City. Morris countered by denying that Court's jurisdiction. It was to no avail, and the Court found for Turneur and Jensen, but assigned damages at only fifty shillings. Nevertheless, Morris sent men to cut hay there the following year, and on Turneur's and Jensen's complaint, the mayor ordered the constable at Harlem to warn Morris. Morris still denied that the Mayor's Court had jurisdiction, and, after the two men appealed to Governor Andros, the colonel replied that he would answer the charges in the Court of Sessions of the North Riding at Jamaica, in whose competence any case involving Broncksland would lie. Consequently, when Turneur tried to cut hay on the island, Morris had him ejected.

At the insistence of Turneur and Jensen, the case came up before the North Riding's Court of Sessions in June, 1683. The two plaintiffs produced the Harlem patent, which specified that Stony Island was in the bounds of that town, and the special patent of 1663 from which they traced their claim. They produced their own witnesses. Adolph Meyer stated that the plaintiff's claim had never been contested for twenty-two years, and that Jensen had cut hay there before the Dutch interlude. Morris countered by claiming that the island did not exist until David Demarest, his own overseer, had dug a ditch in the time of the Dutch interlude, thus creating Stony Island. The jury, however, found for the plaintiffs. Morris's attorney then pled for an arrest of the judgment, which was not only granted, but the verdict was quashed, and the plaintiffs ordered to pay all the court costs.

Undeterred, Turneur, acting alone, appealed to the governor and his Council to be allowed to try the case before the Court of Assizes, asking for damages of £40. Receiving permission, Turneur began his case there in October, 1683. Morris submitted a written reply to the Court, recounting the ownership of the property from the time of Jonas Bronck, contending that he remained in possession from 1668 until the Dutch seized his slaves and the land. At that time, he again contended, the ditch was dug creating the island. He stated that he returned to his property with the peace in 1674, and had his ownership to the land confirmed by Andros's patent of 1676. To enhance his argument, there were witnesses who testified in his favor. Engeltie Burger, who was the widow of Burger Joris, who was an immigrant from Sweden, who had known Jonas Bronck, and who was, in 1683, very old and blind, testified that Bronck had cut hay on the meadow there three times about forty years earlier, that he had built a bridge over the marshland there, and that he had grazed his cattle there. Thomas Hunt, Sr., remembered seeing the fences and the bridge there, and stated that the land was always called Broncksland, and that Stony Island was a new name. Thomas Hunt, Jr., testified that Morris's brother had purchased the land, and that Turneur himself had once shown him a map that included the disputed territory as part of Broncksland. John Archer stated that Harlem received its patent to the land in an underhanded manner, claiming that the Harlemites had obtained Peter Stuyvesant's permission to cut hay there because they had pretended they had no meadow, and that they had proceeded to cut hay until the rightful owners had warned them off. The Fordham proprietor also said that Richard Nicolls had given Harlem the patent to Stony Island without knowing the facts about it. Both Mr. Osborne, Morris's overseer, and

Thomas Waddell stated that they had cut hay on that site under orders from Lewis Morris's deceased brother, and, at that time, there was no ditch there to make it an island. Despite this heavy weight of testimony, the Court of Assizes found for Turneur, ordering Morris to pay £4 15s. 6d. in costs. Morris immediately petitioned for a review of the case by a jury of the neighborhood, which was granted, provided half the jury was from New York, and the other half from Long Island.[66]

It was at this juncture, however, that a significant event occurred that affected not only the future of Stony Island, but all the settlements on the mainland north and east of Manhattan Island. The duke's government of the colony was highly centralized, with the governor's permission needed for many things. Moreover, except for the right of petition, there was no way a farmer or a merchant could exercise any influence on the making of laws or regulations. The farmers at the eastern end of Long Island and the merchants of New York City objected to this, and their objections were becoming ever more vocal as the 1680s wore on.

There is no evidence that the small communities on the mainland had conveyed any such objections to the lack of political expression on the colonial level. Compared to settlements along the Hudson connected with New York City by the great river highway, and the towns on Long Island, which were not far from the city's great sea lanes, Westchester and Eastchester were relatively isolated. The people there were more concerned about the disposition of land within their towns and other local matters than anything else. It is true that at least three people of prominence were living on the mainland. John Archer, with his friendship with Cornelis Steenwyck, a prominent New York City merchant, had risen high enough to be appointed sheriff of New York City. John Pell was a justice of the North Riding, and, as such, had the right to be at all meetings of the riding's Court of Sessions and with the governor and his Council at the Court of Assizes. Lewis Morris, who not only successfully obtained title to Broncksland, but who purchased a tract in New Jersey, had grown prominent enough in 1680 to accompany Governor Andros on a journey across the Hudson to meet with the neighboring governor there to iron out certain differences between the colonies.[67] Significantly, these were the largest landowners in the area, and their properties had among the fewest people of all the nearby settlements.

Yet, from what happened, we can infer that the people living in

Westchester and Eastchester, and probably Pell's manor, Fordham, the Yonker's land, and Broncksland, had found it inconvenient that their area should be divided between the jurisdictions of New York and Jamaica. It is true that the people of Fordham did not find it inconvenient to go down to New York City to press a case against John Archer before the Mayor's Court, despite the fact that they could obtain no satisfaction there. Similarly, the people of Westchester and Eastchester, and most certainly Justice John Pell and Colonel Lewis Morris, had no difficulty proceeding to Jamaica to attend the Court of Sessions. On the other hand, there must have been some feeling, either unexpressed publicly or in documents undiscovered or since destroyed, that if all the settlements on the mainland were placed under the same jurisdiction, the courts would be nearer to them. The closest expression of such a sentiment that exists is Lewis Morris's plea to the Court of Assizes that the case of Stony Island be tried once again, but this time by a jury of his neighbors.

Because of the increasing discontent in his colony, in 1682, the duke of York appointed Colonel Thomas Dongan to replace Edmund Andros as the governor of New York. Dongan, like the duke, was a Catholic, and he was destined to be the first, and only, Catholic ever to serve as governor of the colony. More significantly, the duke instructed the new governor that, with the advice of his council, he should call a representative assembly of all the freeholders to debate and to propose laws for the colony not prejudicial to the duke's rights. The duke pledged to agree to such laws.[68]

Dongan arrived to take up his post, landing in August, 1683, at the eastern end of Long Island, where he observed the discontent firsthand. Shortly thereafter, he issued writs to the sheriffs in the colony to summon the freeholders to choose their representatives.[69] In the North Riding, each town meeting chose representatives to meet at Jamaica, which, in turn, selected the riding's delegates. Unfortunately, the records of the debates of the first New York Assembly have been lost, but its accomplishments are recorded. It met in October, 1683, and, by early November, its first acts were completed. It did create a Charter of Liberties and Privileges, which outlined a constitution for the colony in the form of a grant of rights by the duke.[70] Ultimately more important for the people of the mainland settlements was a measure enacted three days later dividing the entire colony into counties. By this act, Westchester, Eastchester, Broncksland, Fordham, Pell's manor, the newer patent of Mamaroneck north and east of Pell's land, Yonkers, "and all the land on the Maine to the Eastward of Manhatans Island . . . and Northward along Hudsons river as farr as the High Land" was erected into the county of Westchester, taking its name from the largest settlement there. Each county would have its own sheriff appointed for a yearly term.[71]

By another act passed the same day, each town would have a court of three commissioners to try small cases to the value of 40 shillings, unless the litigants requested a jury trial. The county would have a Court of Sessions to try criminal and civil cases presided over by at least three of the justices of the peace in the county, with the Court meeting the first Tuesday in June at Westchester and the first Tuesday in December at Eastchester. There would also be a Court of Oyer and Terminer to try capital crimes and civil cases of a value of £5 or more presided over by a judge assisted by four justices of the peace. This court would meet the first Wednesday in every December, with the facts in every case determined by a jury of twelve men of the neighborhood. The governor and his Council would constitute the Court of Chancery to determine cases of equity.[72] In order to prevent constant law suits involving contested rights to grants and patents, the Assembly decreed that all landholdings had to be re-registered at the office of the new county recorders.[73] The members of the Assembly, no doubt with the secret urging of Thomas Dongan, also passed an act providing for a voluntary gift for the new governor, and John Pell, Walter Webley, William Richardson, and John Archer were deputized by the act to collect the sum in the new Westchester County.[74]

Because of this Assembly's work, the people of the mainland settlements would be closer to the courts that affected their lives. Now they resided in the new Westchester County. All the area that would one day become The Bronx was to be, for the following 190 years, the southernmost portion of it, and it was in this new county that its people would shape their destiny.

CHAPTER IX

REBELLION

1684 TO 1691

The creation of the new county system in the colony was quickly implemented by Governor Dongan's appointment of county officials. In November, 1683, Benjamin Collier, who then lived in the town of Westchester, was appointed as the first sheriff of the new Westchester County.[1] In early May of the following year, he was also commissioned the county collector of the quit-rents.[2] John Rider became the first county clerk and register of deeds a few days later.[3]

The county's creation also meant the abolition of the old court system and the establishment of another. This disruption of the legal process affected several cases in progress, including the heated one over the ownership of Stony Island.

To shore up his own case, Colonel Lewis Morris called together several Indians from the vicinity to sign a deed that not only confirmed the original sale of the property to Jonas Bronck, but also legitimatized Morris's possession of the increased acreage granted to him by Governor Andros in 1676. In early February, 1684, the new deed, duly signed and witnessed in the English manner, was concluded.[4]

Undeterred, Daniel Turneur petitioned the Council. He argued that the review of the case regarding Stony Island could not take place in the Court of Assizes because that tribunal had been abolished. He demanded possession of the property. Morris countered with a writ of error, which was granted, and petitioned instead for the case to be heard in the Court of Oyer and Terminer of Westchester County. He probably felt that he would find the officers of that Court more favorable to his views. Possibly the Council thought this as well, and, in fairness to Turneur, hit upon a unique solution. Probably recalling the fact that Stony Island was a matter in dispute between the jurisdictions of the old North Riding (much of which had included the new Queens County) and New York City, the Council decided that the case would be heard by a special jury of twelve men each from the city and Queens. Consequently, writs were sent out to the sheriffs of the two areas to summon the men.[5] The case was tried in New York in October, 1684, and, although the records of the trial are lost, it is evident that the decision went against Morris, since he had to pay the court costs in November.[6]

Although the loss of Stony Island might have embittered Colonel Morris, it was probably not as bitter to him as the constant arguments and frustration he experienced in caring for his young nephew, Lewis, orphaned son of his brother, Richard. The boy, now in his teen years, showed evidence of having a quick and brilliant mind. He was easily angered, however, and, as he grew aware of the circumstances of his life, his anger became directed against his uncle.

At first, the boy's anger was manifested in harmless adolescent pranks. Colonel Morris, who had converted to Quakerism, hired a fellow Quaker, Hugh Coppathwait, to teach his nephew. Coppathwait was a zealot in his religion, and, one day, his student took the opportunity to ridicule him. The orphan hid in a tree and, when his teacher passed within earshot, pretended to be a celestial voice calling upon the Quaker to preach the Gospel among the Mohawks. Taking the voice to be genuine, Coppathwait was about to set off for the Mohawk country when young Lewis Morris's trick was discovered.[7] Aside from being an example of adolescent frivolity, the incident was also an indication of the growing differences between the nephew and his uncle. As his life was to show, young Lewis Morris completely rejected his uncle's religion and became a firm supporter of the Anglican faith.

Far more serious were young Lewis Morris's accusations against his uncle. No doubt as soon as he discovered that his father and uncle in 1668 had invested in the Broncksland property together, that he had a rightful claim to part of it, and that somehow his uncle had been able to receive an official patent that cheated him of what he regarded as his rightful inheritance, young Lewis turned on the colonel. He demanded his rights, and was refused.[8]

Young Lewis, filled with righteous anger, consorted with men of whom his uncle disapproved, and he ultimately ran away from home. He walked all the way to Virginia and, from there, sailed to the island of Jamaica in the West Indies, where he was employed as a scrivener. A few years later, Lewis, perhaps wiser, and certainly older, probably realized that this course would not lead him to receiving his property, and he decided to return.[9]

This view of Lewis Morris's voyage first became public in a book written about a century later by William Smith, Jr., a Tory in the American Revolution and a political opponent of the Morris family. Another version of the episode comes from contemporaries of Lewis Morris, who told it to Benjamin Franklin, who, in turn, related it to John Jay decades later. According to this version, young Morris's voyage was the idea of his uncle, who sent the young man to the West Indies with a ship and cargo. Once the cargo was sold, young Morris spent all the proceeds.[10]

Both versions of the story, although related long after the event, have a ring of truth, and each is suspect for different reasons. It is true that Lewis Morris was frequently willful and headstrong, and both versions of the episode freely admit that he was a wild youngster. The Tory, William Smith, Jr., could tar his contemporary Morrises, his opponents in the Revolution, with bearing the seeds of rebellion in their ancestry. The Franklin-Jay version, on the other hand, suffers from being recorded third-hand, and no one can be sure if the facts related were altered in the retelling. Franklin even relates an anecdote about the wedding of young Morris that cannot be true. While specific facts about the voyage are in dispute, it is clear that the younger Morris did journey to the West Indies, stayed there for a time, and then returned to the home of his uncle.

Meanwhile, the public business of the colony and the county went forward. In October, 1684, the second session of the Assembly met, and promptly addressed several questions that came to the fore since it had decreed the creation of the county system. The Assembly decided that each town could choose its own constables, as they had all done before, in the beginning of April. It also decreed that each town could make its own regulations regarding marking cattle and fencing fields so long as they were registered at the next Court of Oyer and Terminer and that the town's meeting and two justices of the peace had agreed to them. In Westchester County, it was discovered that the courts of Sessions and of Oyer and Terminer were scheduled by law to convene at the same time. Since this was a hardship, the Assembly decreed that the Court of Sessions would meet on the first Tuesday in November, one full month before the original date. In addition, the Assembly allowed the monthly town courts to have jurisdiction over cases involving amounts up to £5, instead of up to only 40 shillings. Cases over 40 shillings, however, had to be tried by jury.[11]

This Assembly proved to be the last ever held under the authority given to Governor Dongan by the duke of York. In February, 1685, King Charles II died. Since he had no legitimate children to inherit the throne, the duke of York, his brother, became King James II. A month later, the new king turned his attention to his colony of New York, which, because he now reigned in London, passed under the jurisdiction of the Crown as a royal, rather than as a proprietary, colony. Since New York was now a royal colony, the new king informed Governor Dongan that all the bills passed by the colonial Assembly had been submitted to the Privy Council for discussion.[12] The Privy Council disallowed the Charter of Liberties under which the Assembly had been operating, but some of its laws were allowed to stand. This decision was to have severe repercussions in a few short years.

Life in the southern part of the new Westchester County continued in large measure as it had before. Johannes Verveelen continued to operate his ferry across Spuyten Duyvil Creek until he died in 1687. At that time, his son, Daniel, petitioned for a renewal of the license to operate the ferry there.[13]

The lack of a resident clergyman in the area was still keenly felt. In 1684, the people of Eastchester, Westchester, and Yonkers joined together to raise £60 in country produce as a yearly salary for Warham Mather, a young man from a family of prominent Massachusetts clergymen, to serve as their minister. Hired only for the year, Mather had to accept his salary in quarterly installments.[14] The arrangement might have been renewed for 1685, but, by that time, the inhabitants of Westchester were finally able to attract the Reverend Morgan Jones to officiate at services in their town, although not on a permanent basis. The men of Eastchester paid his expenses by raising the money among themselves.[15]

Eastchester, in particular, was still trying to attract some professional men to live in the community. In August, 1685, Richard Shute wrote to Edward Gilliam, a blacksmith, that the town would give him some upland and meadow provided he lived there for seven years.[16] By 1686, the first merchant is recorded seeking a site in the town. In August, the Eastchester men granted John Butler, a merchant, two acres (about four-fifths of a hectare) of meadow to live there, but part of the meadow west of the creek could never be sold by him, but had to be returned to the town if he had no further use for it.[17]

The area, however, was producing its own merchants. Horse trading became a profitable occupation, and, as early as 1683, the Westchester County sheriff had to be ordered to warn all persons not to ship off any wild or unmarked horses.[18] In 1686, Robert Hunt and Matthew Pugsley of the town of Westchester amassed a herd of horses by purchasing one each from a number of owners. Rarely were they able to obtain more than one horse from any seller because few owned more than one. They bought them from people in their own town, Eastchester, and Rye, shipping them from Hunts Point for resale elsewhere.[19]

The two towns were also growing. In August, 1685, the inhabitants of Eastchester agreed to erect a town house 14 feet (about 4.2 meters) long by 12 feet (about 3.6 meters) wide near the road between the homes of William Haiden and Richard Shute.[20] This building was meant to be the civic center of the community.

In 1686, in response to the growing herds of sheep, the townspeople of neighboring Westchester took a significant step in voting to establish a sheep pasture. This land was held in common by the owners of the property abutting it. Each landowner had shares in the sheep pasture determined by the size of his farm, but, in time, these shares were bought and sold independently of the ownership of the contiguous property. Of course, other livestock were allowed to graze on this common land, but the fact that it was called the sheep pasture indicates the use for which it was intended. In fact, the townsmen considered this step so important, they forbade future residents ever to divide the land unless every freeholder and inhabitant gave his consent to the act.[21]

Soon afterward, the people living in southern Westchester County were engaged in trying to renew the patents to their lands. Not only did the recent Assembly decree that all landholdings be recorded anew by the county authorities, but Governor Dongan discovered that the quit-rents due to the king on several tracts of land were merely nominal. Dongan vowed to have the patents renewed bearing a higher quit-rent. He succeeded in many cases by discovering tracts within a grant that had not been purchased from the Indians. These lands could, in theory, be taken away from the current occupants and be given by the king to others.[22] In December, 1686, John Pell received a license to purchase all Indian lands within his patent,[23] a privilege he gradually put into practice. Before a year passed, Pell requested Dongan to provide his patent with a more full and firm grant under the royal seal, which the governor was happy to do in return for imposing a quit-rent on the property of twenty shillings in New York money each year. It was in this patent that Pell's land received the official title of manor of Pelham.[24] Meanwhile, Thomas Hunt's property on Throggs Neck, called Grove Farm, was confirmed by the governor with the provision that it carry a quit-rent of one bushel (just over 35 liters) of winter wheat a year.[25]

Dongan's strategy in renewing patents not only involved land claimed by individual inhabitants, but land included in grants made to towns. In December, 1683, the townsmen of Eastchester chose Nathaniel Tomkins, John Drake, and Richard Shute to go into the woods with the Indians to mark out the land lying within the boundaries of the community. They also ascertained how much the Indians would take to sell the land they claimed was theirs. Once that was determined, Will Haiden, Philip Pinckney, Samuel Drake, Sr., and Moses Hoit, along with those who had marked the boundaries, negotiated with the Indians to purchase the property. The inhabitants assessed themselves according to the size of the farms they already held to pay for the purchase.[26]

Receiving a deed of purchase from the Indians meant that Eastchester did not have to worry about increased quit-rents due to the Crown. It did not make the town immune from the continuing controversy over the boundary with neighboring Westchester, however. In March, 1686, Will Haiden and Moses Hoit, Sr., were chosen to treat with the Westchester men in defense of the land granted to them by patent. The matter went to the county's Court of Sessions for a decision, but the Court's scribe did something which offended the Eastchester representatives. The matter came to the attention of Governor Dongan, who, in November, requested to see the town's patent. Both the patent and supporting documents were sent to the governor, but, because the Court of Sessions was meeting, no person was available to accompany these papers.[27]

While Dongan was considering the Eastchester claims, in January, 1687, he reconfirmed the patent of the town of Westchester. The bounds set in this renewed grant included all lands not otherwise disposed of by patent which had been, or would be, purchased from the Indians or others extending from the western boundary of Broncksland near the Harlem River to the manor of Pelham, and from Long Island Sound and the East River "and so run upon a parallel line, for the east and west limits, north into the woods without limitation, for range of cattle and other improvements."[28] Such an open-ended vaguely worded boundary line practically invited conflict between Eastchester and Westchester.

The Eastchester inhabitants were in the process of appealing action on their patent before the king's Court of Exchequer when the Westchester men took their first move to settle the boundary in their favor. In April, 1687, William Richardson, Richard Ponton, and Joseph Palmer were chosen by Westchester to run the line between their town and Pell's land. Meanwhile, John Ferris, William Barnes, Richard Ponton, Thomas Baxter, and John Hunt, or any three of them, were given the authority to lay out the land between the Eastchester line and the Bronx River. But where was the line located? To discover that, Joseph Palmer, William Barnes, and Richard Ponton were selected to lay out the line between the two towns.[29]

Palmer, Barnes, and Ponton, in order to avoid complaints from Eastchester, worked with John Pell to appoint a mutually agreed upon time to survey the line with Eastchester. In early May, Pell and the Westchester survey team met and readily agreed on the boundaries between their two patents, but the Eastchester men refused to have the line run along their boundary, claiming that the surveyors would run the line over Eastchester land. It was clear that the townsmen of Eastchester were in a violent mood, and Pell immediately stepped in, suggesting that Eastchester also appoint a survey team that would meet with the Westchester men the following day so that the line could be run jointly. This was agreed upon, but, at the appointed time, the Eastchester men were willing only to survey the northwest border of Westchester near the Bronx River, but not the other lines. The Westchester team immediately thought that the reason for their rivals' refusal to run the other lines between the two towns was that the Eastchester men knew that they had fenced and planted on Westchester town property.[30]

Determined to run the line with Eastchester, the Westchester Board of Trustees reappointed Palmer, Barnes, and Ponton to complete the survey. They also sent Edward Waters, who was permitted to take someone with him, to the governor to complain about the actions of the Eastchester men, entreating Dongan that, if Eastchester sent a complaint against them, that he should notify the people of Westchester so that they could defend their actions. They also requested the governor not to issue a new patent to Eastchester.[31] The Westchester men were extremely perceptive, for, in early July, the Eastchester inhabitants chose, by majority vote, to send John Butler, Philip Pinckney, and Richard Shute to New York to see the governor, or, in his absence, a member of the Council, to issue a patent to their town with all the privileges appertaining.[32] No new patent seems to have been issued.

By October, 1687, the controversy seems to have died down. Westchester sent out John Ferris, Sr., and Joseph Palmer to run the northwest line with Eastchester, and then it laid out twenty lots in that area known as Long Reach. At the same time, Joseph Palmer and Edward Waters were sent to the Indians to show them the line between the two towns, and also the line between Pell's land and Westchester,[33] a practice first started by Thomas Pell when he purchased the land from the Siwanoy.

If the controversy between Westchester and Eastchester was prolonged and sharp, it paled in comparison to the one that broke out over the ownership of the manor of Fordham. In 1684, John Archer, the Fordham proprietor, suddenly died.[34] In normal circumstances, the heir to the huge manor would have been his son, John Archer, Jr., who, in March, 1685, petitioned Governor Dongan's Council to appoint an administrator for his father's estate with the authority to try the title to the Fordham lands.[35] Before the week was out, Cornelis Steenwyck sent his own petition to the governor requesting that he receive the letters of administration for the manor, that the land be surveyed by the surveyor-general, and that persons be appointed to appraise its value.[36] Steenwyck, of course, held the mortgages on the property, and Archer had still owed him the unpaid balance. Moreover, John Archer, Jr., was also indebted to him, albeit for a much smaller sum.[37]

On the merits, then, Cornelis Steenwyck, the New York City merchant and one of the wealthiest men in the colony, obtained control of Fordham. That claim was soon disputed, however, not by John Archer, Jr., but from the unlikely source of the town of Westchester. According to the town's patent, its westernmost boundary was on the Harlem River and included all lands not otherwise disposed of by patent or purchase. Since the Fordham patent belonged to John Archer, who was dead, Westchester made its claim. In November, 1684, the town's trustees ordered Richard Ponton, Joseph Palmer, and William Barnes to go to Spuyten Duyvil to meet with surveyor Philip Wells to run the boundary between Fordham and Yonkers.[38]

Steenwyck and his wife Margarieta, obviously felt that Fordham was theirs to do with as they wished, for soon after the Westchester survey team was ordered to go to Spuyten Duyvil, they made their wills in which they bequeathed the manor to the Dutch Reformed Church in New York with the proviso that the church hold it forever and the lands never be alienated, the proceeds going toward the maintenance of the Church's ministers.[39] Before a year passed, Steenwyck was dead and his widow named executrix of the estate.[40] The leaders of the Dutch Church indicated they would accept the legacy of Fordham, but they requested Margarieta Steenwyck to clear the manor of Westchester's claims to the property before they would actually take possession.[41]

The widow's first step toward this goal was to eliminate John Archer, Jr.'s, claim to the manor. This proved to be fairly easy because of the youth's financial difficulties. Not only was he indebted to her late husband, but the Westchester County sheriff obtained a warrant to seize his goods for non-payment of quit-rents.[42] Probably because of his need for money, in October, 1685, young Archer sold his title to Fordham to the widow.[43] On the following day, in return, the young man received a deed from Margarieta Steenwyck for his house, a home lot, forty acres of upland, and a portion of meadow, all lying within the manor.[44] Thus, he would still retain his own home and sufficient land to make his way in the world. In November, John Archer, Jr., formally turned over possession of the manor of Fordham to John West, the widow Steenwyck's attorney.[45] West had previous experience on the manor, having once served as John Archer's steward. In April, 1686, Margarieta Steenwyck appeared before Matthias Nicolls, the secretary of the colony, to acknowledge the execution of the deed she gave to John Archer, Jr.[46] She never forgot that the ownership of the remainder of the manor's property was meant to be invested in the Dutch Reformed Church. Indeed, in October, the widow remarried, becoming the wife of Dominie Henricus Selyns, a minister of the Dutch Church in New York.[47]

Nothing was done affecting Westchester's claim to Fordham for over a year, but events in both Europe and the colony were to have a bearing on the controversy. In April, 1688, King James II implemented a plan to amalgamate the colonies of Massachusetts,

Plymouth, New Hampshire, Rhode Island, Connecticut, New York, and New Jersey under the title of the dominion of New England. Commissioned the governor of the new dominion was the former governor of New York, the recently knighted Sir Edmund Andros, who would rule from Boston. Appointed as his lieutenant governor was Captain Francis Nicolson, who would be stationed in New York.[48] Thus, the ultimate authority over the fate of Fordham now rested with officials in far away Boston, not nearby New York City.

While these changes were in the process of being made, word came to Westchester that Nicholas Bayard, a wealthy New York merchant and influential man in both colonial and in Dutch Reformed Church affairs, was in Fordham, probably to grant leases on behalf of the Church. The town immediately appointed Richard Ponton, Robert Huestis, and Edward Waters to meet Bayard at Fordham to warn him not to dispose of the land belonging to Westchester on the west side of the Bronx River.[49]

Bayard, however, was not a man to be put off by such tactics. In May, he met with John Pell at Spuyten Duyvil to resolve the dispute. Since Pell was a justice of the county, evidently plans were made to call a jury to decide the matter. Immediately, the town sent a delegation to confer with the merchant, and Bayard proposed to them that the matter be settled by arbitration[50] using seven honest men. The Board of Trustees of the town accepted the arbitration proposal, dispatching Joseph Palmer to Long Island to obtain the names of men who would be good arbiters. Meanwhile, William Richardson, Edward Waters, and Joseph Palmer were appointed to go to New York to confer with Henricus Selyns and his wife, offering a bond of £500 to stand by the arbiters' award. In doing so, they were not to yield the town's rights nor to enter into any other agreement with them. They were also given permission to see Nicholas Bayard.[51]

The arbitration plan was never implemented, however. At the end of May or the beginning of June, 1688, the men of Westchester took direct action. Edward Waters and Richard Ponton went to Fordham and forcibly ejected two of the tenants, Aert Pieterse Buys and Ryer Michielsen, from their farms, installing Roger Barton, Sr., and his son, Elijah, in their places on behalf of Westchester.[52] Hearing of this act, an outraged Bayard, in July, rushed to Fordham accompanied by Ryer Michielsen, one of those evicted, and Nicholas Stephenson, Teunis De Kay, Johannes Kipp, Isaac van Vleek, Michael Bastiensen, his wife and sons, Henrick Kiersen and his wife, Jacques

Tourneur, and the wife of John Odell. Their object was to oust the Bartons. Hearing of the expedition, the town of Westchester sent Edward Hubbard to intercept them.[53]

Roger Barton, Sr., was ensconced in the former home of Aert Pieterse Buys to retain possession for Westchester when Bayard and his party arrived at about 3:00 o'clock in the afternoon. The door was locked, and Nicholas Stephenson tore a pole from the fence, using it to try to force the door. He was not successful. Teunis De Kay took the pole from him and requested Bayard's permission to use it to break open the door, a request which the merchant quickly granted. De Kay succeeded in breaking the door open, but the sixty-year old Barton, using all his strength, was able to shut it again. Johannes Kipp then rushed to help De Kay, breaking down the door. Both men then seized the elderly Barton and hauled him out of the house, kicking him in the breeches. Kipp grabbed the pitchfork with which Barton was defending himself, and told him to go. Beaten and probably dazed, the elderly man started on the road toward the town of Westchester, only to find his way barred by a man with a sword, who was most likely De Kay. Turned back from the path, Barton had to make his way through the woods.[54]

Bayard and his party then turned their attention toward the other house, the one which had been in the possession of Ryer Michielsen, but which was now occupied by twenty-year old Elisha Barton and his friend, Andrew Davis. There, Michielsen himself took the lead in evicting the old man's son, and with the help of Teunis De Kay, he broke open the locked door. The door swiftly swung inward, striking young Barton in the left eye, severely hurting him. Michielsen and De Kay quickly entered the house, threw out the two defenders, locked the door once again from the inside to secure it, and rejoined their companions by creeping out the window.[55]

While Bayard and his party were attending to Elisha Barton, Edward Hubbard, sent from Westchester to secure the property on behalf of the town, arrived at the house where Roger Barton, Sr., had been so recently evicted, finding parts of the fence at the side of the house broken and the door missing. A half hour later, Bayard returned with his party following him. Seeing Hubbard now on the site, Bayard demanded to know what he was doing there. When Hubbard told him his mission, the New York merchant ordered him to leave. Bayard's companions immediately set upon the hapless Hubbard, hauled him out of the yard into the roadway, held him by his hair and shoulders, and kicked him.[56] Teunis De Kay even drew his sword on the Westchester emissary.

At this point, Thomas Statham and Robert Hudson were passing nearby on their way to Valentine Claessen's house. Hearing the commotion, they rushed toward the noise in time to see Hubbard being kicked and abused. Statham, hailing Bayard, demanded to know what was going on, and inquired if they were murdering a man. Bayard, who must have recognized the voice, asked if it were Statham who was speaking, and when he received an affirmative reply, he told his inquisitor to go about his business. Undeterred, Statham stood his ground, pointing out that he was on the king's highway, and, thus, not trespassing. Bayard then turned toward Statham demanding that he tell him who owned the land. Statham replied that it belonged to the town of Westchester, and that he knew it by virtue of his own purchase a few years earlier. The reply angered Bayard, who then threatened him and accused him of being deceitful. Once again, Bayard insisted that Statham go about his own business.[57]

As a result of this incident, a few days later, John Palmer and William Richardson, both Westchester residents and both justices of the peace, issued a warrant directing Westchester County Sheriff Benjamin Collier to arrest Nicholas Bayard and those who assisted him and to bring them to trial. Although most of those who committed the deeds were not apprehended, a grand jury did issue an indictment charging Bayard and his companions with riot and forced entry.[58] Roger Barton, Sr., evidently shaken by the incident, made his will, leaving the land he stated was his by virtue of the Westchester claim to the west side of the Bronx River to his son, Elisha.[59]

The forces of the Dutch Reformed Church were not idle either. Henricus Selyns petitioned to remain in quiet possession of the manor of Fordham against the claims of Westchester,[60] but the petition was denied, probably because a court case concerning the matter was already calendared for trial. Just before the Westchester County Court of Sessions was to meet, the Consistory of the Dutch Reformed Church at New York requested Dominie Selyns and his wife to defend their rights to Fordham, promising to pay all costs.[61] It was impossible, however, for the Church to obtain a fair trial from a court whose justices and jury were so intimately affected by the outcome, and the Church lost. Quickly, Nicholas Bayard requested an appeal to the court at Boston.[62]

In the meantime, the town of Westchester was busy asserting

its claim to the manor. In September, Nicholas Bailey surrendered his land on the west side of the Bronx River to the jurisdiction of the town.[63] There was a clamor by several town residents to divide all that tempting unimproved land in Fordham among themselves, and, finally, the Board of Trustees gave in. Even before the results of the trial involving the Dutch Church was held, the trustees decreed that as many freeholders who had a right might fence and clear as many of the lots on the west side of the Bronx River as they wished as long as they began at one end, occupying the lots in order one after the other, with Elijah Barton having lot number one.[64]

After the verdict in the Westchester County Court of Sessions was handed down, the town began to levy assessments on the property in Fordham. All those living there had to pay £30, one-third in money and two-thirds in corn and winter wheat.[65] In April, 1689, the house and land of Aert Pieterse Buys, where the eviction of Roger Barton, Sr., had occurred, was assigned to John Hadden, while Robert Huestis and Samuel Palmer were sent to Spuyten Duyvil to warn those found trespassing on that land to give Hadden possession.[66] Bastiaen Michielsen, a long-time resident of Fordham, petitioned the Westchester trustees for fifty acres near the Harlem River for nine years. It was agreed that Michielsen would pay one bushel (just over 35 liters) of wheat for each of the first two years, three bushels (almost 105.7 liters) for the third year, and £5 10s. in wheat and corn for the final six years.[67]

Thus, pending the Dutch Church's appeal to Boston, the town of Westchester took firm control of the manor of Fordham. Events in Europe, however, would conspire to block the Church's appeal, and the outcome of those events would place Westchester's claim in jeopardy.

Ever since James II's accession to the throne, the new king showed favoritism toward the public worship of his own Catholic religion and toward his co-religionists. In addition, he attempted to rule without Parliament, even to the extent of trying to change laws without parliamentary approval. These actions lost him the support of the leaders of the kingdom, many of whom began to correspond with William, the prince of Orange, the Dutch stadtholder to whom the residents of the colony of New York had to swear allegiance during the Dutch interlude. William was married to Mary, James's eldest daughter by his first wife, the Protestant Anne Hyde, and heir to the throne of England.

The Protestant English resentment against James reached a

high point in July, 1688, when Mary of Modena, the king's second wife and a Catholic, gave birth to a son, who would supersede Mary as heir and provide the possibility of an endless succession of Catholic monarchs. Thirty days later, a group of prominent political leaders in England invited William of Orange and his wife to come with an army and restore their liberties. After gathering an army and a fleet, William landed at Torbay in Devonshire in November. Almost everyone in the kingdom rallied to William's banner. In December, James II fled the country to safety in the France of Louis XIV.

In the new year, a convention called by the prince of Orange met and resolved that the throne was vacant. In February, 1689, William and Mary were proclaimed king and queen, respectively, to rule jointly.

In the meantime, Louis XIV, in one of his maneuvers to enlarge the territory of France, declared war on the League of Augsburg, an anti-French alliance of Spain, Sweden, the Netherlands, and several German states, augmented by Savoy and the pope. With a Dutchman as king, and hoping for some commercial advantage, England joined the war against France in May, 1689.

It took time for news of all these events to cross the Atlantic, and with thousands of miles separating them from these occurrences, no one in the colony of New York could know if the intelligence first received reflected what really happened. In February, King William appointed a committee of the Board of Trade to prepare the drafts of proclamations of his accession to be sent to the colonies and of his desire that those who held office there continue in their places.[68] News of William's landing in England in November, 1688, reached New York City only at the beginning of March, 1689, however. The members of the Council in the city, Mayor Stephen van Cortlandt, Frederick Philipse, and Nicholas Bayard, knew that such an account would cause unrest among the populace, and they resolved to keep the communication secret.[69]

The leaders of Massachusetts, however, felt no such compunction, and the people of Boston rose up, jailed Governor Sir Edmund Andros, and took steps to dissolve the dominion of New England. Rhode Island and Connecticut soon restored their governments as well.[70]

Lieutenant Governor Nicolson and his Council in New York heard of the revolt in Boston by early May, and they immediately wrote to the justices of the peace and the military officers of the several counties, including Westchester, to come to the city to advise them. Since John Pell had been appointed a captain of a troop of horse in 1687,[71] it is certain he was there, and all those summoned from Westchester County, led by Captain Richard Ponton, appeared on the appointed day and promised to keep the peace.[72] Unfortunately, it was about this time that rumors of war with France reached New York,[73] and that was to prove one of the major causes of the undoing of the agreement so recently made.

The rebellion started in Suffolk County at the eastern end of Long Island. The people there ejected the office holders, including all the magistrates and military officers, from their positions. Queens County followed suit, and shortly thereafter, the people of Westchester County. By the middle of May, 1689, a militia at Jamaica was marching on New York City, and the city merchants were openly protesting the payment of the customs duties, alleging that they were illegally established.[74]

By early June, Jacob Leisler, the commander of the militia of New York, augmented by six captains and 400 men, and by a company of 70 men from Eastchester, had taken control of the fort in the city. The men mutually agreed to hold it for the prince of Orange.[75] Complaining of the rebelliousness of Leisler and those who assisted him, Lieutenant Governor Nicolson set sail for England, leaving the members of his Council to deal with the situation.[76]

Eager for accurate information, at the end of June, Nicholas Bayard and Stephen van Cortlandt left New York City to intercept a Major Gold who was on his way to New York City from Connecticut with a proclamation announcing the accession of William and Mary. Unfortunately, they did not find him, and the two councilors stayed the night at the house of Colonel Lewis Morris.[77] Two days later, Gold and his companion arrived in the city bearing a printed paper with the news that William and Mary now reigned in England. Upon receiving the news, Leisler had the drum beaten and proclaimed them king and queen. The militia commander then went to City Hall, demanding that Mayor Stephen van Cortlandt duplicate the ceremony there. The mayor refused to do so because Leisler had already done it, whereupon Leisler performed the ceremony again, and proceeded to manhandle the members of the Council there, including van Cortlandt and Nicholas Bayard.[78]

Two days after this violent incident, Stephen van Cortlandt received the printed proclamation from the king and queen confirming all parties in their offices.[79] When confronted with this evidence of their authority the following day, Leisler violently beat van Cortlandt, Bayard, and Frederick Philipse, the members of the Council, and announced he was taking control of the fort as the captain appointed to secure it on behalf of William and Mary.[80]

By early July, Leisler had appointed a Committee of Safety consisting of two men each from New York City, Brooklyn, Flatbush, Esopus, Newtown, Staten Island, Essex in New Jersey, and Westchester.[81] He seems to have called it on the advice of some of the principal inhabitants and officers with whom he was in contact.[82] It is interesting to note that under Leisler, for the first time, residents of such small towns as Westchester were given weight in the counsels of the colony. Previously, only wealthy merchants and landholders from New York City and Albany had ever been extended the privilege. Serving on the new Committee was Thomas Williams from Westchester. By mid-August, the Committee of Safety conferred the title of commander-in-chief upon Leisler, giving him authority to administer oaths and issue warrants.[83]

In December, 1689, a letter written in London in August arrived in New York addressed to Lieutenant Governor Nicolson (who had fled the colony months previously), or "in his absence to such as for the time being take care of preserving the Peace and administering the Lawes. . . ." It called upon the person addressed to take the title of lieutenant governor and commander-in-chief, and to take the burdens of the colony's government upon himself. Since Jacob Leisler was obviously the man who was administering the laws, he took the letter, and, from that time, adopted the title of lieutenant governor, using the communication as the official authorization for his acts.[84] Two days later, the Committee of Safety decided that the new lieutenant governor should have a Council, and recommended nine men for the position. Thomas Williams, who was present, found himself nominated to the new Council as a representative for Westchester County.[85]

With his new Council, Leisler promptly appointed new officers for Westchester County, naming Thomas Statham sheriff, Joseph Pudway, Joseph Ponton, Andrew Tauvert, Edward Waters, and Thomas Williams justices, and Edward Collier clerk. Williams was commissioned to give the oath of office to the county justices.[86] Most of these men lived in the town of Westchester. The first act Leisler required the new county justices to perform was to proclaim William and Mary joint monarchs in the town of Westchester as the principal settlement in the county.[87]

By January, 1690, Leisler moved to consolidate his power by

issuing a proclamation ordering those who had held civil or military commissions under either Governor Dongan or Governor Andros to surrender them.[88] This was a direct strike at the members of the old Council that Leisler had deposed. A letter did exist, it will be recalled, that had confirmed them in the positions they had held. If they surrendered their positions, however, they would be acknowledging Leisler as the duly constituted authority. Led by Nicholas Bayard, the members of the Council wrote a letter to London detailing the events that had occurred, and, since they realized that any ship departing New York for London bearing such a letter would immediately come under Leisler's scrutiny, they decided to place the communication on a packet to Boston to be transshipped from there. Leisler, however, suspected that maneuver, too, and appointed Daniel Turneur to intercept any such letters on their way to Boston, giving him the authority to search any house along the route. When the packet bound for Boston stopped at Colonel Morris's house, it was searched, and the letter discovered. A warrant for the arrest of Bayard, Stephen van Cortlandt, and others involved was soon issued.[89]

The eclipse of Bayard, the man in the forefront of pushing the claims of the Dutch Reformed Church to the manor of Fordham, probably convinced those who upheld the Church's cause that their struggle was hopeless. Certainly, Ryer Michielsen, whose house had been one of those seized by the Bartons in 1688, and who accompanied Nicholas Bayard in the expedition to evict them, gave in to the claims of Westchester. In early May, he petitioned the town's trustees to rent land on the west bank of the Bronx River. The trustees gave him the lot on which his house stood, which had formerly belonged to Perigreen Turner, and a ten-acre lot formerly belonging to Thomas Vail for four years in return for one cock and other consideration. At the same time, Matthias Valentine received twenty acres for four years in return for 7s. 6d. a year.[90]

Leisler's policy was to reintroduce the laws established under the duke of York which the Privy Council had disallowed after the duke became king. Therefore, the courts to try small causes for Westchester County were commissioned in accordance with the Act of 1683, and, in April, 1690, writs were issued for election of representatives to a new Assembly.[91]

The circumstances of Leisler's coming to power, however, made the new lieutenant governor and his followers the foes of all Catholics, and of all those who had previously run the colonial government. It was for this reason that Thomas Statham, the new county sheriff, was issued a warrant to arrest all papists, disaffected persons, and all those who had held commissions under Dongan and Andros.[92] Nevertheless, it must be said that this action was not taken until after news was received that a party of French and Indians had attacked Schenectady in February, 1690.[93]

With the attack, the colony was at war. Requests were sent to the various counties to raise men for an expedition to be sent to fight the invaders at Albany,[94] and Richard Ponton was raised to the rank of major in the county militia.[95] In March, Ponton, assisted by John Williams, called out the militia company of the town of Westchester. The commander appealed for volunteers to fight the French at Albany. Gabriel Leggett spoke up, however, saying that anyone who went was a fool, and asked who would give them an arm or a leg if any of them lost one. Ponton angrily told him to keep his silence, but Leggett continued to shout out, calling Williams the father of rogues, and heaping further abuse on him.[96]

Gabriel Leggett, in fact, had a personal feud with John Williams. Leggett had married Elizabeth, the daughter of John Richardson, one of the original settlers of West Farms. Richardson had built a grist mill and a saw mill on the Bronx River in 1671, and Leggett took care of some of the business of running the saw mill. Richardson, however, in his will of November, 1679, left his property to his wife, Martha, to use during her lifetime. After his death, the widow married Thomas Williams. Since the widow was comparatively wealthy, Leggett undoubtedly felt cheated in not receiving a portion of the wealth as Richardson's son-in-law, and probably palled at the prospect of that wealth being used by Williams. Indeed, Leggett tried to evict Williams from the Richardson house, but failed.[97]

The immediate cause of Leggett's outburst against Williams in March, 1690, when Ponton was appealing for troops to fight the French, was a stolen hog. Probably out of frustration, Leggett stole the hog from Williams. Leggett's tirade before the town's militia company, coming soon after the theft, provoked Williams, now a member of Lieutenant Governor Leisler's Council. Williams was further inflamed when the two men later drank together at William Barnes's house. Leggett, in his cups, denounced Williams as a thief, murderer, and a liar, saying he could prove it. Williams promptly went to the county clerk, Edward Collier, to obtain a warrant, and Leggett was arrested, refused all offer of bail, spent the night in jail, and was hauled into court held at Thomas Baxter's house. Williams's wife, who was also Leggett's mother-in-law, however, appealed to her husband to forgive her son-in-law for her daughter's sake. She also obtained the aid of Samuel Hitchcock to intercede with her husband. The pleas worked, and Williams declared that he would not press charges if Leggett returned the hog, paid all court costs, and acknowledged that he had been wrong. Leggett agreed to these conditions, apologized to Williams, and the two shook hands.[98] The incident, however, was to cause further problems in the future.

Gabriel Leggett's public sentiments against Leisler's call for military service in Albany were reflected in the actions of several militiamen who had no feud with John Williams. The call itself was unpopular with many who had no desire to endanger their lives so far from home. By the summer, an order had to be issued to the constables of Westchester, Eastchester, Rye, and Bedford to arrest deserters from the French expedition.[99] This was the first time any of Leisler's followers refused to follow him, and this split probably made it easier for those Leisler had deposed to be restored to power in the colony when, in February, 1691, the lieutenant governor appointed by King William arrived in New York harbor.

Major Richard Ingoldsby, upon landing, introduced himself as the duly appointed lieutenant governor, and requested the keys to the fort at New York, which Leisler refused to surrender until Ingoldsby showed him his commission. Taking affront at such a request, Ingoldsby refused to comply. The details of the struggle over the transfer of the colonial government need not concern us here, only that the actions of Leisler and his associates in greeting the king's new appointees were not those that would invoke a feeling of trust and confidence in their loyalty. After the arrival of Governor Henry Sloughter near the end of March, Leisler was persuaded to surrender the government, and both he and members of his Council, including Thomas Williams, were taken prisoner.[100]

Some historians have examined Leisler's Rebellion to understand why it occurred and who supported the cause. There is no doubt that the first incident of defiance of the authority of the appointees of James II came from Suffolk County on Long Island, and it has been said that the prime cause of their disaffection with the existing order was New York City's monopoly on the inspection and packing of flour for export.[101] In the context of the southern part of the county of Westchester, this explanation will not suffice completely. There were only two grist mills located in the area, one in Eastchester and another in Westchester, and it is true that the

Eastchester militia was one of the first units to come to Leisler's side in holding the fort at New York, while Thomas Williams of Westchester, who held possession of that town's mill as the husband of Martha Richardson, became a member of Leisler's Council.

Although some wheat was grown in the area, that its importance was increasing, and that the mills would grind it into flour, the main economic activity was livestock raising, not making flour for export. The theory of a reaction against the monopoly held by New York City cannot fully explain why many of the residents of the town of Westchester supported Leisler so ardently.

Another reason advanced by historians for Leisler's Rebellion is rooted in the ethnic diversity of New York City. The less wealthy Dutch inhabitants of the city resented the rule of the wealthier English elite, and it is they who followed Leisler's standard in an attempt to restore the prominence of the Dutch in the affairs of the colony.[102]

There are no grounds for upholding this view when examining the area that would one day become The Bronx. The center of Leisler's support in the area was the town of Westchester, and all of his prominent supporters were of English heritage. Moreover, the social structure of the time really did not indicate that there was a local ruling elite. Only two large landholders whose property was located substantially within the area could be considered in that category, and neither was the target of local enmity.

Colonel Lewis Morris, a prominent Quaker, clearly preferred those opposed to Leisler, for he was Bayard's and van Cortlandt's host when they wanted to intercept Major Gold's news of the accession of William and Mary. He had no quarrel with the inhabitants of the town of Westchester, however. Indeed, the only major controversy with him involved the town of Harlem over the possession of Stony Island. Over all, he took no active part in the events of the rebellion, and he was to die in 1691 before Leisler's arrest.[103]

John Pell of the manor of Pelham also had good relations with the ruling elite of the colony. Under Andros and Dongan, he was a justice, first of the North Riding, and then of Westchester County. He did have a quarrel with Eastchester over fences separating the town from his manor, but he was also married to the daughter of one of the town's first settlers. Pell had no substantial argument with the people of Westchester, and he often presided at their town meetings. The inhabitants of the town frequently turned to him for advice and arbitration, as shown in his actions over the boundary disputes between Westchester and Eastchester. Although Leisler may have suspected that his sympathies did not lay with his cause, since a warrant was issued in February of 1690 to search his manor for several barrels of gunpowder in his possession,[104] Pell also had some amicable dealings with Leisler. In July, 1687, Pell had agreed to sell the New York militiaman a large tract in his manor, and the sale was finally consummated in September, 1689, when Leisler was in power.[105] This purchase was the origin of the town of New Rochelle. In November, 1690, Leisler also named Pell a justice of Westchester County.[106]

It will be recalled that the rebellion, breaking out in Suffolk County, spread to Queens County, and then to Westchester. There was always a strong connection between the settlements on the mainland and the English towns on Long Island since the Dutch days, and they both had been combined in the North Riding before the creation of counties. Therefore, it might be expected that events on Long Island would have an influence on the inhabitants of Westchester. Nevertheless, this does not fully explain why they followed the lead of the Long Islanders so readily.

The answer most probably lies in the dispute over the ownership of the manor of Fordham. The man in the forefront of upholding the rights of the Dutch Reformed Church to the property was Nicholas Bayard, one of the men of the Council ousted by Leisler, and one of the militiaman's chief antagonists. Bayard had a face-to-face confrontation over the ownership of lots in Fordham with Thomas Statham, who became Leisler's sheriff of Westchester County, and over the running of the boundary line with Richard Ponton, who became Leisler's major of the county militia, and with Edward Waters, who became one of Leisler's county justices. All of the town of Westchester could hope to profit from possession of the manor, and the town's inhabitants supplied most of Leisler's prominent followers in the county.

Of course, there were personal reasons why men chose sides in the events of the day. Gabriel Leggett opposed Leisler's expedition to Albany more from his personal enmity toward his step-father-in-law, Thomas Williams, than from personal conviction. Simply by marrying his mother-in-law, Williams appeared to preclude Leggett from participation in the lucrative mill business Martha Richardson Williams had inherited. Since Williams was in such a high position sitting on Leisler's Council, Leggett opposed anything that Williams supported. It is likely that this element of personal enmity was present in more people than this one instance, and the political development of the area that would one day become The Bronx, and even the entire colony and state of New York, would be henceforth marked by factionalism based upon the personal feelings of one leader toward another.

In the meantime, with the fall of Leisler, Bayard and the other members of the old political elite returned to help govern the colony, but now under the auspices of William and Mary. Those who supported Leisler now had to face the consequences of their actions.

CHAPTER X

CONSEQUENCES

1691 TO 1696

With the fall of Jacob Leisler and his government, the men he deposed returned to their former prominence in the colony. Joseph Lee petitioned to be restored as Westchester County's clerk,[1] replacing Edward Collier. Benjamin Collier returned to his old position as county sheriff with the removal of Thomas Statham. Leisler and his Council, including Thomas Williams, were thrown into prison.

The prisoners immediately petitioned for a hearing and for an opportunity to prepare their defense. They also vainly asked to be relieved of the inconvenience of their confinement.[2] The governor's Council then appointed Nicholas Bayard and Stephen van Cortlandt, two of their number who were previously humiliated by Leisler, to act with William Pinhorne to prepare evidence against the prisoners.[3] In early April, 1691, the grand jury indicted Thomas Williams, along with three other Leisler supporters, for high treason.[4] Pleading not guilty at his trial, Williams admitted he had been a councilor, but stated he had been persuaded to go along with Leisler's actions. This explanation did not sway the jury, which found him guilty of the charge, but which also found that he had no property to their knowledge that could be confiscated.[5] Eleven days after the conclusion of his trial, Williams, in the company of Jacob Leisler and the other members of his Council, found himself before Chief Justice Joseph Dudley to be sentenced. Leisler and his son-in-law, Jacob Milbourne, when asked if they had anything to say why the death sentence should not be imposed, stated that they would not answer until the king determined the authority under which they had acted. Thomas Williams and the other erstwhile councilors, on the other hand, merely stated that what they had done was for the welfare of the province. Neither statement stayed Dudley from imposing the supreme penalty, death by being drawn and quartered.[6]

Leisler and Milbourne were quickly executed, but the only hope of salvation for Thomas Williams and the others lay in some form of clemency by the new colonial Legislature, by the governor, or by the king and queen. A new representative Assembly had been elected soon after Leisler's fall. Although the sole representative elected for Westchester County was John Pell, a man who was trusted by Leisler's supporters in the southern part of the county and who had held office under the deposed lieutenant governor, the majority in the new Assembly had opposed Leisler. On the same day that Thomas Williams was sentenced to death, the Assembly unanimously resolved that the actions of Leisler and his supporters were illegal.[7] It would have been impractical to try everyone in the colony whose actions, no matter how slight, could have been interpreted as supporting Leisler. Therefore, the Legislature, one month after the conclusion of the trial, passed a law pardoning all New Yorkers of all charges of treason, sedition, libel, and similar crimes committed before Leisler's surrender of the fort in New York City. Thirty people, however, were specifically excluded from the effect of this act. Thomas Williams and Richard Ponton, both of the town of Westchester, were among them.[8]

Governor Sloughter, after ordering the execution of Leisler and Milbourne, must have realized that the subsequent execution of Thomas Williams and the five remaining former councilors would have accomplished nothing, and he appealed to the king and queen in England to pardon them.[9] By April, 1692, the matter came before the committee of trade and plantations, which recommended their pardon to the Privy Council. At a subsequent Privy Council meeting, Queen Mary declared that she would pardon the men once they asked for it and would also restore whatever estates had been confiscated.[10] Pending their personal plea, in May, 1692, the Queen in Council ordered Governor Benjamin Fletcher, who had succeeded the deceased Sloughter, to release Thomas Williams and the other former councilors.[11]

In early September, 1692, the six Leisler advisors were still in prison, and they still had not petitioned the queen for a pardon. Instead, they petitioned Governor Fletcher, asking him to make the application for them, and to release them until word arrived from England.[12] Fletcher refused to do either, advising them to send their own petition.[13] This, they finally did. Thomas Williams and his colleagues, as unbending as ever, asserted in their petition to Queen Mary that they had faithfully served the king and queen and were unjustly tried and condemned for some pretended high treason. Asserting that the queen had declared her intention of pardoning them, they then requested such a pardon.[14]

The document, however, seems never to have arrived in England. The condemned men remained incarcerated until King William ordered Governor Fletcher to set them free in 1693. Thomas Williams and his colleagues, however, were still under the sentence of death, and, until October of that year, the governor asked that they be either pardoned or executed. The committee of trade and plantations noted that, even though the prisoners had never applied for it, the queen had resolved to issue a pardon. The members voted to lay the matter before the Privy Council with the recommendation that the pardon be granted. The Privy Council agreed with the recommendation, and the royal pardon was issued in March, 1694.[15]

A pardon, however, still indicated that Thomas Williams and his fellow former councilors had committed treasonable acts, but had been forgiven. None of Leisler's advisors were willing to admit that any of their acts had been treasonable. On the other hand, their opponents were not as forgiving as the officials in distant England, and not all their property was restored. Therefore, after the death of Queen Mary in 1695, Jacob Leisler's son, on behalf of himself, Jacob Milbourne's widow, and the six former councilors, petitioned King William to fully restore their estates and to give them permission to apply to the English Parliament for a law that would reverse the attainder of treason, thus wiping the slate clean.[16] In early March, 1695, the Privy Council, considering the petition, referred the question to the committee on trade and plantations, but gave the petitioners the right to apply directly to Parliament to have their attainders reversed.[17]

On the heels of this decision, a petition signed by Leisler's son and by one of the former councilors on behalf of all involved was sent to the House of Lords requesting a reversal of their attainder of treason.[18] In April, 1695, such a bill passed the House of Lords, and survived unchanged in the House of Commons the following month. It became law with King William's assent the day following its final passage.[19] Thus, four years after his initial arrest, finally it had been determined that Thomas Williams had committed no crime.

While Williams was fighting for his life, both he and other Leisler supporters in the town of Westchester had to face the enmity of those who opposed the rule of the erstwhile lieutenant governor. Soon after the new colonial Assembly declared the actions of Leisler and his associates illegal, Gabriel Leggett, in May, 1691, sued Thomas Statham, the erstwhile county sheriff, for £200 for assault and false imprisonment.[20] Leggett, it will be remembered, had been arrested by Statham for stealing Thomas Williams's hog. Richard Ponton, now reduced from the rank of major he held under Leisler to his former position of captain, posted Statham's bail. Sometime afterward, it was agreed that Statham would pay Leggett £25, but Leggett would not accept the former sheriff's bond without further security. Ponton and Statham's brother-in-law, William Chadderton, then stepped forward offering to sign another bond with Statham so that any one of the three men would be liable for the full amount. Leggett readily accepted this.[21]

This agreement did not quench the smoldering enmity that had built up over the years between Gabriel Leggett and his step father-in-law, Thomas Williams. With Williams then in prison under the sentence of death, Leggett hounded Statham and Ponton to pay what they had promised in their bond. The quarrel had so upset the town that, by October, 1692, the county Court of Sessions called upon Justice of the Peace William Barnes to collect depositions from all involved to try to get to the bottom of the differences among Ponton, Statham, and Leggett, three of the town's prominent citizens.[22] Nevertheless, Leggett brought the case to the Supreme Court in New York City, suing Ponton instead of Statham for the £25. It will be remembered that Richard Ponton stood by Thomas Williams's side in March, 1690, when Gabriel Leggett denounced Leisler's military expedition against the French. Ponton, however, never even appeared to make a plea, and the Supreme Court ordered that, without a plea, the judgment would go against him.[23] Ponton was ordered to pay Leggett £50 levied against his estate. Richard Ponton, in turn, sued Thomas Statham in Westchester County's Court of Common Pleas to recover at least some of the sum, and, in December, 1692, the Court ordered the former sheriff to pay Ponton £40 plus court costs. Statham was ruined. He could not pay the amount. He was jailed and faced the danger of having the sheriff seize his land for sale. To save himself, he appealed for relief to Governor Fletcher, who, in turn, referred the matter to Caleb Heathcote,[24] a man who was to assume increasing importance in the town's affairs.

Gabriel Leggett, however, was not to continue unchallenged. Once Thomas Williams was released from jail in 1693, he pressed his criminal case against his step son-in-law concerning his stolen hog, which was one of the foundations of the dispute between them. In December, the case came before Westchester County's Court of Sessions. Leggett brazenly announced to the Court that he had, indeed, stolen Thomas Williams's hog, but pointed to the Legislature's act of May, 1691, pardoning all New Yorkers for crimes committed during Leisler's Rebellion, stating that the law covered this case. In addition, Leggett maintained that there were errors in the indictment. The Court, examining the law, announced that the Legislature's act did not cover actions committed before Leisler's Rebellion, and that Leggett had stolen the hog while King James II was still on the throne. Leggett was sentenced to pay the court charges and to pay a year's security for his good behavior or to be remanded to the sheriff's custody in the county jail.[25]

Undeterred, Gabriel Leggett appealed to the colony's Supreme Court, insisting that there were errors. He alleged that the indictment was not written in the proper form, that Thomas Williams, who had been convicted of high treason, was sworn as a witness to testify against him, that the indictment (falsely as it turned out) placed the time of the hog's theft during the period when Williams was attainted for treason and was not entitled to own any property, and that, by law, Leggett should have to be set free. After postponing the matter for a year, the justices finally entered their decisions in October, 1696. Since a majority of the Court's justices also had served on the court that had condemned Thomas Williams in the first place, it is not surprising that they reversed the judgment against Leggett.[26] Thus, Gabriel Leggett, who had confessed to the crime in an open court, was able to avoid punishment, and Thomas Williams, his hated step father-in-law, had to suffer the consequences of his close connection with Jacob Leisler and his rebellion.

Richard Ponton, who had been an avid Leisler supporter along with Thomas Williams, was another target for those who had suffered under the one-time lieutenant governor. The means of attack was an act passed by the new Assembly in early October, 1691, by which commissioners were appointed in each county to receive and investigate charges of personal and property damages performed by officials of Leisler's administration. The commissioners were empowered to assess the damages and order offenders to pay the cost. The act named John Palmer and John Hunt, both of the town of Westchester, John Drake of Eastchester, and Joseph Theale and Jonathan Heart to be commissioners for Westchester County.[27] Ponton, of course, would have to answer for his actions when he had been a militia major under Leisler.

The Westchester County commissioners appointed by the act met in the town of Westchester to begin their work in January, 1692. Richard Ponton and a large number of Leisler's supporters met them there, forming what seemed to the commissioners to be an angry mob. Ponton loudly proclaimed that the seal on the commissions was a forgery and that the commissioners actually had no authority to sit. Outraged, the commissioners ordered the undersheriff to arrest him for sedition. At that point, Robert Bloomer of Mamaroneck and Thomas Baxter of Westchester threatened the hapless lawman, daring him to arrest Ponton, and threatening that the county jail would be broken into by the mob and Ponton freed if arrested.[28]

This incident was a clear disturbance of the peace, and justices John Pell, John Palmer (who was also one of the appointed commissioners), and William Barnes immediately set themselves to the task of collecting affidavits from witnesses to the incident. By March, 1692, they completed their work, and communicated the information to James Graham, the attorney general in New York City. At the same time, they informed Graham that Richard Ponton was the head of a number of people in the county who denied the authority of the government and were aiming for a new rebellion. To prevent further trouble, they requested Graham to take Ponton, Bloomer, and the principal ringleaders to the jail in New York.[29] Graham, who was more level-headed about prosecuting Leisler's former adherents than many in the colony, took no action. In June, however, the Westchester County grand jury did indict Ponton, along with Robert Bloomer and Thomas Baxter, for disturbing the peace. Upon conviction, Baxter wisely paid the necessary fees and was discharged.[30]

Ponton, however, had the additional difficulty of being attainted for treason, and, along with Thomas Williams, of being specifically excluded from the 1691 legislative pardon extended to most of Leisler's adherents. In spite of this, Queen Mary, acting in the Privy Council in May, 1692, ordered Governor Benjamin Fletcher to release all those who had court cases pending for adhering to Leisler's cause. Ponton, along with some in a similar position, was summoned before the governor's Council and was informed that the grand jury's indictment of treason against him had been dropped.[31]

The pardon, however, did not affect the case involving the disturbance of the peace, which finally came to trial in December, 1693. Two weeks prior to the sitting of the county's Court of Sessions, Richard Ponton had been in jail, largely because he did not have enough cash to obtain his release. Out of sympathy for one of the town's leading citizens, who was also one of the handful of original settlers, the Westchester Board of Trustees attempted to raise funds to obtain his bail. William Barnes proposed to lend the board £6 for the purpose in exchange for the use of some land under its jurisdiction. The Board agreed to this proposition.[32] Thus, Ponton was a free man when he and Robert Bloomer appeared for their trial before the Court of Sessions. The defendants pleaded not guilty to the charge. However, at their request, the trial was delayed until the following sitting of the Court to afford them the opportunity to reach a settlement in the matter.[33] A settlement was reached, since the Court of Sessions never took up the case again, and Ponton was to serve on its grand jury a year later.[34]

Nevertheless, Ponton's difficulties were far from over. The Supreme Court had ordered Richard Ponton to pay Gabriel Leggett £50 when Thomas Statham could not pay Leggett the sum he owed for false arrest. As late as 1695, however, Ponton still had not paid this debt. To obtain his money, Leggett sold Ponton's debt to Thomas White, who, in turn, took the case to the colony's Supreme Court once again, and, in October, 1695, the Court for a second time ordered Ponton to pay.[35] Richard Ponton also faced financial ruin because of his adherence to Leisler's cause.

The opponents of Jacob Leisler, now returned to power, were extremely sensitive to any action that could be interpreted as a revival of the rebellious spirit, even if it were committed by someone previously uninvolved with the incidents surrounding Leisler's Rebellion. In January, 1695, Queen Mary died, leaving King William the sole English sovereign. By May, the news spread throughout the colony of New York, and, in the town of Eastchester, at John Pinckney's house, the matter came up during a conversation among Pinckney, his brother, Thomas, one other person, and Peter Chock, who acted as an attorney in several of the colony's courts. Chock made the comment that the queen's death invalidated Governor

Benjamin Fletcher's commission, and he thought the Assembly should have him recalled. Chock then argued against a number of actions Fletcher had taken, saying that if the king of England had done such things, he would be beheaded. He did not hesitate to call Fletcher the worst governor New York ever had.

Alarmed, John Pinckney informed Attorney General James Graham of Chock's words, and Graham, in June, placed the matter before the grand jury in Westchester County. In Peter Chock's presence, Pinckney was sworn and told his story. After hearing it, the Court of Sessions declared Chock's words to be highly criminal, but not within its cognizance. They ordered Sheriff Benjamin Collier to take Chock to jail in New York for trial there. Chock, however, offered bail, which James Graham accepted to guarantee his appearance before the Supreme Court.

Twenty days later, William Pinhorne and Justice of the Peace William Barnes, accompanied by justices John Hunt, James Mott, and William Chadderton, met at the town of Westchester to constitute an auxiliary sitting of the Supreme Court. Attorney General Graham had examined the case further and found no real sedition attempted. No prosecution was made, and Peter Chock was cleared.[36]

It was in this tense atmosphere following Leisler's Rebellion, however, that the controversy between the town of Westchester and the Dutch Reformed Church in New York over the control of the manor of Fordham was renewed. In May, 1691, the newly-elected Assembly, in one of its first acts, reconfirmed all charters, patents, and grants made in the past, but any person could dispute a claim if he began his case within five years.[37] By early October, the Westchester trustees noted that a number of suits had been instituted against the town that would infringe on its rights and privileges, and they resolved to defend them. These suits were instituted by Henricus Selyns and his wife, Margarieta, acting on behalf of the Dutch Church. To raise the funds to pay the costs of these law suits, William Barnes offered to buy two pieces of meadow on Throggs Neck for £3 18s. The trustees accepted the offer and sent Barnes and Samuel Palmer to New York City to obtain legal counsel.[38] Three days later, it was obvious that the money raised would not be enough, and the trustees sold the common meadow on the east bank of the Bronx River at auction, which William Richardson purchased for £4. Similarly, the common meadows within John Ferris's ditch leading to Eastchester field was sold, which William Barnes obtained for £6.[39] Thus, fortified with £13 18s., the town of Westchester awaited the legal onslaught of the Dutch Reformed Church.

Four days after the town raised the money, the case began in the Supreme Court in New York. By record, it was simply the case of Andries Marschalk as a tenant lessee to dispossess William Richardson, who held the land in dispute. Everyone knew that Selyns and the Dutch Church were the principal plaintiffs behind Marschalk and that the town of Westchester was the principal defendant behind Richardson. Witnesses and documents were introduced on behalf of both sides, and the jury found in favor of the defendant. The town of Westchester had won the case.[40]

At the same time, the Supreme Court considered another suit instituted by Selyns against Thomas Statham. It will be remembered that Statham purchased land in Fordham before Leisler's Rebellion and loudly upheld to Nicholas Bayard the claim of the town of Westchester to the manor. Part of the reason for Statham's support of the Westchester claim may have come from the fact that he purchased his Fordham property with his bond, which, if the Dutch Church had no jurisdiction, he would not have to pay. Statham was ordered to show cause why judgment should not be made against him, and, two days later, the Dutch Church asked that the judgment be executed.[41] Considering Statham's previous appointed position as Leisler's Westchester County sheriff and the anti-Leisler attitude of the Court's justices, it is likely the Supreme Court ordered Statham to pay.

Nevertheless, a court jury found that the town of Westchester had jurisdiction over Fordham, and the town's trustees were not slow to exercise their rights. In early November, 1691, they resolved to make leases with those who held the town's land on the west side of the Bronx River.[42] A number of those in that area, however, refused to sign a lease with the town or to recognize its jurisdiction. Consequently, the trustees decided to sue to eject Frederick Shurmer, Hendrick Corson, John Odell, and Thomas Bailey in the county's Court of Common Pleas, and assigned William Richardson to retain the eminent attorneys, Edward Antill and James Emott, to act for the town.[43]

The Dutch Church, however, stung by the jury's verdict in the Supreme Court, considered the matter in its Consistory in March, 1692. The Church spent £1,200 on the property and felt that Westchester was able to take Fordham because the jury had not understood the case well. The members of the Consistory debated their options, even the possibility of appealing to a court in England. In the end, they resolved to bring up the case again as if it were completely new, authorized the deacons to spend money from the treasury for it, and entrusted the whole business to the capable Nicholas Bayard.[44]

This time, it was arranged that the Dutch Church's case be brought to suit in the name of John White, and the Westchester trustees responded by appointing William Richardson and William Barnes to hire another attorney in New York City to act on behalf of the town. The case came before the Supreme Court in April, 1692, both sides agreeing that a special jury be impaneled to decide it.[45]
While this case was pending adjudication, the town once again faced the prospect of raising funds to pay for it. Thus, in early May, the Westchester trustees voted to tax those who had rights on the west side of the Bronx River 18s. 7d. each. With the question in doubt, a number of them were reluctant to part with the sum, and, in August, the trustees voted that those holding out had to pay the bill in January at Justice William Barnes's house in cash or in merchandable corn or winter wheat. The tenants also doubted Westchester's claim, and, by January, three of them refused to pay their rent to the town.[46]

The question was finally argued before the Supreme Court in its session of October, 1692. Some difficulty arose when one member of the jury did not appear. Both parties, however, consented to proceed without him. The Dutch Church then produced Governor Lovelace's patent for Fordham as evidence that the property belonged to it, while Westchester showed Governor Nicolls's patent for the town, arguing that it provided for including Fordham within its borders. The Church, thereupon, agreed that Westchester's evidence was true, but contended that it was inadequate as proof that Fordham belonged to the town. This was a question of law to be decided by the justices, not a question of fact to be left to the jury. In reply, Westchester moved to extend the case to the Court's next term to give its attorney a chance to argue the point. The motion was granted. The question of adequacy was then argued in April, 1693, and the Supreme Court justices decided in favor of the Dutch Church.[47]

After the question was decided, the trustees of the town of Westchester tried to make an arrangement to salvage something from the outcome. In early August, 1693, they agreed to send William Barnes, John Hunt, Samuel Palmer, Joseph Palmer, John Ferris,

Thomas Baxter, Richard Ponton, Edward Waters, Robert Huestis, Jr., Josiah Hunt, and Edward Collier, or any seven of them, accompanied by as many of the town's freeholders who wished to go, to meet with Henricus Selyns or his agents on the west side of the Bronx River to come to terms.[48] Nothing seems to have come from this attempt. Therefore, at the end of August, the trustees sent Samuel Palmer and Thomas Baxter to New York to consult directly with Selyns and his wife, Margarieta.[49] Little progress seems to have been made at this time. In early October, however, Selyns appeared ready to offer some propositions, and Palmer and Baxter were sent to him again.[50] In early November, 1693, the trustees of Westchester, for an unspecified sum of money, signed a quit claim deed releasing to Henricus and Margarieta Selyns all possession of the manor of Fordham.[51]

Nevertheless, the town's trustees were reluctant to surrender their claim. By early May, 1694, they complained of the great cost the court cases had been to Westchester, and indignantly discovered that Samuel Palmer and Thomas Baxter received £25 from Henricus Selyns for the quit claim deed and had not turned the money over to the town. They resolved to send Joseph Palmer and Josiah Hunt to New York City to examine the records of the Dutch Reformed Church to determine the facts.[52] Nothing came from the intimation of bribery in the final settlement of the Fordham property, but Westchester's claim of jurisdiction would be revived periodically in the future, and would not be laid to rest until the middle of the eighteenth century.

In January, 1695, Henricus Selyns and his wife, Margarieta, finally completed the transfer of ownership of the manor of Fordham to the Elders and Overseers of the New York City Dutch Reformed Church to be held by it forever to support its ministers. Included in the deed was the stipulation that the land could never be alienated.[53] In April, it was decided that only persons belonging to the Church would be commissioned to let out lands in Fordham, make leases there, or to examine and settle disputes over the property.[54] Leases would be made for eight, ten, twelve, or twenty years, and, in an attempt to quash disputes as to boundary claims, the committee chosen to make the leases was empowered to erase all existing lines and to make new ones in the presence of two impartial surveyors.[55]

At the same time, the Dutch Church, noting the favorable circumstances, resolved to incorporate the institution, the church buildings and lands, and the manor of Fordham, and appointed a committee to approach Governor Benjamin Fletcher and his Council to obtain whatever useful privileges they could.[56] In June, 1695, a petition to the governor was presented,[57] and, in May, 1696, a charter of incorporation was granted to the Minister, Elders and Deacons of the Reformed Protestant Dutch Church of the City of New York. It noted the properties held by the Church, including Fordham with its boundaries delineated, reaffirming its rights to them.[58] For this, the consistory resolved in June to present Fletcher with a present of silver plate worth £75 to £80. The deacons were expected to lend the Church the money for the present and were to be reimbursed in time from revenues from Fordham or other sources.[59]

While it may have been true that Westchester's legal claim to Fordham was weak, the town's argument was not bolstered by its recent past when it had been one of the centers of Jacob Leisler's strength and home of some of his strongest supporters. The case for the Dutch Church was managed by Nicholas Bayard, an outspoken Leisler opponent, and many of the Church's officials agreed with Bayard's views. The town's initial success in the colony's Supreme Court in retaining control of Fordham came at the hands of a jury. The final decision in the second case, however, turned on a matter of law, which excluded the jury from deliberation, and rested upon the findings of the justices, a majority of whom had sat in judgment on Leisler and his Council. Thus, the town's loss of jurisdiction over Fordham could have been another consequence of Leisler's Rebellion.

Although he did not start it, another of Leisler's legacies was the war with the French, which the erstwhile lieutenant governor supported and prosecuted, called the War of the League of Augsberg in Europe and King William's War in the colonies. One of the first acts of the newly established Legislature was to regulate the militia. Under these regulations, every man between the ages of 15 and 60 had to register with his local militia captain within a month after his arrival in the area or pay a fine of twenty shillings for each month he failed to do so. Members of the governor's Council, justices of the peace, sheriffs, coroners, court officers, ministers, schoolmasters, physicians, and surgeons were exempt from serving. The arms and equipment for each soldier and horseman were detailed, and, once a year, the colonel had to order his inferior officers to inspect his men to see if they had complied with these regulations. In addition, each captain was to provide drums, colors, trumpets, trumpeters, and banners for his unit. Each company had the right to elect its own officers.[60] It was in accordance with these regulations that the

Westchester County militia was organized.

The fighting in the war against the French never touched the southern part of Westchester County, but the war took its toll in the contributions in men and money the county had to supply as its quota in the war effort. Men were needed to protect the Albany frontier, and, periodically, the colonial Legislature ordered a number of troops to go there from Westchester County to serve for a few months.[61] In September, 1692, 25 men were raised within the county for such service. By early May, 1693, the entire county militia consisted of six companies of foot soldiers with a total of 283 men.[62] Ten of these men were ordered to Albany for the winter months in early November, 1694.[63] This did not mean, however, that the war was any more popular with the men affected since the time Gabriel Leggett voiced his protest in the town of Westchester in front of Leisler's representatives. In May, 1693, the governor's Council had to urge the colonels of the Suffolk, Queens, and Westchester County militias to forward their men to reinforce Albany. A similar order had to be issued in June, 1695.[64] Clearly, there was resistance to the prospect of journeying to a far-away place endangering life and limb.

The cost of the war also proved to be burdensome. Generally, the Legislature specified the sum to be raised to cover the cost of the number of men sent to Albany, apportioning the amount among the several counties. It was left to the local assessors in each subdivision to levy the assessment as they saw fit. In the laws passed between May, 1691, and September, 1696, Westchester County's share of the military burden amounted to £1,609 4s. 6d.[65] That sum would come to more than £5 per family in five and a half years, which, if assessed equally among them, would have pushed several to the edge of bankruptcy considering the general poverty of many in the county then. Certainly, the men of Eastchester complained early that they were being overtaxed. In early October, 1692, the inhabitants at a town meeting chose Samuel Casling and Thomas Pinckney to address the justices at Westchester on the matter.[66] In September, 1693, John Drake was sent to Westchester to meet with others in the county to try to petition the governor to equalize the assessments.[67] The attempt must have succeeded, since the county's monetary quota for the following year was a more reasonable £143.[68] By November, 1695, the cost of the war was being felt throughout the colony, and the Legislature voted to raise £1,000 to send attorney William Nicoll to the Privy Council in England to attempt to obtain an English contribution to ease the monetary burdens felt by all New Yorkers.

Westchester County's share in the endeavor was £52 14s.[69]

Despite all of these consequences of Leisler's Rebellion, the few years following the fall of the erstwhile lieutenant governor did mark some significant advances in the southern part of Westchester County. In 1693, an effort was made to extinguish the last Indian claim to lands within the town of Westchester, and, in May, arrangements were made for John Hunt to put up four Siwanoys for the night, entertaining them with an Indian supper and a gallon (almost 4 liters) of cider. The following day, the Siwanoys, Hunt, and John Ferris, Sr., viewed the property, and, in early April, two sachems sold all the land from the east side of the Bronx River to the head of Rattlesnake Brook and the border of John Pell's property for two guns, two coats, two shirts, two bottles, two adzes, one barrel of cider, and six bits of money.[70] Later, it was agreed that William Barnes would provide the kettles, Hunt and Ferris would contribute a coat each, William Richardson would give the shirts, and Joseph Hunt, the adzes and the money. Samuel and Joseph Palmer volunteered to share the cost of one of the guns, as did Robert Huestis and Thomas Baxter, while Josiah Hunt would provide the cider.[71] Once the Siwanoys received these goods, all the land in the town would be controlled by the descendants of Europeans for the first time.

Indeed, some of the advances in these years came from the Legislature, which was firmly in the hands of Leisler's opponents. In November, 1692, a law established a public and open market every Wednesday at the town of Westchester, probably because it was the county seat. At the market, people could sell their cattle, grain, provisions, or merchandise from eight o'clock in the morning until sundown without paying a toll for the privilege. Although the town itself would gain no monetary reward from the weekly market because no tolls were charged, the townsmen would benefit. The site of sale was not too far from their doors, and the location would save them time and much of the cost of transportation. Moreover, the same considerations applied if any of them wished to buy anything. In addition, the operator of the local tavern would certainly profit from those who wanted to eat and drink while attending the market.

The same law that established the market also decreed that each county hold a fair twice a year. In Westchester County, the fair was to be held at the town of Westchester for four days starting at the second Tuesday in March, while another was to be held in Rye in October. In effect, there would be little difference between a market and a fair, except that the fair would last for four days and that the law specifically provided for the sale of horses at fairs, although it did not forbid such sale at markets. The governor appointed the rulers of the fairs from among the county's residents to make the rules and to constitute the Court of Piepowder to adjudicate disputes arising there. A toll of 9d. was charged for the sale of every horse, half paid by the buyer and half by the seller, and the sale had to be registered in a book kept for the purpose.[72]

The avowed purpose of the law was to encourage trade and commerce, and both Eastchester and Westchester took steps at this time toward the same end. The inhabitants of Eastchester continued the policy of offering land for a limited period to attract craftsmen to their town. In early January, 1693, they granted Edward Avery a home lot of three acres (just over one hectare) on condition that he would practice his trade as a tanner and shoemaker for three years starting in April.[73] In February, 1694, the trustees of the town of Westchester voted to build a fourteen-foot (4.2 meter) wide cart bridge over Westchester Creek to replace the one originally built on the site, which must have either fallen apart or have washed away in a flood.[74] Once again, Throggs Neck would be connected commercially with the center of the town. Moreover, in September, William Richardson was given the right to erect a grist mill on Westchester Creek to grind the grain of the town's inhabitants, charging them a fourteenth part of the whole for his service. He was also permitted to cut timber and build a sawmill there.[75] Eastchester also had plans to build a sawmill, and, in March, 1695, Thomas Pinckney and John Drake were chosen to pick a site for one.[76]

Nevertheless, the southern part of Westchester County not only remained overwhelmingly rural, but it had sections of wilderness. In 1692, the trustees of the town of Westchester had to impose fines on the owners of hogs found wandering on the roads and in the sheep pasture.[77] Indeed, some black slaves made it a practice to hunt hogs lost in the woods, and this so disturbed the owners of the hogs that the county Court of Sessions issued an order forbidding slaves to carry guns, dogs, or staves when off their masters' farms.[78] It is not known how much of a loss could have been attributed to wolves in the woods, but when the Legislature ordered each town to have two wolf pits to capture them, the Court of Sessions, in December, promptly put the order into effect.[79] John Jennings requested from the Westchester trustees permission to build one of the town's wolf pits if he could keep whatever profit obtained from it, obviously the bounty offered for the wolves. The trustees readily agreed to the proposition.⁸⁰

Nowhere was the poor, raw, and rural state of the area so evident than in the continual difficulty in obtaining resident ministers to conduct church services. Caleb Heathcote, who rapidly rose in power and influence, was as shocked at the conditions he beheld when he arrived in Westchester as any recent immigrant from a more settled and genteel England could be. He thought the people "rude and heathenish," since they used Sundays for sports and diversions that appeared lewd to him. He thought the frontier rudeness of the inhabitants intolerable, and was determined to correct it. Upon his appointment as colonel of the Westchester County militia, he issued a command to his captains to call their men together and threaten them with constant military drill every Sunday unless each town appointed readers to hold religious services. Since there was no great desire for military activity in the first place, it was unanimously agreed that readers be chosen.⁸¹

Heathcote's opinion of the state of religion was not entirely accurate. In the past, both the towns of Westchester and Eastchester attempted to attract resident ministers with varying degrees of success, and there are records of readers leading Sunday services in their absence. Therefore, it was not difficult for the inhabitants of Eastchester at a town meeting in early January, 1693, to choose Richard Shute and Samuel Casling to read the Bible and sermons.⁸² A few days later, the Westchester town meeting agreed to hire an orthodox (by which they meant Puritan) minister as soon as possible for £50 a year. The residents agreed to get Heathcote to procure a man for the job on one of his many visits to New England, but, failing that, William Barnes was to hire the man.⁸³ Eastchester went one step further and began the process of building the first structure designed for religious services in the county, which they called a meeting house. In May, 1693, the Eastchester inhabitants agreed on its dimensions and to assess themselves to pay its cost according to the value of their property. This provision came into force when a carpenter was hired in December. In early February, 1695, they laid out half an acre (about one-fifth of a hectare) lot near the village green upon which to build a parsonage.⁸⁴

Caleb Heathcote, of course, was aware of Governor Benjamin Fletcher's first proclamation issued in 1692 to suppress vice and to observe the Sabbath. undoubtedly, he was instrumental in initiating its execution in Westchester County. At a Westchester County Court of Sessions held in September, 1693, over which Heathcote presided, regulations for the observance of the Sabbath were issued. He noted that a complaint had been made about disorder and profaneness in the county on Sundays, but most likely it was he who had registered the complaint. He noted that public worship was neglected and children and servants grew up without fearing the Lord because several places in the county lacked the funds to pay for a minister to instruct the people. Therefore, in conformity with the governor's proclamation, the Court ordered the readers to read two sermons out of good books every Sunday, one between 9:00 and 11:00 o'clock in the morning, and one between 2:00 and 4:00 o'clock in the afternoon. Anyone who dared deride such public worship was to be placed in the stocks for an hour or fined ten shillings to be used for poor relief. In addition, on Sundays, drinking at a tavern, traveling without permission from a justice of the peace, fishing, shooting, hunting with horses, and other sports were forbidden, but strangers in town were allowed to buy meat and drink.[85]

In early October, 1693, the colony's Legislature passed an act to settle a ministry in New York City and in Richmond, Queens, and Westchester counties. Subtly worded, it was the basis upon which the Church of England would become the establishment in the four counties, although it was not perceived that way by the vast majority of the inhabitants of the southern part of Westchester County who were overwhelmingly of other religious sects. The law called for Protestant ministers to be called to officiate in defined parishes within one year. Westchester County was to have two parishes, with Westchester, Eastchester, Yonkers, and Pelham forming one of them. By the law, each of Westchester County's parishes was to pay £50 in country produce to support its minister. The county justices were empowered to summon the freeholders of each parish each January to elect ten vestrymen and two church wardens. The justices and vestrymen were empowered to levy taxes collected by the constable to support the minister. Each minister was to be paid quarterly in equal installments. The vestrymen and church wardens were empowered to choose the minister, but all former agreements with ministers would remain in force.[86]

No matter what the law stated, finding a minister was still a difficult task. In early September, 1694, John Drake and Henry Fowler, Sr., were chosen by the Eastchester town meeting to go to Westchester to consult with others chosen in the parish about providing a minister.[87] Nothing seems to have come of that meeting.

In May, 1695, however, the freeholders and inhabitants of the parish of Westchester, Eastchester, Yonkers, and Pelham agreed that Warham Mather be chosen as minister for one year or longer, and that Edward Waters as churchwarden, along with John Hunt and William Barnes with as many vestrymen as could be assembled, were to make an agreement with him.[88] Mather had previously served as a minister for Eastchester, Westchester, and Yonkers in 1684, and, thus, was well-known. He was originally from Massachusetts, and did not fit the description of a minister according to Caleb Heathcote or Governor Fletcher. Not only was Mather not ordained as a minister in the Church of England, but he was not ordained at all. He never rose above the position of a divinity student for all his years of preaching.[89] Yet, for the first time, southern Westchester County had a resident minister chosen by the process established by law.

In a sense, the establishment of a church organization by law was part of a profound change coming over the area that would one day become The Bronx. In part as a consequence of Leisler's Rebellion, in the last decade of the seventeenth century, society and government were becoming more structured and formal. The first generation of settlers in the region were growing older, and some prominent ones would die in this decade or the next. The men who would replace them would be like them in their drive and insistence upon their rights. Some of the rough edges that existed in the frontier generation, however, would be refined, and the effort of the younger people only now coming into prominence would be bent not only to recreating part of the life they had known in England, but to attempting to recreate all of it, even the aspects of gentility, privilege, and power that were the hallmarks of the English aristocracy.

One of those in the forefront of this development was a member of the older generation, Frederick Philipse. He arrived when the colony was first under Dutch rule and Anglicized his name following the English conquest. Over the years, he amassed a fortune as a merchant, using some of his profits to purchase land, much of which was in Westchester County. It will be remembered that he was one of the first to purchase part of Adriaen van der Donck's land from Elias Doughty. By the last decade of the seventeenth century, he was powerful enough to be a member of the governor's Council and wealthy enough to own vast tracts of land, almost unbroken by anyone else's property, between the Hudson and Bronx Rivers from the Croton River to a point just south of today's Bronx-Westchester border.

Philipse wanted to have his landholdings in Westchester County erected into a manor, such as Pelham and Fordham. His petition of January, 1693, for this purpose, however, also meant to serve the twin goals of extending his property and of providing him and his heirs with a good investment procured at little expense. For many years, the idea of building a bridge across Spuyten Duyvil Creek to replace the Verveelen ferry was broached. Philipse now proposed to build the bridge in return for obtaining title to the island of Paparinemin and for the right to charge tolls on the span.

As a member of the Council, Philipse was in constant contact with Governor Fletcher, who was not averse to granting huge tracts of land to those who requested it, and, who, in the common practice of the time, expected a valuable present in return for the favor. Accordingly, in June, 1693, in a long and wordy document describing each purchase, Frederick Philipse's Westchester County lands were confirmed in his possession and erected into the manor of Philipsburgh for the nominal payment of £4 12s. a year. Added to his lands was the island of Paparinemin, and the document specifically empowered Philipse to build a bridge over Spuyten Duyvil Creek, enumerating the tolls. In New York currency, each man and each cow was to be charged 3d., while every 20 hogs, calves, or sheep were to be charged 12d., and each cart, coach, or sleigh was to be charged 9d., as was to be any watercraft that caused the bridge's draw to be raised. After sunset, special night rates were to be levied, with each passenger paying 2d.; each man and horse, 6d.; and each watercraft, 2s.[90] When built, the span was called the King's Bridge, and people began calling the land on each side of it by the same name.

Not only was the manor of Philipsburgh far larger than the older manors of Fordham and Pelham, but a monopoly right to build a bridge and to charge tolls for it was included in such a patent in the area for the first time. Unlike Verveelen's ferry, whose franchise had been limited to a specified number of years, no such limit applied to the King's Bridge. Moreover, the right to the bridge and its tolls was hereditary. The farmers of Westchester County using the new facility might discover travel to their markets in New York City more convenient than before, but they would be paying generations of Philipses for the privilege for decades to come.

Among the members of the younger generation who was to emulate Frederick Philipse in several ways was Lewis Morris, whose guardian, the Quaker colonel, Lewis Morris, died in 1691. The will, drawn up by William Bickley, reflected the differences that the colonel had with his nephew. The old Quaker declared that he had previously intended to make young Lewis his sole executor, but, because he had been constantly disobedient, had frequently absented himself from his house without cause, and had associated with people of whom he had disapproved, he made Lewis's aunt, his own wife, Mary, the sole executrix. The colonel, after bequeathing small parts of his valuable property in Monmouth County, New Jersey, to various legatees, left the bulk of that estate, including an iron works, to his nephew, but only on condition that he not challenge the provisions of the will. If young Lewis Morris did challenge them, then that property would be left to the colonel's widow, Mary, and her heirs. It will be remembered that young Lewis had a right to the property in southern Westchester County which had been the cause of the dispute with his guardian. Yet, the old Quaker, after making some small bequests from that property, boldly left it all to his wife.[91]

The proof that young Lewis Morris had a right to the property in Westchester County was contained in the articles of agreement between the old Quaker and his brother, Richard, by which the surviving children would inherit the estate. Richard's son was the sole survivor. Young Lewis had his father's copy of the agreement, but not his recently deceased uncle's, which was held by William Bickley, who had drawn up the will, but which had mysteriously disappeared. The clause of the will prohibiting challenge on pain of losing the New Jersey property was clearly designed to prevent young Lewis from claiming the Westchester lands by using his evidence of ownership.

A series of fortuitous circumstances, however, then occurred. Mary Morris, the old colonel's widow, followed her husband to the grave one week after his death. The will then lacked an executor to carry out its provisions. Of the six overseers the old Quaker named in his will, one, Miles Foster, then informed young Lewis Morris that the document contained some erasures and words added between the lines in those clauses affecting the Westchester property. The young man's anger then rose to the surface. The provisions of the will now looked like a conspiracy on the part of Mary Morris and her heirs to deprive him of his rightful inheritance. He seethed at what looked like an underhanded attempt to deprive him of what was rightfully his, and his anger at this development and those he felt responsible for it remained for the rest of his life. Fortunately, with his Aunt Mary deceased, with no executor for the will, an administrator had to be appointed by the governor and his Council, and, at that time, the opportunity for young Lewis to question the provisions by calling attention to the erasures and interlineations would present itself. Ostensibly, he would not be questioning the provisions of the will, only how it was drawn up. Thus, he would not be in danger of losing the New Jersey property his uncle bequeathed him.

The will was probated before the governor and his Council in May, 1691, and the alterations were pointed out. The six witnesses to the will were called to discover if they knew anything, but only two were willing to testify under oath, and they said they knew nothing about them. William Bickley, who drew up the will, stated that he had made the alterations, but that he did not know why they were made. The testimony did not appear credible because the will had been drafted only three months earlier, and there was no great elapse of time for the people involved to forget such things. Most of those present thought that the portions erased must have had a different meaning from the words interlined. Since no one would admit the reasons for the change, Governor Henry Sloughter granted the administration of the estate to young Lewis Morris.[92]

Morris, however, was also ordered to make an inventory of his uncle's far-flung possessions, and, in early November, Richard Ingoldsby, who took over the administration of the colony following Sloughter's death, ordered Stephen van Cortlandt and Nicholas Bayard of New York City, along with John Pell of Pelham and William Richardson of the town of Westchester, to appraise their value. The appraisal of the Morris lands in Westchester County was submitted in February, 1692. The total value of such merchandise as cloth, iron, sugar, and ginger, which the elder Morris could have sold at a profit, together with wheat, livestock, farm implements, slaves, odd coins and jewelry, and debts to be paid to him, came to an enormous £9,078 17s. 1d. This sum probably included the value of the lands as well.[93]

As administrator of this huge estate, Morris could have retained possession of it all, especially in light of questions raised about the legitimacy of the bequest to Mary Morris and her heirs. Nevertheless, Lewis Morris was legally bound by the terms of the will, and his aunt's heirs could have brought him to court to force him to execute those terms. In November, 1691, while the entire estate was being inventoried, however, the young man married Isabella Graham, the daughter of James Graham, the speaker of the Assembly and the colony's attorney-general. This combination of circumstances probably left Mary Morris's heirs no recourse but to surrender their claim to the Westchester County lands to young Lewis. The marriage now placed him in a position of great influence in the colonial government, and opposition to the newlywed's assertion that he was the rightful heir to the property would have been futile. To keep things both legitimate and quiet, Lewis Morris, within a year or two of his uncle's death, purchased releases from his deceased aunt's heirs. He would hold the property without opposition for more than fifty years.[94]

It was clear that, in young Lewis Morris, the use of privilege and power was combined with landed wealth on the model of the English aristocracy. With him, the younger generation of Westchester County entered a new era. Unlike his deceased uncle, who was a Quaker, this Lewis Morris was a firm member of the Church of England, and would, in later decades, seek to extend its membership and influence. Unlike John Pell, who married a local girl, the daughter of one of the early settlers of the town of Eastchester who brought with her little or no wealth and not a scintilla of political influence through family connections, Lewis Morris made a politically advantageous match. Through his father-in-law, the speaker and attorney general, he would be able to meet members of the Assembly from all over the colony and to engage socially with the governor and members of the Council. Political connections could lead to obtaining advance information to increase his wealth, and could also lead to holding political office. These results, in turn, could increase his own influence to the point where he could become a major factor in shaping events.

The quintessence of the younger men emerging with privilege and power, however, was Caleb Heathcote. Heathcote, the sixth of seven sons of a mayor of Chesterfield in England, came from a distinguished merchant family. After spending the first quarter century of his life in his homeland, he made the fateful decision to seek his fortune in the colony of New York. His reason may have been the marriage of the woman he loved to an older brother. On the other hand, Caleb Heathcote's merchant brothers maintained mercantile interests in many parts of the world, often residing in foreign parts or a British colony. With the decease of his father, clutching his share as one of the heirs, and possessing a letter of introduction to Governor Henry Sloughter, who had, unknown to him, died earlier, Caleb Heathcote set sail for New York, arriving in 1692. In the city, he became a merchant, adding to his inherited wealth by trading goods from one section of the empire to another.[95]

Heathcote's rise to prominence was extraordinarily rapid. Certainly, he was intelligent and industrious. In his dealings with others, he had the unusual ability of obtaining his object while using a combination of tact, charm, and logic to dissipate any resentment by those who opposed his views. He had the capacity for leadership. In the content of the times, his increasing wealth and family connections were distinct assets, presaging activity in government.

It is likely that Caleb Heathcote's letter of introduction to Henry Sloughter was ultimately delivered to Benjamin Fletcher when he arrived to take over as governor. It is certain that, within a month after the new governor's arrival in August, 1692, Fletcher appointed Heathcote a member of his Council, the highest honor then open to a resident of the colony. Because the members of the Council were named in his commission, Fletcher proposed to the Lords of Trade that Heathcote be added. Unfortunately, several ships carrying the request never made it to England, and, in early June, 1695, Fletcher restated the proposal, noting that Heathcote was very serviceable and forward on all occasions. By August, the Lords of Trade recommended the appointment, although the proper papers did not cross the Atlantic until the summer of 1697. By that time, Heathcote had been acting as a member of the Council for almost five years.[96]

The war against the French proved advantageous to Caleb Heathcote, both commercially and politically. Through the years, probably aided by his presence on the Council, he received contracts for providing the army with watchcoats, bedding, blankets, and other supplies, and for furnishing materials to repair the fort in New York. Politically, Heathcote was given primary responsibility for military affairs in Westchester County when he was appointed colonel of its militia before the end of 1692.[97] It was an admirable choice to attempt to use a man of Heathcote's ability and temperament to bring order and obedience to a county known as one of the leading centers of Leisler's Rebellion.

By 1693, Heathcote was made a judge of the county's Court of Common Pleas and president and judge advocate of the county's Court Martial.[98] As a member of the Council, he exercised his right to preside at sittings of the county's Court of Sessions since December, 1692.[99] Thus, in his person, he combined the judicial authority over civil suits, criminal acts, and military infractions.

It was clear to those living in the southern part of Westchester County that Caleb Heathcote was a man of power and influence to be reckoned with, and, as a consequence, John Pell's position slipped from its height of preeminence. Of course, Pell was still respected and trusted. He was chosen by the people of the county to represent them in the Assembly, and he was still a justice of the peace, entitled to a seat as one of the judges of the Court of Sessions. In the Assembly in April, 1692, Pell chaired a committee to devise a way to raise 200 men to reinforce the frontiers at Albany, and, while the process continued toward its successful conclusion, he was named a major in the county militia.[100] Yet, as a man who accepted office under Leisler, he was not completely trusted by those who ruled the colony. Heathcote, a man more to Governor Fletcher's liking, was named Pell's superior as colonel, although, before the year was out, Pell was promoted to lieutenant colonel, but still under Heathcote's command.[101] Thus, if inhabitants of the area had to appeal to a higher authority for a favor, Caleb Heathcote, who had influence, was the man to whom to turn, not John Pell.

For his part, Heathcote, by both commanding the militia and presiding over the courts, came to know the people of Westchester County, especially those of the town of Westchester, the county seat. As a merchant, with a keen eye for profit, he must have seen opportunities for investment in the area, especially the banksides of such streams as the Bronx and Hutchinson rivers and Westchester Creek. A few mills had already been erected along these waterways, but a man of Heathcote's great financial resources could afford to build and operate many more and to make a significant impact on the overwhelmingly rural economy of the region. Certainly, by 1696, Heathcote entered into partnership with William Ward, who had purchased land along Westchester Creek in December 1693, and they began construction of a mill there.[102]

By early 1696, the people of the town of Westchester had some cause for worry because of their previous adherence to Leisler's side, which alienated the rulers of the colony. Prominent residents of the town were harassed and sued to the point of poverty, and the Dutch Reformed Church successfully challenged the town's claim to Fordham on the grounds that Westchester's patent was inadequate. Moreover, the Dutch Church applied for incorporation that would include the Fordham lands. Clearly, the town needed a new charter for its own protection.

It is likely that Caleb Heathcote suggested the possibility that the town ask for incorporation so that Westchester's boundaries could be confirmed and any special privileges attained. With an investment in the town, and a vision of greater economic possibilities,

Heathcote could benefit from such assurances, and, with his wealth, he could hope to dominate the new municipal corporation. What is certain is that in March, 1696, the town's trustees, realizing they had few friends with sufficient influence in the colonial government, unanimously agreed that Heathcote intercede with the governor on behalf of the town for a better confirmation of its former patents and to seek whatever rights and privileges that could be obtained. They also agreed to draw up a petition, and, three days later, William Barnes, as president of the trustees, signed one asking the governor to incorporate the town under a mayor, aldermen, and common councilmen.[103]

In April, 1696, one month after Barnes signed the petition, Governor Benjamin Fletcher issued a new charter to the town of Westchester. It recited the town's boundaries in the Nicolls and Dongan patents, and then redefined them once more. Grants made by previous governors, however, were to remain in the hands of those who held them. This provision took care of the question of Fordham. In addition, grants made by the town's trustees were also to remain in force, and Heathcote's joint venture in building mills of Westchester Creek was specifically mentioned. For this confirmation, the town was to pay 30s. a year in New York currency to the colony's treasurer. In addition, twelve freeholders were to be chosen as trustees, as before, every first Monday in May with the power to dispose of the town's undivided lands.

To this point, Westchester's new charter was largely unexceptional. The rest of its provisions were highly unusual, however. All the town's lands, with the exception of the lands belonging to Lewis Morris, were created into a borough called the borough and town of Westchester. Morris's lands were excluded, probably because of the countervailing influence of James Graham, Lewis Morris's father-in-law and speaker of the Assembly and attorney general, who was living on the property while his son-in-law took care of the more valuable New Jersey estate. Uniquely for a rural area, Westchester, with the status as a borough, was assured of having municipal self-government.

The charter provided for a mayor, six aldermen, and six assistants or common councilmen. Caleb Heathcote was named in the document as the first mayor, while William Barnes, John Hunt, William Willett, Thomas Baxter, Josiah Hunt, and John Bailey were to serve as the first aldermen, and Israel Honeywell, Robert Huestis, Samuel Huestis, Samuel Ferris, Daniel Turner, and Miles Oakley were named as the first common councilmen. All were to serve for one year until the first Monday in May. Acting for the borough, they could make contracts and grants; they could make, receive, and take gifts, grants, and purchases; and they could sue and be sued. They were to have a seal of their own design and build a town hall where they could meet. Together, as a free commercial association, they could establish ordinances, statutes, orders, and by-laws not repugnant to the common law or statutes of England or New York. They had a right to establish a ferry to Long Island over Long Island Sound and to take its fees for the use of the borough. A ferry had previously been established, but its control was now vested in the mayor, aldermen, and common councilmen. Similarly, they had the right to choose the town clerk, but he had to be learned in the law. This automatically excluded Edward Collier, who had served as county clerk under Leisler and had been the town clerk since then. It is likely that this provision was designed to exclude Collier because of his past, something upon which Governor Fletcher might have insisted. The tactful wording that is not aimed specifically at Collier, however, is typical of Heathcote. Moreover, Heathcote, seeking to recreate the environment of his native Chesterfield, might have insisted on a more knowledgeable town clerk. The mayor, aldermen, and common councilmen also had the right to name the sergeant of the mace and other inferior officers customarily found in a borough. Moreover, they had the right to keep the town market every Wednesday, a practice previously sanctioned by law, and two fairs, one starting the first Tuesday in May, as previously authorized by law, and a second new one beginning on the last Tuesday in October. Each fair, however, was to last three days instead of four. On the other hand, instead of the governor, the mayor, aldermen, and common councilmen were given the authority to establish the Court of Piepowder at the two fairs, along with all fees, court costs, tolls, and other charges.

In addition to all this, the mayor and aldermen alone had the right to admit people as freemen of the borough to enjoy all the privileges, franchises, and immunities of the town. If the mayor were absent from the town, which in the case of Heathcote might be frequent, the mayor and aldermen could appoint a deputy mayor to act for him. Moreover, the mayor and at least two aldermen constituted a Mayor's Court, meeting the first Tuesday of every month, to consider civil suits up to the value of £20 and to inquire into any public fight, riot, or bloodshed, and to punish the guilty party according to English and New York law. Within the limits of the town, the mayor and aldermen were also justices of the peace. Thus, Westchester was to have its own local court, rather than resorting to others in the county with similar jurisdiction. Moreover, such a court would likely attract New York lawyers and more legal business, adding to the town's prosperity.

The charter also provided for the mayor alone to license annually all tavern keepers, inn keepers, sellers of wine, beer, and liquor, and victualizers within the town for a fee not to exceed twenty shillings to be used for the public good. In addition, he was to be the coroner and the clerk of the market.

Similar privileges could be found in such cities as New York and Albany, and some small towns in England, so they were not unprecedented. These provisions of the charter are unusual because of the privileges of self-government they conferred upon a small rural town.

Two provisions, however, were astounding. The most startling aspect of the charter was the clause providing for the election of the mayor, aldermen, and common councilmen every year on the first Monday in May by the freeholders and inhabitants of the borough. Neither the mayor of New York City nor the mayor of Albany were elected. Each was appointed by the governor. The borough of Westchester, however, far smaller than either in population or commercial significance, was to have an elected mayor. Moreover, the franchise was not restricted to freeholders, those who held property worth at least a specified amount, as was universal. Inhabitants, those who held no land at all, also had the right to vote. This, in fact, may have made the town of Westchester the first place in the world to enjoy officially sanctioned universal male suffrage.

The second astounding provision gave the borough the right to send one representative to the colony's Assembly to act in framing and voting upon laws on an equal basis with other assemblymen.[104] Boroughs with such a privilege could be found in England, several of which were controlled by powerful local aristocrats who sent themselves or cronies to Parliament. Certainly, in terms of population or economic importance, Westchester did not deserve to have its own assemblyman. Perhaps, Caleb Heathcote envisioned himself in the position of the powerful English landlord controlling the seat. Whatever the reason, the town would be overrepresented in the Assembly, wielding a larger influence there than it otherwise would have.

When the town's trustees saw the new charter in May, 1696, they immediately accepted it and voted to thank Caleb Heathcote for his prudent care in getting such privileges for the town. The cost of obtaining the document was £45, part of which, no doubt, wound up in Governor Fletcher's pocket, and to raise the sum, the trustees levied an assessment on those who held privileges in the sheep pasture.[105] In June, they granted the mayor and aldermen a section of the town green to erect a market house to act as the focal point for the weekly market and, perhaps, the semi-annual fairs.[106] The following day, Caleb Heathcote swore in three of the aldermen and five of the common councilmen,[107] and the new borough and town of Westchester began to function.

With the establishment of Westchester as a borough as well as a town, the settlement that began 42 years earlier with fifteen men from Connecticut entering a wilderness inhabited only by Indians fully entered the new era. Controversies with central colonial authority could no longer be met with the brash obstinacy of a Richard Ponton, but could be manipulated only through persons of influence, such as Caleb Heathcote. Merit and a great landholding would continue to be important factors in establishing colonial leadership, as it had been with John Pell, but alliances by marriage with other ruling families, as in the case of Lewis Morris, would become increasingly significant. The tenants of Fordham no longer dealt with a volatile John Archer as a landlord, but with a highly organized, well-connected church corporation. The crossing at Spuyten Duyvil was no longer controlled by a small businessman operating a ferry on a limited franchise, but by a powerful merchant, highly placed in the colonial government, adding lands to his holdings, and who held the crossing by a grant that was hereditary. The town of Westchester, in becoming a borough, entered this new era where people were trying to recreate an aristocratically-dominated English society in New York, and it joined in the rush for privilege, power, and influence.

CHAPTER XI

PERSPECTIVE ON THE BRONX FRONTIER

1609 TO 1696

Much had happened in the 87 years between the time Henry Hudson first sighted the hills of The Bronx in 1609 and the creation of the borough and town of Westchester in 1696. There had been a wholesale change in the people who occupied and ruled the territory, several changes in the manner in which they governed themselves, changing perspectives on the way they viewed each other, and a change in economic activity and in social structure.

Certainly, the greatest change involved the Indians. Despite the sparseness of their settlements and their semi-nomadic way of life, they easily outnumbered the newcoming Europeans and were able to overcome them at first. The Indians who defied explorer Thomas Dermer, expelled the Throckmorton settlement, murdered Anne Hutchinson, and frightened settlers on Adriaen van der Donck's land to cause them to flee to the safety of the fort in New Amsterdam obviously could take care of themselves. This latter incident, however, 46 years after Henry Hudson's arrival, proved to be the last serious threat to the European settlers.

Even before 1655, the Indians became increasingly dependent upon the Europeans, trapping and trading furs for settlers and merchants in return for trinkets and valuable metal products that the tribes could not make for themselves. Eventually, the Indians became dependent upon the superior weaponry of European rifles, which proved to be their doom. Their only source of supply was the Europeans who were contending with them for control of the land.

Yet, for a considerable time, the Indians were feared and respected by the settlers. Thomas Pell and the inhabitants of the town of Westchester deemed it prudent to survey annually the bounds of their purchases with the Indians, a concession to the Indian view of landholding. In 1665, an Indian stole one of Edward Jessup's children, and the constable of Westchester was ordered to find a fit person to talk to the sachems to ask for the child.[1] A punitive expedition was not contemplated. With incidents such as this as background, it is no wonder that only ten years later, King Philips's War in New England caused a wave of terror among the European settlers in the area.

By the time the seventeenth century reached its three-quarter mark, an attitude of increasing contempt for the Indians began to manifest itself. Despite some objections by John Pell, the colonial government deigned to issue orders concerning where the Indians in the southern part of Westchester County could reside, and denied them the use of canoes during the emergency of King Philip's War. Most telling was the promise of the sachems to give the governor notice of any disturbance in return for receiving notice from him of any intention he might find to harm them. The Indians not only became dependent upon the settlers, but they now feared them.

During the last quarter of the century, the Indian population dwindled, and increasing amounts of land were purchased from them by the settlers. Indians continued to reside in the area for decades to come, but the final indignity arrived when some of the Indians were enslaved. By 1698, James Graham, who lived on Lewis Morris's land, owned an Indian woman named Mary and a girl, Margaret, who was probably her daughter, as slaves.[2]

The first Europeans who succeeded in establishing a permanent settlement were able to do so, in part, by securing the friendship of the Indians and by adapting to some of their customs. Lonely outposts, such as those of Jonas Bronck and Anne Hutchinson, failed, as did settlements, such as Throckmorton's and Cornell's, because the residents refused to adapt. Van der Donck's patroonship, a medieval fiefdom on the frontier, did not survive the death of its proprietor because it suffered from the prolonged absence of its owner whose attention was diverted to causes, thus interfering with his management of the land.

Yet, no matter how well the Europeans adapted to Indian ways to survive, their model remained what they had previously known and what was comfortable. Both the towns of Westchester and Eastchester each established a government by town meeting, which elected town officers, especially a Board of Trustees to make and enforce local rules and regulations, particularly concerning the distribution of land. Since their inhabitants originally came from New England, it is no surprise that the system of local government followed the New England model. Even the huge rural estates, such as Pelham, Fordham, and Philipsburgh, erected into manors, followed closely the pattern of the English countryside.

There were differences, however. The winning of the wilderness was no easy task, and the people who did it were forceful, rough, and resilient in overcoming adversity. Perhaps nowhere but on a frontier could a man like Richard Ponton rise to prominence. Violent, direct, intolerant of any authority that crossed his path, Ponton had a personality that drew people to him and made him a leader. He was illiterate, signing all documents with a mark rather than a signature. Yet, his fellow townsmen in Westchester did not hesitate to elect him to their Board of Trustees or to entrust him with such special missions as surveying a boundary line, negotiating an agreement, hiring legal counsel, or being their captain of militia. Under such frontier conditions, his abrasive acts become understandable, and his qualities were those needed for survival.

John Archer, of course, had similar traits. Possessed of the same violent temper as Richard Ponton, he frequently displayed it in his running feud with Johannes Verveelen, in evicting recalcitrant tenants, and in enforcing the peace as sheriff of New York. Time and again, when faced with reverses, he managed not only to survive, but to hold onto his huge landholdings.

Yet, Ponton and Archer came from two different national traditions: English and Dutch. When Archer was a resident of the town of Westchester, the two clashed, in part because of Archer's Dutch background and of Ponton's previously demonstrated antipathy toward Dutch rule. Certainly, Ponton and his fellow English townsmen preferred English rule and the company of Englishmen, while John Archer had close connections with the Dutch town of Harlem and with Cornelis Steenwyck.

It was difficult in that wilderness, however, to maintain national exclusivity. Under Dutch rule, so few natives of the Netherlands migrated to the colony that many national groups lived there. Even in the beginning, Jonas Bronck's party consisted of Scandinavians, Germans, and Dutch. Both John Archer and Adriaen van der Donck married English wives. By June, 1688, Thomas Statham and Robert Hudson of the town of Westchester were friendly enough with Valentine Claessen to journey to his house on no particular business and to be expected to be received by him. Members of the two groups were learning to live together, beginning the process of adaptation and assimilation that would ultimately forge a new nationality and which would enable people from many backgrounds to come into the fold.

For the time being, one group, aside from the Indians, stayed out of the fold because of its status. The overwhelming number of blacks in the colony were slaves, and this included the few in the southern part of Westchester County.

By far, the largest slaveholder at that period in the area was Colonel Lewis Morris, who took control over the slaves his brother, Richard, had imported from Barbados, and who used them to cultivate the land. The evidence indicates, however, that the Morris brothers treated their human property humanely and with more respect than did several others in the colony in a similar position. It is significant that Anthony and Sussanah, who were seized by the authorities and sold to Louis DuBois during the Dutch interlude, not only ran away from DuBois after the English regained control, but headed back to the Morris property where they would still be considered slaves. The motive for such extraordinary action could only have been that they were treated better under Morris's ownership than under that of DuBois. Bess, who the Dutch sold to Peter Aldrich and who Walter Webley recovered for Lewis Morris, was eventually placed on the New Jersey lands the Quaker colonel had purchased. There, she had several children, and managed to outlive her master.[3]

At first, slaves were given legal standing in the frontier period. In 1686, when Edward Collier, the Westchester town clerk, registered the marks on the dozen horses that Robert Hunt and Matthew Pugsley shipped from Hunts Point, three witnesses to the act were recorded. There were Thomas Hunt, Jr., Gabriel Leggett, "and Ned[,] Col[one]l. Morrises Negro."[4] Despite his status as a slave, Ned's worth as a witness was considered the equal of each of two of the town's prominent citizens.

As slave ownership became more widespread, more restrictive measures were imposed. To keep things in perspective, it should be emphasized that only Lewis Morris in the southernmost portion of the county, and Frederick Philipse, whose property just managed to edge its way into the area that would one day become The Bronx, owned large numbers of slaves before the end of the seventeenth century. A scattered number of people owned slaves in the town of Westchester, in Fordham, and in the lower part of Yonkers near the new King's Bridge, but few of these owned more than one, and the total amounted to about ten percent of the population by 1698.[5] Yet, this small proportion appeared to be enough for the Westchester County Court of Sessions to forbid slaves from carrying guns, dogs, or staves to prevent them from hunting hogs in the woods.

Because slaves were considered property, they could, of course, be bought and sold. Colonel Lewis Morris, in his will of 1691, disposed of his slaves as he did the rest of his possessions, even giving one of the children of Bess to one new master, while she and the rest of her children were inherited by another, the colonel's nephew.[6]

Yet, slaves could be freed, and free blacks could live among other inhabitants in the area, apparently without difficulty. In his will, Lewis Morris also states that, following his wife's death, Nell would have her freedom; and "Toney," who had made barrels for the colonel, was given a stipend of forty shillings a year for life "besides his usual accommodation."[7] Nell may have left the Morris lands following the death of Mary Morris, or she may have died soon afterward, for her name does not appear on the list of inhabitants there in 1698. Toney's name does not appear there either. It is possible, however, that he may have been freed subsequently. Certainly, he could have made his own way in the world as a cooper making barrels. It is possible he may have moved to Fordham or the area near the King's Bridge, for an "Antone the neger" is recorded as living there in 1698 along with his wife, Diana, and three children.[8] Which makes this family the first free blacks to be recorded as residing in the area that would become The Bronx.

The blacks brought into the southern part of Westchester County most likely came from the West Indies. Richard Morris, who introduced them, probably brought them with him from Barbados. It is also possible, however, that a small number of blacks in the early years came directly from Africa. Frederick Philipse amassed a considerable fortune, in part, from the slave trade, and his ships were known to pick up human cargo on the African coast.[9]

On the other hand, the European inhabitants migrated into the area from closer locations. Few followed the example of Jonas Bronck, Jochem Kaller, Carsten Pieter, Jacob Gever, Pieter Andriessen, and Laurens Duyts in settling in the area directly after the voyage from Europe. Usually, a settler arrived at another location, lived there for a period of time, and then moved again to settle on a farm or in a town in the southern part of Westchester County. Anne Hutchinson, John Throckmorton and his settlers, and Thomas Cornell all arrived from Rhode Island. Adriaen van der Donck came down from Rensselaerswyck, and John Archer moved northward from Virginia. There were three primary sources of immigration into the area, however: Connecticut, Long Island, and Manhattan.

Connecticut was the source of the first large-scale movement of Europeans into the area. Thomas Pell of Fairfield persuaded the first fifteen settlers of the village of Westchester to move into the territory from Connecticut, and the settlers of Eastchester, who purchased the land from him, came from there, too. The southern New England colony even claimed control over the area until the duke of York's grant placed it under his rule. Correspondence and human contact continued between Eastchester, Westchester, and Pell's lands and Connecticut during the Dutch interlude despite the efforts of Dutch authorities to prevent them. Afterward, Warham Mather came from New England to conduct religious services at Westchester.

Long Island contributed immigrants into the area from the beginning. Cornelis Jacobsen Stille agreed to accompany Jonas Bronck to the mainland while he was the owner of a farm on Long Island. Adriaen van der Donck married a woman from Flushing. The original inhabitants of Westchester early established close ties with the English towns on Long Island, warning them of the danger of an Indian attack in 1655. They borrowed some needed funds from those living in those towns, as well. Perhaps, one result of these initial contacts was the migration of people from the island to the mainland, which continued beyond the English conquest of the Dutch colony. Morgan Jones, who performed religious services in both Eastchester and Westchester, came from Newtown. Roger Barton resided in Setauket, representing that town in a meeting with the governor at Hempstead in March, 1665,[10] but later moved to the town of Westchester and claimed title to land in Fordham. Contact with Long Island was enhanced by the establishment of a ferry service to there from the town of Westchester.

Manhattan Island proved to be the third major source of

European immigration into the area. John Archer sought settlers for Fordham from Harlem. Frederick Philipse, who purchased some of van der Donck's old property, was a prominent merchant in New York City, and Caleb Heathcote lived in that city for a few years before moving to the town of Westchester. Through the years, Manhattan's influence would grow to be far greater than either Connecticut's or Long Island's.

Yet, it was by no means certain in those early years that Manhattan would prove to be the strongest influence of the three, since ties with Connecticut and Long Island were initially closer. Connecticut's political influence was eliminated by the duke of York's grant, but Long Island's was enhanced by the creation of the system of towns and ridings that placed all of the mainland but Fordham within the North Riding of Yorkshire with a number of Long Island towns. The creation of Westchester County and the placing of the mainland settlements within it, certainly did not eliminate the economic and social ties the inhabitants continued to maintain with Long Island.

On the other hand, it was difficult to ignore Manhattan Island, and, especially, New York City. Even under the old towns and ridings system, Fordham was placed under New York City's courts, at least until the manor was created. Every item imported for use on the manors, farms, or towns of Westchester County came through the port of New York, and the thriving commercial city at the tip of Manhattan was a major market for the county's products. Livestock was driven over the roads to Verveelen's ferry, and, later, to the King's Bridge, to be sold in the city. Wheat grown in the area was sent there for export, usually in the form of flour. Wood for the fort in New York was cut from the timber in the area and sent to the city by wagon and raft. The Dutch Reformed Church, one of the city's major institutions, obtained control of a large portion of the territory in southern Westchester County. Moreover, the city, as the seat of the colony's government, had to attract anyone living in the area that would one day become The Bronx if he had business with the governor, his Council, the Assembly, or the high courts.

Southern Westchester County in the frontier years was overwhelmingly rural, however. It is likely that fur trade with the Indians of the area was established soon after the European explorers mapped the land, but there are few incidents of settlers actually trading with the Indians for furs. Lumber from clearing the land for farming became the first major commodity the inhabitants sold. Wood from Jonas Bronck's farm was sold for fence posts in Harlem. Adriaen van der Donck established a sawmill, and so did William Richardson. Toney, the slave of Lewis Morris, made barrels, undoubtedly with wood from the Morris property.

    Livestock raising grew to be the major economic activity of the frontier years, with cattle taking the lead, probably for the beef. Van der Donck had an Indian tending his cattle, while the settlers of Westchester had theirs feed on the marsh grass in the northern reaches of Westchester Creek. Hogs ran in the woods, and were used for domestic consumption, although any surplus could have been sold to New York. The introduction and spread of sheep raising in the town of Westchester was significant, not only because of the mutton sheep could provide, but also because of the wool. That would become more important in the following century. Horses were not numerous and horse trading was not that important. Oxen were the preferred beasts for pulling plows.

    When the land was cultivated, it took some time before the farmers hit upon a successful cash crop. Jonas Bronck obviously thought that tobacco would bring him money, but the future did not belong to that weed. He grew rye and barley also, but the cultivation of wheat was to grow in importance. Both Eastchester and Westchester had grist mills to grind the grain into flour, and, in the absence of hard coin, wheat was readily acceptable in lieu of money as the seventeenth century progressed. Despite all this, livestock continued to be the most valuable possession of the settlers, other than land. Thomas Hunt of the Grove Farm on Throggs Neck, for instance, had 37% of his wealth in cattle and oxen when he died in February of 1695, but only less than 3% in wheat, rye, and corn.[11]

    Other crops were grown as well. Such garden vegetables as peas were used at home, rather than sold. Orchards were common on farms, and the fruit produced by the trees was also consumed at home. An exception was probably the apple, since apples could be pressed into cider, a process that would be performed increasingly in the following century.

    Despite this growth, the vast majority of the inhabitants of the southern part of Westchester County were far from wealthy. Cash was always difficult to obtain. The original settlers of the town of Westchester often engaged in barter to get what they needed. Payments of rent for leasing land in Fordham from John Archer or the town of Westchester, and for quit rents payable to the government for a grant of land, were often stated in terms of agricultural products or livestock. Archer's loans were in the form of wampum or beaver skins, and the Fordham proprietor paid his steward, John West, in firewood. John Hunt was told he had to accept wheat in payment for his services in operating the first tavern in the area in 1681.

Few people in this rural society were not primarily farmers. Eastchester inhabitants were particularly active in attempting to attract such necessary professional people or craftsmen as ministers, millers, blacksmiths, or tailors. The attraction, however, remained the land, the only item of great value in the gift of the settlers. Thus, it is unlikely that those they attracted lived entirely on the income provided by their profession or craft, and it is most probable that a tailor or a miller devoted a good part of his time to the pursuits of agriculture.

It is because of the value of the land, as well as the newness of the settlements, that there were seemingly endless disputes as to boundaries. The controversies over the dividing line between Eastchester and Westchester, and between Westchester and the Dutch Reformed Church over the possession of Fordham, involved primarily the income the governing authority could derive from the land in question by either sale or lease. The announcement by the Dutch Reformed Church that it was going to redraw the lines between farms provides the evidence that even the tenants on the Fordham property argued over the boundaries of the lands they rented, since the income derived from the disputed territory would add to the meager wealth of the leaseholder. This consideration is also the foundation of the controversy between Lewis Morris and the township of Harlem over the possession of Stony Island.

Because of disputes such as these, as well as the Indian menace of the earlier years, settlers in the area were prone to direct action and violence. Jonas Bronck's home was well armed, and the original inhabitants of the town of Westchester had firearms ready in greeting Peter Stuyvesant's messenger. No doubt, the vast majority of farmers in the area emulated Thomas Seabrooke of Castle Hill, who, in 1676, had his arms and ammunition ready in his home, and who was a member of the local militia. The tales of the attempt by the Westchester townsmen to retain control of two farmhouses in Fordham from the assault of Nicholas Bayard and his party, and of the effects of Leisler's Rebellion in Westchester County, are replete with examples of individual and organized violence.

This violent tendency, however, manifested itself chiefly in the defense of home. In case of the possibility of Indian attack (such as in King Philip's War), of the threat of opposing military force (such as in Stuyvesant's attempt to oust the original settlers of the village of Westchester), or of the threat of harm to person, family, and property, men with their firearms, swords, pikes, and fists were at the ready to face the danger. On the other hand, if the threat were distant, the settlers were loathe to risk their lives. Leisler's call for military aid to relieve the residents of the Albany region from attack met with great opposition. King William's War against the French was greeted with reluctance to send militia members up the Hudson and with complaints about the level of taxation to carry on the fighting.

People living in the area were not only violent, but they were restless. All members of the frontier generation came from long distances to settle in southern Westchester County, several living in more than one place before arriving there. For a great many of these people, the area that would one day become The Bronx was not the last stop, but one of several places in which they would reside before reaching their final rest. Jonas Bronck's family and servants scattered after his death to Long Island, Manhattan, Hog (now Roosevelt) Island, and Rensselaerswyck. John Throckmorton and Thomas Cornell both returned to Rhode Island, Throckmorton dying while on a visit to his children in New Jersey. Adriaen van der Donck's widow, who came from Long Island, remarried and moved to Maryland. John Archer came from Virginia to Westchester, then resided for a short time in Connecticut before returning and moving to Fordham. Lewis Morris, the nephew of the Quaker colonel, walked to Virginia and lived in Jamaica before returning to his uncle's home.

In the town of Westchester alone, in the eight years between 1675 and 1683, almost 22% of the inhabitants moved elsewhere, judging from the disappearance of their family names from the tax rolls in that time period. In the fifteen years between 1683 and 1698, when a full census was taken, more than 27% of the settlers moved out of the town. This figure is derived from noting the family name in the tax roll of 1683 and its absence in the census of 1698.[12]

Yet, with all this constant movement, the vast majority of the families who moved into the area decided to stay, and the population grew. Over 800 men, women, and children, including slaves, lived in the area that would become The Bronx in 1698, and they constituted over 75% of the inhabitants of Westchester County at that time. Of the total, 517 were officially counted as residents of the town of

Westchester, and 110 of Eastchester.[13] For another century and a half, the center of population would continue to be east of the Bronx River.

Moreover, the population was a young one. In the town of Westchester, the number of free children outnumbered the free adults by just over 41%. The population of children was even greater in Fordham and in that part of Yonkers near the King's Bridge where the number of free children was larger than the number of free adults by almost 44%.[14]

As was usual in a rural area, most youngsters were reared with the object of aiding in the operation of the farm and the home. Their formal education must have been rudimentary, since no schools existed in southern Westchester County and no schoolmasters came there, despite a single attempt by the town of Eastchester to attract one. Wealthy men could provide a tutor for a child, such as Colonel Lewis Morris did in engaging Hugh Coppathwaite to teach his young nephew. Most of the inhabitants living there, however, could not afford such an expense, and it is probable that parents taught their own children the rudiments of reading and mathematics.

Certainly, few books were available to read. Jonas Bronck's large library was unusual, and only Colonel Lewis Morris in the later years is known to have amassed a number of books, a collection that he ultimately bequeathed to his nephew.[15] The original settlers of the town of Westchester are known to have had with them a book of sermons from which Robert Bassett read each Sunday, and similar volumes must have continued to exist for the county's Court of Sessions to order sermons to be read out of such books in 1693. No other printed books are known to have been used in the area at the time, however.

In such surroundings as existed on the frontier, pleasures were few and simple. Diversion happened at family events, such as weddings. In the absence of ministers, of course, no religious ceremony could be performed in the area. With the establishment of a settled civil government, however, justices could perform civil ceremonies, as did Justice John Palmer when he married the cooper, Joseph Boyle, to Eleanor Rawson in 1686, and as did Justice John Pell when he married Matthew Pugsley and Mary Hunt at John Hunt's house in 1683.[16]

Special events, such as a town meeting or market day, would break the monotony of everyday life. These were the times when the local taverns in Westchester and Eastchester would be filled with men drinking heartily and engaging in ribald conversation. On occasion, such as happened with Gabriel Leggett, a man in his cups could make remarks, as he did about John Williams, that could lead to feuds or continuing animosity between men.

If Caleb Heathcote is to be believed, Sundays were used by many people for disorder and profaneness. It appears, however, that the inhabitants of the region used the day to drink at the taverns, to go fishing, to hunt animals or birds, or to travel, all to vary the order of their lives. What appeared to shock Heathcote is that so few residents used the day for worship, a condition he attributed to the absence of a settled ministry.

The society that had developed in the area was fairly democratic. With the exception of a few men, most of those who moved into the area that would one day become The Bronx were of modest means and would remain so. Jonas Bronck, the Pells, and the Morrises were the exceptions, not the rule. The inhabitants of the two towns met in town meetings as equals and fought each other's claims as equals. Except under Dutch rule, no distinction was drawn between those of Dutch and English descent.

Nevertheless, to call that society democratic may be overstating the case. Beside the obvious class division between slaves and free inhabitants that developed after the introduction of slavery by Richard Morris, other divisions did exist. Jonas Bronck had indentured servants working for him, and Adriaen van der Donck had certain rights as a patroon which the settlers on his land were not legally permitted to exercise. The original inhabitants of Westchester acknowledged the rights of overlordship by Thomas Pell, which, it is true, he returned to them. Both John Pell and John Archer had their lands erected into manors which gave them special privileges. It appears that Archer was the only owner of a manor to have actually established a court for his tenants, a maneuver those who tried to sue him apparently disliked, but which effectively protected him from mounting litigation. John Pell was looked to as an arbiter of the area's affairs not only for his judicious temperament and fairness, but for his social standing as well. It is significant, however, judging from the population statistics, that most people in the area chose to live in the two towns and not on the manors or on the Morris lands.

On the other hand, the people living in southern Westchester County were never the sole masters of their own destiny, but felt the repercussions of events happening, and of decisions made, elsewhere.

An Indian uprising provoked by incidents elsewhere practically depopulated the area in 1655, and conditions in New England caused King Philip's War, frightening the inhabitants. Decisions made by King Charles II and the Connecticut Assembly led to the change of sovereignty over the area from the Dutch to the English. A bloodless revolution in England, the outbreak of war in Europe, and incidents in New York City led to Leisler's Rebellion, which had so much consequence for the people of southern Westchester County. The establishment of the boundaries of the North Riding of Yorkshire and of Westchester County were not made by those living there.

Even in what might seem purely local matters, such as the ownership of Stony Island, the establishment of Verveelen's ferry, the building of the King's Bridge, and the award of the ownership of Fordham to the Dutch Reformed Church, the decisions were not made by the local inhabitants, although in each case they tried to influence the outcome. The settlers could not afford to ignore the world outside their own vicinity, since that world had an impact that would cause change. The town of Westchester survived and thrived because its people adapted to changing circumstances, and, as the seventeenth century was drawing to a close, the circumstances were changing once again.

The values and the methods of the outside world were beginning to encroach upon the frontier settlements. Fordham was already owned by the Dutch Reformed Church, an influential institution based in New York City. Frederick Philipse, a city merchant with important government connections and one of the wealthiest men in the colony, had his Westchester County lands erected into a manor and secured a hereditary monopoly of the tolls on the King's Bridge. Young Lewis Morris obtained control over the lands of his deceased uncle, and began to display several attitudes and thoughts different from the Quaker colonel's. Westchester County became one of the four counties in the colony to obtain public financing for a settled ministry, and one parish was designed to include almost all of the area that would one day become The Bronx.

In short, a world of social stratification, of privilege for men of wealth, of personal economic advantage through government connection, and of an official religion arrived in the area and would overlay with a patina of aristocratic gentility and propriety the violent and restless, somewhat democratic frontier society which had hitherto existed. Elements of that earlier society would never disappear, but, if the people living in the area were to survive in the new conditions as the frontier generation passed from the scene, they had to adapt to the world of privilege, and, if possible, obtain privileges that would protect them. They turned to Caleb Heathcote, a man of the new generation, and had received undreamed of privileges because of his close connections in high colonial government circles. With the establishment of the borough of Westchester, the inhabitants of the area entered into this new society. As Caleb Heathcote guided them in this unfamiliar situation of power and privilege, he came to dominate the beginning years of the new, aristocratic, era.

NOTES

CHAPTER I THE ADVENT OF MANKIND

1. William A. Ritchie, *The Archaeology of New York State* (Garden City, 1965), pp. 3-5, 9-11, 15; U. Vincent Wilcox, "Prehistory of the New York City Area," 1970, typescript in the New York City — Antiquities Collection, Library of the Museum of the American Indian; *Indian Archaeology of Long Island*, The Nassau Museum of Natural History Education Leaflet 17 (n.p., n.d.) pp. 1-2; Robert E. Funk, "Post Pleistoscene Adaptations, *Handbook of North American Indians*, Vol. XV, *Northeast*, ed. William C. Sturtevant (Washington, D.C., 1978), pp. 16-17; James E. Fitting, "Prehistory: Introduction," in *Ibid.*, p. 14.
2. Funk, pp. 19-20, 23; Fitting, p. 14.
3. Ritchie, *Archaeology*, pp. 32-34; Wilcox typescript; *Indian Archaeology of Long Island*, pp. 3-4; Funk, p. 19.
4. Wilcox typescript; Wilcomb E. Washburn, *The Indian in America* (New York, 1975), p. 9; *Indian Archaeology of Long Island*, pp. 4-5; James A. Tuck, "Regional Cultural Development, 3000 to 300 BC," in Sturtevant, p. 41.
5. Wilcox typescript; Alanson Skinner, *Exploration of Aboriginal Sites at Throgs Neck and Clasons Point, New York City* (New York, 1919), pp. 70-72, 119; *Indian Archaeology of Long Island*, p. 6.
6. Wilcox typescript; Reginald Pelham Bolton, *Early and Indian Remains on Throg's Neck Borough of The Bronx City of New York* (n.p., 1934), p. 11.
7. Wilcox typescript; Skinner, p. 73; Reginald Pelham Bolton, *Indian Paths in the Great Metropolis* (New York, 1922), pp. 90-91, 97-98, 111, 112; James E. Fitting, "Regional Cultural Development, 300 BC to AD 1000," in Sturtevant, p. 44.
8. Bolton, *Indian Paths*, pp. 92, 106-07, 112, 115-116, 119, 122, 123; E.M. Ruttenber, *History of the Indian Tribes of Hudson's River* (Port Washington, N.Y., 1971), pp. 72-82; Allen W. Trelease, *Indian Affairs in Colonial New York: The Seventeenth Century* (Port Washington, N.Y., 1971), p. 8; Reginald Pelham

Bolton, *New York City in Indian Possession* (New York, 1920), pp. 233, 239, 248, 259; Bolton, *Early History*, p. 5; Ives Goddard, "Delaware," in Sturtevant, p. 214.
  9. Trelease, p. 1.
  10. *Ibid.*, p. 2; Carlyle Shreeve Smith, *The Archaeology of Coastal New York, Anthropological Papers of the American Museum of Natural History*, XLIII, part 2 (New York, 1950), p. 116; Ives Goddard, "Eastern Algonquin Languages," in Sturtevant, pp. 72-73; Dean R. Snow, "Late Prehistory of the East Coast," in *Ibid.*, p. 64.
  11. Trelease, p. 3; Ruttenber, pp. 45-56; Reginald Pelham Bolton, *Indian Life of Long Ago in the City of New York* (New York, 1934), pp. 4-5.
  12. Washburn, pp. 1-5.
  13. Trelease, p. 3; Ruttenber, p. 47.
  14. Trelease, pp. 9-10; Ruttenber, pp. 29, 47.
  15. Trelease, p. 10; Ruttenber, p. 48.
  16. Trelease, pp. 2, 10-11; Ruttenber, p. 49.
  17. Bolton, *Indian Life*, pp. 83-85; Smith, *Archaeology*, pp. 116-117.
  18. Bolton, *Indian Life*, pp. 81, 137-143; Smith, *Archaeology*.pp. 116, 117, 121; Ritchie, *Archaeology*, pp. 269-270; Skinner, pp. 64, 86, 117-119, and *passim*; Julius Lopez, "The Milo Rock Site, Pelham Bay Park, Bronx County, N.Y.," *Pennsylvania Archaeologist* XXVIII (December, 1958), 128, 134 n. 7.
  19. Bolton, *Indian Life*, pp. 72-73, 76, 77-78; Ritchie, *Archaeology*, p. 270; Smith, *Archaeology*, p. 121; Skinner, p. 70.
  20. Bolton, *Indian Life*, pp. 65-66, 80, 103-104; Ritchie, *Archaeology*, p. 270; Smith, *Archaeology*, p. 117; Trelease, p. 11.
  21. Bolton, *Indian Life*, pp. 33-36.
  22. *Ibid.*, pp. 35, 66; Trelease, p. 9.
  23. Bolton, *Indian Life*, pp. 70-71; Skinner, p. 72; Ritchie, *Archaeology*, p. 270.
  24. Skinner, p. 120; Ritchie, *Archaeology*, p. 271; *Indian Archaeology of Long Island*, p. 6.
  25. Aliens often remarked on their stature. See Adriaen Van der Donck, *A Description of the New Netherlands* (Syracuse, N.Y., 1968), p. 72, first printed, 1655; and Charles Wolley, *A Two Years' Journal in New York and Part of Its Territories in America* (Cleveland, 1902), p. 31, first printed, 1701.
  26. Bolton, *Indian Life*, pp. 93-94.
  27. Trelease, p. 11.
  28. *Ibid.*, pp. 11-12; Bolton, *Indian Life*, p. 11.
  29. Skinner, pp. 72-73; Ritchie, *Archaeology*, p. 270; Wilcox typescript; Lopez, p. 128, 134 n.; Smith, *Archaeology*, p. 121; Bolton, *Indian Life*, p. 111.
  30. Bolton, *Indian Life*, pp. 99-100.
  31. *Ibid.*, pp. 72, 88.
  32. Bolton, *Indian Paths*, pp. 90-128.
  33. Ruttenber, p. 31.
  34. Bolton, *Indian Paths*, p. 90.
  35. *Ibid.*, pp. 90-128 *passim*.

CHAPTER II THE AGE OF EXPLORATION

1. E.B. O'Callaghan, *History of New Netherland; or New York Under the Dutch* (New York, 1846-1848) I, 32-33.
2. J. Franklin Jameson, ed., *Narratives of New Netherland: 1609-1664* (New York, 1909), p. 6; also in [Samuel Purchas], *Purchas. His Pilgrimes.* (London, 1625) III, 581. That part of Purchas dealing with Hudson's four voyages has been reprinted from the original as *Henry Hudson's Voyages* (Ann Arbor, 1966).
3. Purchas, III, 584-591; Jameson, ed., *Narratives of New Netherland*, pp. 16-21.
4. Jameson, ed., *Narrative of New Netherland*, pp. 22-23.
5. Jameson, ed., *Narratives of New Netherland*, pp. 25-26. O'Callaghan, *History of New Netherland*, I, 41, states the shelter is near Hoboken, and Jameson, p. 27 n. 1, says parts of the description fit the Hoboken site. He points out, however, that the narrative makes it clear that it is at northern part Manhattan. His qualm is that the wind directions do not square with later happenings if that is the site. Since Robert Juet wrote the description sometime after the voyage ended and at the end of a long written manuscript, a mistake could have been made in the wind direction. William A. Tieck, *Riverdale, Kingsbridge, Spuyten Duyvil: New York City* (Old Tappan, N.J., 1968), p. 3, appears to accept Spuyten Duyvil Creek as the site.
6. Jameson, ed., *Narratives of New Netherland*, pp. 26-27.
7. *Ibid.*, pp. 7-8, 26-27.
8. *Ibid.*, pp. 8, 22, 25; O'Callaghan, *History of New Netherland*, I, 41; Alice P. Kenney, *Stubborn For Liberty: the Dutch in New York* (Syracuse, N.Y., 1975), pp. 15-17.
9. Jameson, ed., *Narratives of New Netherland*, pp. 8-9, 38; Kenney, pp. 15-17; O'Callaghan, *History of New Netherland*, I, 68; E.B. O'Callaghan and B. Fernow, eds., *Documents Relative to the Colonial History of the State of New York* (Albany, 1856-1883) I, map between pp. 10 and 11. John Romeyn Brodhead, who discovered this map in the Royal Archives in The Hague in 1841, conjectured that the map could be dated 1614 or 1616. There is no date on the map, but a note on it states it was drawn with information from an expedition by a man named Kleynties and his comrades and from two rough drafts. This is the earliest map of the area thus far discovered and is extremely crude compared to a map definitely dated 1616 found between pp. 12 and 13. It may be that the first map could have been drawn earlier than 1614.
10. O'Callaghan, *History of New Netherland*, I, 68-69; Kenney, p. 17.
11. O'Callaghan, *History of New Netherland*, I, 69-71; O'Callaghan and Fernow, eds., *Documents*, I, 5-6.
12. O'Callaghan and Fernow, eds., *Documents*, I, 11.
13. *Ibid.*, I, 12 and map between pp. 12 and 13; Jameson, ed., *Narratives of New Netherland*, pp. 39, 41, 42, 44, 50, 51; O'Callaghan, *History of New Netherland*, I, 73-74; Kenney, p. 17; Hendrick Van Loon, *Adriaen Block: Skipper, Trader, Explorer* (New York, 1928), pp. 46-63. Van Loon makes several minor

statements for which there appears no supporting evidence in the documents. His statement on p. 5 that the 1616 map was based on first-hand information supplied by Block, however, seems to be accurate insofar as the territories explored by Block are involved.

14. O'Callaghan and Fernow, eds., *Documents*, I, 11-12; Kenney, pp. 18-19; O'Callaghan, *History of New Netherland*, I, 74-76.
15. O'Callaghan and Fernow, eds., *Documents*, I, 21-25; O'Callaghan, *History of New Netherland*, I, 81.
16. Purchas, III, 1778-1779.
17. O'Callaghan and Fernow, eds., *Documents*, I, 24-25.
18. O'Callaghan, *History of New Netherland*, I, 30-31.
19. *Ibid.*, I, 89-91; the complete text of the charter can be found in Arnold J.F. Van Laer, ed., *Van Rensselaer Bowier Manuscripts* (Albany, 1908), pp. 86-135; Kenney, p. 19.
20. Kenney, pp. 19-20; O'Callaghan, *History of New Netherland*, I, 95-96.
21. Kenney, pp. 20-22; O'Callaghan, *History of New Netherland*, I, 100-101, 103-104.
22. Kenney, p. 23; O'Callaghan, *History of New Netherland*, I, 110-112.
23. Van Laer, ed., *Van Rensselaer Bowier Manuscripts*, pp. 136-153; another translation in O'Callaghan, *History of New Netherland*, I, 112-126.
24. Kenney, p. 23.
25. Jameson, ed., *Narratives of New Netherland*, p. 73.
26. *Ibid.*, pp. 106-107.
27. See, *e.g.*, Van Laer, ed., *Van Rensselaer Bowier Manuscripts*, p. 379.

CHAPTER III THE FIRST EUROPEAN SETTLERS

1. See "Bronck, Jonas," *Dansk Biografisk Leksikon* (1934), IV; the article by Joost Dahlerup in *Politiken*, January 4, 1914; N. Andersen, "Jonas Bronck og Jochem Pietersen Kuyter eller Kayser," *Personalistorisk Tidsskrift* 6th Series, V (1914), 73-75; *Danes in America: Sketches of Emigrants*, The Press and Cultural Relations Department of the Danish Ministry of Foreign Affairs (n.p., 1976), section entitled, "Jonas Bronck, Peacemaker," no pagination; and the chapter on Jonas Bronck in Janus Øssurson's reader, *Føroysk Lesibok* II, published in 1955.

2. See the publication of the banns for the marriage of Jonas Bronck in DTB nr. 449 p. 118, in which the village is given as "Coonstay," and Not. Arch. 1332 fol. 44, in which the province is given as "Smolach in Sweden." Both documents are in the Gemeentie Archief in Amsterdam. Since the references are in Dutch, and spelling was not yet uniform, the closest Swedish equivalents listed by the Institute for Place Name Research (Ortnammsarkivet) in Uppsala, Sweden, are Komstad and Smaland. Bronck signed his name Jonas Jonassen Bronck, indicating that he was the son of Jonas.

3. Bror Olsson, *Ett Bildverk om Smaland*, Serien Allhems Landskapböker (Malmo, 1964), p.53.

4. *Sverige: Geografisk, Topografisk, Statistik, Beskrienning*, ed. Karl

Ahlenius (Stockholm, 1917) II, 126; [Rutgerius Hermanides], *Deliviae Sive Amoenitates Regnarum Sueciae* (Leyden, 1706) I, 425-426.

5. Arnold J.F. Van Laer, tr. and ed., *New York Historical Manuscripts: Dutch*, (Baltimore, 1974) II, 121-122. The same material can also be found in Leo Hershkowitz, ed., "Select Documents Relating to Jonas Bronck," *The Bronx County Historical Society Journal* I (July, 1964), 54-55. Another translation is in E.B. O'Callaghan and B. Fernow, eds., *Documents Relative to the Colonial History of the State of New York*, (Albany, 1856-1883) XIV, 42-43.

6. Not. Arch. 1332 fol. 44, Gemeentie Archief, Amsterdam.

7. Samuel Puffendorf, *The Compleat History of Sweden*, trans. anon. (London, 1702), p. 411.

8. Michael Roberts, *Gustavus Adolphus: A History of Sweden, 1611 - 1632* (London, 1953) II, 63, 124.

9. Michael Roberts, *The Early Vasas: A History of Sweden, 1523 - 1611* (Cambridge, England, 1968), p. 25.

10. *Den Svenska Historien*, ed. Jan Cornell (Stockholm, 1967) IV, 74, 173ff.

11. DTB nr. 449 p. 118, Gemeentie Archief, Amsterdam.

12. *Idem.*

13. Van Laer, ed., *New York Historical Manuscripts: Dutch*, I, 212-214. Van Laer vehemently denies Teuntie Jeuriaens had any Danish origin; see his note I, 213.

14. *Ibid.*, I, 194; also Hershkowitz, ed., *Bronx County Historical Society Journal* (July, 1964), p.52; James Riker, *Revised History of Harlem (City of New York.)* (New York, 1904), p. 129.

15. O'Callaghan and Fernow, eds., *Documents*, I, 38, 50-52, 105, 106, 107.

16. Arnold J.F. Van Laer, ed., *Documents Relating to New Netherland 1624-1636 In the Henry E. Huntington Library*, (San Marino, California, 1924), p. 10.

17. O'Callaghan and Fernow, eds., *Documents*, I, 107, 113-114, 150; E.B. O'Callaghan, *History of New Netherland; or New York Under the Dutch* (New York, 1846 - 1848) I, 200-203; Alice P. Kenney, *Stubborn for Liberty: the Dutch in New York* (Syracuse, N.Y., 1975), p. 26. It is interesting to note that the States-General had some reservations about the new company regulations and forced a reconsideration. New regulations were adopted in 1640 reaffirming the rights of patroons, but stating that any colonist bringing fifteen people to New Netherland for fifteen years would be granted 100 morgens (over 210 acres or just over 85 hectares). Free trade was reaffirmed also, subject to payment of customs duties at New Amsterdam. See O'Callaghan and Fernow, eds., *Documents*, I, 114, 115, 119-123.

18. O'Callaghan, *History of New Netherland*, I, 205-206; Adriaen Van der Donck, *A Description of the New Netherlands*, ed. Thomas F. O'Donnell (Syracuse, N.Y., 1968), p.129.

19. O'Callaghan and Fernow, eds., *Documents*, I, 96-100, 119-123.

20. *Ibid.*, I, 107, 100-114, 119-123.

21. Van Laer, ed., *New York Historical Manuscripts: Dutch*, II, 121-125;

also found in Hershkowitz, ed., *Bronx County Historical Society Journal* (July, 1964), pp. 54-57; and in another translation in O'Callaghan and Fernow, eds., *Documents*, XIV, 42-44.

22. Not. Arch. 1332 fol. 44, Gemeentie Archief, Amsterdam.

23. Hershkowitz, ed., *Bronx County Historical Society Journal* (July, 1964), pp. 44-47.

24. *Ibid.*, pp. 47-49.

25. *Ibid.*, p.45, shows the servants were expected to board at Texel; O'Callaghan and Fernow, eds., *Documents*, XIII, 5 (also Van Laer, ed., *New York Historical Manuscripts: Dutch*, I, 196-197) has convincing evidence, when coupled with the documents Bronck signed in Amsterdam, that Bronck sailed aboard *De Brant Van Troyen*; David Peterson De Vries, *Voyages from Holland to America, A.D. 1632 to 1644*, tr. by Henry C. Murphy (New York, 1971), shows that the ship was at New Amsterdam on July 16, 1639, laden with cattle for Jochem Pietersen Kuyter.

26. O'Callaghan and Fernow, eds., *Documents*, XIII, 5; another translation in Van Laer, ed., *New York Historical Manuscripts: Dutch*, I, 196-197.

27. Lloyd Ultan, ed., "Document Relating to the Ursuline Convent at East Morrisania", *The Bronx County Historical Society Journal* VIII (July, 1971), 67. The figures for acres and hectares are based on calculating a morgen using the Amsterdam, rather than the Rhineland, measure.

28. Van Laer, ed., *New York Historical Manuscripts: Dutch*, I, 194; also in Hershkowitz, ed., *Bronx County Historical Society Journal* (July, 1964), p. 52; Carl Horton Pierce, *New Harlem: Past and Present* (New York, 1903), p.6.

29. Pierce, p. 6; Riker, p. 129.

30. De Vries, p. 128; O'Callaghan, *History of New Netherland*, I, 206-207; Pierce, p. 7; O'Callaghan and Fernow, eds., *Documents*, XIV, 53 n; Riker, p. 134.

31. Van Laer, ed., *New York Historical Manuscripts: Dutch*, I, 194-195; IV, 53; see also Hershkowitz, ed., *Bronx County Historical Society Journal* (July 1964), p. 52.

32. O'Callaghan and Fernow, eds., *Documents*, XIII, 5; another translation in Van Laer, ed., *New York Historical Manuscripts: Dutch* I, 196-197.

33. Van Laer, ed., *New York Historical Manuscripts: Dutch*, I, 215-216; Hershkowitz, ed., *Bronx County Historical Society Journal* (July, 1964), pp. 53-54.

34. Van Laer, ed., *New York Historical Manuscripts: Dutch*, I, 63-64, 121-122, 181-182.

35. *Ibid.*, I, 212-214.

36. *Ibid.*, I, 340.

37. *Ibid.*, IV, 89.

38. *Ibid.*, II, 121-125; also Hershkowitz, ed., *Bronx County Historical Society Journal* (July, 1964), pp. 54-55; and O'Callaghan and Fernow, eds., *Documents*, XIV, 42-43.

39. See *e.g.* C. Alexander Rhodes, "Biographies and Geneologies of the Shuneman Family, Van Bergen Family, Bronck Family, Witbeck Family, Finch Family, Perks Family for 800 Years", MSS, 1915?, microfilmed November 7, 1941, New York Public Library, pp. 105, 107. See also Peter Bronck's will and power of attorney in Van Laer, ed., *New York Historical Manuscripts: Dutch*, II,

176-177, 345, 236; also in Herskowitz, ed., *Bronx County Historical Society Journal* (July, 1964), pp. 57-59.

40. See *e.g.* William Miller Collier, *Casper, a Collier, Hallenbeck, Conyn Name with Memoranda as to Bearers of it and Incidental References to Collers named Jochem (Jehoiakem), Michael and Isaac* (Auburn, N.Y., n.d., 1951?), pp. 29-31.

41. See the Vingboom Map of New York City, 1639, Library of Congress.

42. Van Laer, ed., *New York Historical Manuscripts: Dutch*, II, 121-125; also Hershkowitiz, ed., *Bronx County Historical Society Journal* (July, 1964), pp. 54-57; another translation in O'Callaghan and Fernow, eds., *Documents*, XIV, 42-44.

43. Van Laer, ed., *New York Historical Manuscripts: Dutch*, IV, 92; Riker, p. 385.

44. Van Laer, ed., *New York Historical Manuscripts: Dutch*, II, 121-125; also Hershkowitz, ed., *Bronx County Historical Society Journal* (July, 1964), pp. 54-57; another translation in O'Callaghan and Fernow, eds., *Documents*, XIV, 42-44.

45. O'Callaghan, *History of New Netherland*, I, 240-244, 249-250; Van Laer, ed., *New York Historical Manuscripts: Dutch*, IV, 124-126; O'Callaghan and Fernow, ed., *Documents*, I, 211.

46. Van Laer, ed., *New York Historical Manuscripts: Dutch*, IV, 396, 399, 408-409; O'Callaghan and Fernow, ed., *Documents*, I, 197, 199.

47. Van Laer, ed., *New York Historical Manuscripts: Dutch*, IV, 110-111; another translation in O'Callaghan and Fernow, eds., *Documents*, XIII, 8.

48. Francis Grimes Sitherwood, *Throckmorton Family History* (Bloomingdale, Ill., 1929), pp. 45-47.

49. Van Laer, ed., *New York Historical Manuscripts: Dutch*, IV, 164-165; another translation in O'Callaghan and Fernow, eds., *Documents*, XIII, 10.

50. John Winthrop, *Winthrop's Journal: "History of New England" 1630-1649*, ed. James Kendall Hosmer (New York, 1908) I, 195-199, 226, 232-235, 263-265, 277, 284, 297, 330-331; II, 7-8, 39-41 gives full details about the theological controversy. There are a number of full biographies of Anne Hutchinson, among which are Winnifred King Rugg, *Unafraid: A Life of Anne Hutchinson* (Boston and New York, 1930); Edith Curtis, *Anne Hutchinson: A Biography* (Cambridge, Mass., 1930); and Reginald Pelham Bolton, *A Woman Misunderstood: Anne Wife of William Hutchinson* (New York, 1931). For some reason, the exact location of Anne Hutchinson's house agitated writers for decades. For instance, Robert Bolton, *The History of the Several Towns, Manors and Patents of the County of Westchester* (New York, 1881) II, 30, places it at Pelham Neck in today's Pelham Bay Park, a view which seemed to gain credence with the article by Reginald Pelham Bolton, "The Home of Mistress Anne Hutchinson At Pelham 1642-3," *New-York Historical Society Quarterly Bulletin*, VI (July, 1922), 43-52, in which he describes an excavation near Split Rock. This site is accepted by Rugg in her biography, p. 244. Careful reading of the contemporary documents, however, indicate that the house was on the west bank of the river, a fact that even Reginald Pelham Bolton has to admit on p. 109 of his biography of Anne Hutchinson, written a mere nine years after the report of his excavation. The entire controversy is summed up in Lockwood Barr, *Ancient Town of Pelham:*

Westchester County, State of New York (Richmond, Va., 1946), pp. 6-11. Curtis, p. 109, it appears, did not do much research on the subject and accepts the statement by Theodore Welde in the preface to what was probably John Winthrop's unsigned work, *A Short Story of the rise, reign, and ruine of the Antinomians* (London, 1644) that Anne Hutchinson had settled near "Hell-gate" to mean that the house was in Astoria, which is way off the mark. It appears that the house was located at or near the site of today's Co-op City.

51. Samuel Niles, "A Summary Historical Narrative of the Wars in New-England with the French and Indians, in the several parts of the Country," *Collections of the Massachusetts Historical Society*, 3rd Ser., VI (Boston, 1837), 197-199. This story is confirmed in more general terms in [Edward Johnson], *A History of New England. From the English planting in the Yeere 1628 until the Yeere 1652* (London, 1654), p. 132.

52. There is no evidence that Anne Hutchinson made any effort to purchase the land either from the Dutch or the Indians.

53. Winthrop, II, 137-138; [Johnson], *History of New England*, pp. 132-133; Welde's Preface to [Winthrop?] *Rise, reign, and ruine of the Antinomians*; Niles in *Collections of the Massachusetts Historical Society*, p. 201, These sources are also used for the biographies of Anne Hutchinson by Rugg, pp. 245-248; Curtis, p. 104; and Reginald Pelham Bolton, pp. 114-115, 123-127. Oliver A. Rich, *Holland on the Hudson: An Economic and Social History of Dutch New York* (Ithaca, N.Y., 1986), p. 221 is wrong stating Hutchinson's death was part of the Indian war provoked by Governor-general Kieft. Contemporary accounts indicate that events on the mainland were not connected with Kieft's actions.

54. Winthrop, II, 138; [Johnson], *History of New England*, p. 133; Rugg, p. 127; Bolton, *A Woman Misunderstood*, p. 123; Sitherwood, p. 48; John Cornell, *Genealogy of the Cornell Family* (New York, 1902), p. 20.

55. Sitherwood, pp. 47-53, also supposes Throckmorton was in New Amsterdam at the time of the Indian attack, but gives no reason for the belief.

56. O'Callaghan, *History of New Netherland*, I, 262-271; Van Laer, ed., *New York Historical Manuscripts: Dutch*, IV, 185-189; O'Callaghan and Fernow, eds., *Documents*, XIV, 10-11.

57. Van Laer, ed., *Van Rensselaer Bowier Manuscripts*, pp. 395, 410, 433-434, 359-461, 549-552.

58. Arent van Curler to Killiaen Van Rensselaer, June 16, 1643, in O'Callaghan, *History of New Netherland*, I, 464-465.

59. *Idem*. The letter, written on June 16th, clearly states the couple was engaged. On June 25th, it is van Curler who executes the lease for Bronck's land. Legally, he could not do so unless he had already married Bronck's widow by that date.

60. Van Laer, ed., *Van Rensselaer Bowier Manuscripts*, pp. 743, 815.

61. *Ibid.*, p. 841.

62. *Ibid.*, pp. 835, 836. Jacob Gever may have been Jacob Hevingh or Hevick mentioned here. Hershkowitz, ed., *Bronx County Historical Society Journal* (July, 1964), p. 60 n. 2, concedes the possibility, and the Dutch pronunciation of Gever and Hevick or Hevingh is close enough to cause confusion in an age when spelling was not uniform.

63. Van Laer, ed., *New York Historical Manuscripts: Dutch*, II, 154-155.

Notes: Chapter IV The English Farmer and the Dutch Patroon 193

64. *Ibid.*, II, 48 n; III, 210-211; O'Callaghan and Fernow, eds., *Documents*, XIV, 63.
65. E.B. O'Callaghan, ed., *Calendar of Historical Manuscripts in the Office of the Secretary of State, Albany, N.Y.* (Albany, 1865-1866) I, 203-204.
66. Van Laer, ed., *New York Historical Manuscripts: Dutch*, II, 126-128, 149.
67. *Ibid.*, II, 139-142.
68. O'Callaghan and Fernow, eds., *Documents*, XIV, 53-54; Riker, pp. 143-145.
69. O'Callaghan, *History of New Netherland*, I, 300-302.
70. O'Callaghan and Fernow, eds., *Documents*, XIII, 18; Van Laer, ed., *New York Historical Manuscripts: Dutch*, IV, 278-280.
71. Van Laer, ed., *New York Historical Manuscripts: Dutch*, IV, 329-330.
72. *Ibid.*, IV, 62, 101, 158, 225, 283.
73. *Ibid.*, IV, 352-253.
74. *Ibid.*, IV, 572-575; O'Callaghan and Fernow, eds., *Documents*, XIV, 101-102.
75. Van Laer, ed., *New York Historical Manuscripts: Dutch*, III, 367-368.
76. Dutch Colonial Manuscripts, Vol. V, p. 381, New York State Library.
77. Van Laer, ed., *New York Historical Manuscripts: Dutch*, III, 373-376.
78. Dutch Colonial Manuscripts, Vol. V, p. 402, New York State Library.
79. Van Laer. ed., *Van Rensselaer Bowier Manuscripts*, p. 835; Ultan, ed., *Bronx County Historical Society Journal* (July, 1971), p. 68. The real estate man who did the search for this abstract of title mistook the Dutch, "Jans," an abbreviation of Jansen, for "Van." This is confirmed by the document reprinted in Riker, p. 384.
80. Van Laer, ed., *Van Rensselaer Bowier Manuscripts*, p. 835; Ultan, ed., *Bronx County Historical Society Journal* (July, 1971), p. 68.
81. Ultan, ed., *Bronx County Historical Society Journal* (July, 1971), p. 68.
82. *Idem.*; E.B. O'Callaghan, *Register of New Netherland* (Albany, 1865), p. 83.
83. Ultan, ed., *Bronx County Historical Society Journal* (July, 1971), p. 68; Riker, pp. 232-233; Thomas H. Edsall, "Notes on Samuel Edsall," copied February 26, 1925, by Gertrude Nelson for Florence Edsall Bryant, typescript in the Local History and Genealogy Room, New York Public Library, pp. 1-2.

CHAPTER IV THE ENGLISH FARMER AND THE DUTCH PATROON

1. John Cornell, *Genealogy of the Cornell Family* (New 1902), pp. 17-18; John Ross Delafield, *Delafield: The Family History* (n.p., 1945) II, 647; Francis Grimes Sitherwood, *Throckmorton Family History* (Bloomingdale, Ill., 1929), p. 48; Winnifred King Rugg, *Unafraid: A Life of Anne Hutchinson* (Boston and New York, 1930), pp. 244, 247; Reginald Pelham Bolton, *A Woman Misunderstood: Anne Wife of William Hutchinson* (New York, 1931), pp. 108, 123; John Winthrop, *Winthrop's Journal: "History of New England" 1630-1649*, ed. James Kendall Hosmer (New York, 1908) II, 138. Thomas Cornell of Essex

is sometimes confused with his son, Thomas, and with another Thomas Cornell, who served as a soldier in New Amsterdam at the same time. See Arnold J.F. Van Laer, tr. and ed., *New York Historical Manuscripts: Dutch* (Baltimore, 1974) IV, 224-225, 247-248.

2. Cornell, p. 20.

3. *Ibid.*, p. 21. A translation of the patent appears on pp. 398-399; also in Robert Bolton, *The History of the Several Towns, Manors and Patents of the County of Westchester* (New York, 1881) II, 270. See also E.B. O'Callaghan and B. Fernow, eds., *Documents Relative to the Colonial History of the State of New York* (Albany, 1856-1883) XIII, 20.

4. Cornell, p. 21; Bolton, *History of...Westchester*, II, 272.

5. Bolton, *History of...Westchester*, II, 272.

6. *Idem.*; Cornell, p. 22. The Indian uprising that drove Cornell off the land seems to have occurred in the early 1650s, considering Cornell's service in Portsmouth in 1653 and 1654. There is nothing in the Dutch records noting what happened, perhaps because the farm was not only isolated from New Amsterdam, but far from it. A possibility exists that Cornell was driven off in the general fright over an Indian war that gripped the Dutch colony in 1655, which is coincidental with Cornell's probable death date. This would not only conveniently explain his death, but also the lack of a Dutch record of the incident. It does not explain, however, Cornell's service in Portsmouth two years before the 1655 incident.

7. Arnold J.F. Van Laer, ed., *Van Rensselaer Bowier Manuscripts* (Albany, 1908), pp. 524, 527.

8. *Ibid.*, pp. 548-552.

9. E.B. O'Callaghan, *History of New Netherland; or New York Under the Dutch* (New York, 1846-1848) I, 338-339.

10. *Ibid.*, I, 355-356, 382; Alice P. Kenney, *Stubborn For Liberty: the Dutch in New York* (Syracuse, N.Y., 1975), pp. 26-27.

11. Adriaen Van der Donck, *A Description of New Netherlands*, ed. Thomas F. O'Donnell (Syracuse, N.Y., 1968), pp. xxv-xxvi.

12. O'Callaghan, *History of New Netherland*, I, 382-383; Van Laer, ed., *Van Rensselaer Bowier Manuscripts*, p. 824; Bolton, *History of...Westchester*, II, 581.

13. O'Callaghan, *History of New Netherland*, I, 382 n. 1.

14. T. Astley Atkins, *Adriaen Van Der Donck: An address delivered before the Westchester County Historical Society* (Yonkers, 1888), pp. 10-11; Bolton, *History of...Westchester*, II, 581.

15. O'Callaghan and Fernow, eds., *Documents*, XIII, 5-6; Bolton, *History of...Westchester*, II, 581; Atkins, pp. 24-25; Van Laer, ed., *Van Rensselaer Bowier Manuscripts*, p. 824; Frank L. Walton, *Pillars of Yonkers* (New York, 1951), p. 53.

16. Bolton, *History of...Westchester*, II, 581; Arnold J.F. Van Laer, ed., *New York Historical Manuscripts: Dutch*, II, 383.

17. Van Laer, ed., *New York Historical Manuscripts: Dutch*, III, 71, 76-77. For the fact that the dwelling was not complete, see Bolton, *History of... Westchester*, II, 581.

18. Kenney, pp. 36-37.

19. *Ibid.*, p. 47; O'Callaghan and Fernow, eds., *Documents*, XIV, 110-114.
20. Kenney, p. 47; O'Callaghan and Fernow, eds., *Documents*, I, 258-318.
21. O'Callaghan and Fernow, eds., *Documents*, I, 258-318.
22. *Ibid.*, I, 379-380, 420-421; Kenney, p. 48.
23. Kenney, pp. 48-49; O'Callaghan and Fernow, eds., *Documents*, I, 422-432, 471, 473.
24. O'Callaghan and Fernow, eds., *Documents*, I, 470-471, 473-478, 485.
25. Kenney, p. 49.
26. O'Callaghan and Fernow, eds., *Documents*, I, 476-478, 485-486; XIV, 210.
27. *Ibid.*, I, 530-533. See also *Ibid*, I, 532-533 n. 1; XIV, 211-212. The latest English language edition of the book was edited by Thomas F. O'Donnell and published by Syracuse University Press in 1968.
28. O'Callaghan and Fernow, eds., *Documents*, XIV, 211-212, 261.
29. *Ibid.*, XIII, 59; XIV, 550; William A. Tieck, *Riverdale, Kingsbridge, Spuyten Duyvil: New York City* (Old Tappan, N.J., 1968), pp. 3-4, shows an excavation of a Dutch house in Van Cortlandt Park, the foundation of which was discovered in 1910. Coupled with van der Donck's expression that he wished to build his home near there, and the landscape's resemblence to Breda's, it is almost certain that, if the excavation were not van der Donck's home, his house was nearby. Thomas F. O'Donnell's 1968 introduction to van der Donck's book, p. xxvii, states that the saw mill was on a stream north of the house, but that Van Cortlandt Park was the site of the corn field. Walton, p. 53, states that the house was on the Nepperhan, but Walton makes minor errors throughout his book.
30. T. Astley Atkins, *Indian Wars and the Uprising of 1655 — Yonkers Depopulated: A Paper Read Before the Yonkers Historical and Library Association* (Yonkers, 1892), p. 12; O'Callaghan, *History of New Netherland*, II, 290-298; O'Callaghan and Fernow, eds., *Documents*, XIV, 550.
31. Thomas F. O'Donnell, ed., in Van der Donck, *A Description of New Netherland*, p. xxxix; Kenney, p. 49.
32. Atkins, *Adriaen Van Der Donck*, p. 25; Walton, p. 54.

CHAPTER V THE RISE OF THE FIRST VILLAGE

1. E.B. O'Callaghan and B. Fernow, eds., *Documents Relative to the Colonial History of the State of New York* (Albany, 1856-1883) XIII, 36. The first record of the names of the fifteen men appears in an entry dated February 23, 1654, when the Town Minutes of Westchester begins. See Borough Town of Westchester, Record of Town Meetings 1664-1691, on microfilm, New-York Historical Society. The dates appended to the title of this manuscript collection are in error, since the Town Meeting minutes before 1664 are also included.
2. Ronald D. Cohen, "The Hartford Treaty of 1650: Anglo-Dutch Cooperation in the Seventeenth Century," *The New-York Historical Society Quarterly* LIII, (October, 1969), 311-332; O'Callaghan and Fernow, eds., *Documents*, I, 611-612.

3. Robert Pell, "Thomas Pell: First Lord of the Manor of Pelham Westchester Co., New York," *Pelliana* New Series, I (September, 1962), 1-26. This article is the most comprehensive work on Thomas Pell, but should not be relied on for incidents surrounding his venture in The Bronx, where several errors appear.

4. Pell, "Thomas Pell," *Pelliana* (September, 1962), pp. 27-44; "Thomas Pell," *Pelliana*, I (May, 1936), 7-11; *Collections of the New-York Historical Society for the Year 1869* (New York, 1870), p. 5.

5. Robert Pell, "Thomas Pell," *Pelliana* (September, 1962), pp. 45-46. Wampage was also known as Ann-Hooke. Several authors assume that he was the man who killed Anne Hutchinson and took her name. Without documentary evidence, this must remain speculation.

6. *Ibid.*, pp. 44, 47-48; "Thomas Pell," *Pelliana* (May, 1936), p. 10.

7. "Deed from the Indians to Thomas Pell," *Pelliana*, I (May, 1941), 3.

8. Robert Pell, "Thomas Pell," *Pelliana* (September, 1962), p. 47.

9. Borough Town of Westchester, Record of Town Meetings, February 23, 1654, on microfilm, New-York Historical Society. Because the English year, following the Julian calendar, began in the month of March at the time, and was then ten days behind the modern calendar, the date in the minutes would correspond to March 5, 1655, on the Gregorian calendar in use today.

10. O'Callaghan and Fernow, eds., *Documents*, II, 161-162; another translation in XIII, 38-39.

11. *Ibid.*, II, 161.
12. *Ibid.*, II, 136.
13. *Ibid.*, XIII, 60.
14. *Ibid.*, XIII, 39-43.
15. *Ibid.*, XIV, 333.
16. *Ibid.*, XIII, 62-63.
17. *Ibid.*, XIII, 63-65.
18. *Ibid.*, XIII, 64-65.
19. *Ibid.*, XIII, 65-66.
20. *Ibid.*, XIII, 66.
21. *Ibid.*, XIII, 67.
22. *Collections of the New-York Historical Society for the Year 1869*, p. 13.
23. Robert Bolton, *The History of the Several Towns, Manors and Patents of the County of Westchester* (New York, 1881) II, 279; E.B. O'Callaghan, ed., *The Documentary History of the State of New York* (Albany, 1849-1851) III, 925.
24. Dixon Ryan Fox, ed., *The Minutes of the Court of Sessions (1657-1696): Westchester County New York* (White Plains, 1924), pp. 1-34 *passim.*; O'Callaghan and Fernow, eds., *Documents*, XIII, 363. Careful comparison of the names of people throughout these two documentary collections will disclose the population movement from Long Island to Oostdorp.
25. Fox, ed., *Minutes of the Court of Sessions*, pp. 1-34 *passim.*; J. Franklin Jameson, ed., *Narratives of New Netherland: 1609-1664* (New York, 1909), p. 398; Hugh Hastings, ed., *Ecclesiastical Records of the State of New York* (Albany, 1901) I, 397-398; O'Callaghan, ed., *Documentary History*, III, 923.
26. Fox, ed., *Minutes of the Court of Sessions*, pp. 1-34 *passim.*

27. Bolton, *History of...Westchester*, II, 280.
28. *Ibid.*, II, 280-281; J. Hammond Trumbull, ed., *The Public Records of the Colony of Connecticut* (Hartford, 1850), pp. 387-388.
29. Bolton, *History of...Westchester*, II, 281-283.
30. E.B. O'Callaghan, *Register of New Netherland* (Albany, 1865), p. 98; O'Callaghan and Fernow, eds., *Documents*, XIII, 392; Bolton, *History of... Westchester*, II, 284-285.
31. Trumbull, ed., *Public Records of the Colony of Connecticut*, pp. 406-407; O'Callaghan, *History of New Netherland; or New York Under the Dutch* (New York, 1846-1848) II, 456; O'Callaghan and Fernow, eds., *Documents*, II, 217.
32. O'Callaghan, *History of New Netherland*, II, 484-487; Trumbull, ed., *Public Records of the Colony of Connecticut*, pp. 411-412. Connecticut documents date the action as October 8th, but that is according to the Julian calendar.
33. Jameson, ed., *Narratives of New Netherland*, pp. 432-434; Trumbull, ed., *Public Records of the Colony of Connecticut*, p. 410.
34. Jameson, ed., *Narratives of New Netherland*, pp. 438, 440-445.
35. *Ibid.*, p. 443; O'Callaghan, *History of New Netherland*, II, 495.
36. O'Callaghan and Fernow, eds., *Documents*, II, 227-229.
37. Trumbull, ed., *Public Records of the Colony of Connecticut*, p. 418; Bolton, *History of...Westchester*, II, 433-434.
38. O'Callaghan and Fernow, eds., *Documents*, XIII, 363-364.
39. Trumbull, ed., *Public Records of the Colony of Connecticut*, p. 427; Bolton, *History of...Westchester*, II, 286-287; O'Callaghan, ed., *Documentary History*, III, 925.

CHAPTER VI THE GREAT LAND GRAB

1. E.B. O'Callaghan and B. Fernow, eds., *Documents Relative to the Colonial History of the State of New York* (Albany, 1856-1883) III, 106.
2. *Ibid.*, XIII, 392.
3. Robert Bolton, *The History of the Several Towns, Manors and Patents of the County of Westchester* (New York, 1881) I, 203. The date on the grant is June 24th, which would be July 4th on the Gregorian calendar. *Records of the Town of Eastchester*, transcribed by the Eastchester Historical Society (Eastchester, N.Y., 1964- —) I, 74-75.
4. Bolton, *History of...Westchester*, II, 271; John Cornell, *Genealogy of the Cornell Family* (New York, 1902), pp. 17, 21.
5. Bolton, *History of...Westchester*, II, 271-273; Cornell, pp. 21-22; John Ross Delafield, *Delafield: The Family History* (n.p., 1945) II, 469 n.
6. Bolton, *History of...Westchester*, II, 266-267; Victor Hugo Paltsits, ed., *Minutes of the Executive Council of the Province of New York: Administration of Francis Lovelace 1668-1673* (Albany, 1910) I, 231-234.
7. O'Callaghan and Fernow, eds., *Documents*, XIII, 402.
8. *Ibid.*, XIII, 403.
9. *Ibid.*, XIII, 404.

10. Bolton, *History of... Westchester*, II, 434.
11. Jerrold Seymann, ed., *Colonial Charters Patents and Grants to Communities Comprising the City of New York* (New York, 1939), pp. 35-36 n. 90, 372-374.
12. *Ibid.*, pp. 432-433.
13. *Ibid.*, pp. 49-50.
14. *Ibid.*, pp. 353-355. The date on the grant is March 9, 1666, which is March 19, 1667, on the Gregorian calendar.
15. *Ibid.*, pp. 386-387; Paltsits, ed., *Minutes of the Executive Council*, I, 232-233.
16. Bolton, *History of... Westchester*, II, 287-288. The date on the grant is February 13, 1667, which would be February 23, 1668, on the Gregorian calendar.
17. Seymann, ed., *Colonial Charters*, pp. 361-362.
18. Harry W.C. Melick, "The First Real Estate Development in The Bronx," *The New-York Historical Society Quarterly*, XXXII (January, 1948), 33; Harry W.C. Melick, *The Manor of Fordham and Its Founder* (New York, 1950), pp. 10-29, 34-46; [Harry W.C. Melick], "Decendants of John Archer of Fordham," typescript in the Westchester County Historical Society, pp. 1-2; Dixon Ryan Fox, ed., *The Minutes of the Court of Sessions (1657-1696): Westchester County New York* (White Plains, 1924), pp. 1-34 *passim*.
19. Melick, *Manor of Fordham*, pp. 46-49; Seymann, ed., *Colonial Charters*, pp. 49-50; Reginald Pelham Bolton, "A Pioneer Settler's Home on Spuyten Duyvil Hill," *The New-York Historical Society Quarterly Bulletin*, V (April, 1921), 15-16; Paltsits, ed., *Minutes of the Executive Council*, I, 195-202.
20. James Riker, *Revised History of Harlem (City of New York.)* (New York, 1904), p. 232-234, 240, 242, 248; Carl Horton Pierce, *New Harlem: Past and Present* (New York, 1903), pp. 37-38, 46.
21. Riker, pp. 243, 249-250; Melick, *Manor of Fordham*, pp. 51-53; O'Callaghan and Fernow, eds., *Documents*, XIII, 421; Paltsits, ed., *Minutes of the Executive Council*, I, 22-23, 203-205.
22. Melick, *Manor of Fordham*, p. 53, believes that the town's position was weak. It was not. If Paparinemin were judged to be outside the New Harlem limits, and, if it were not in the O'Neale patent, Westchester, by virtue of its own patent, could claim it. For his part, Archer stated that the land in question was not part of his purchase from O'Neale.
23. *Ibid.*, pp. 53-55; Paltsits, ed., *Minutes of the Executive Council*, I, 25-26, 205-207.
24. Melick, *Manor of Fordham*, pp. 58-59. Richard Betts is recorded in the Council records, but was not a member of the immediate family of William Betts, owner of the property in the Yonker's land. There was a Richard Betts living on Long Island at the time, however. See O'Callaghan and Fernow, eds., *Documents* XIV, 619, 685. It is possible the secretary made an error and wrote Richard Betts for William Betts. See Paltsits, ed., *Minutes of the Executive Council*, I, 210-211.
25. Riker, pp. 253-256; Paltsits, ed., *Minutes of the Executive Council*, I, 222-229.
26. Melick, *New-York Historical Society Quarterly* (January, 1948), pp. 35-37. Melick in *Manor of Fordham*, p. 41, believes that the village name is derived

from the Reverend Robert Fordham of Hempstead, whom, he insists, Archer must have admired. Bolton, *History of... Westchester*, II, 503, states that it comes from a parish in Norfolk. Both explanations seem far-fetched. Melick in *Manor of Fordham*, p. 58, rightly states that an English name, such as Fordham, would not be natural for a Dutchman. Yet, in the same place, he points out that the earliest mention of the name is not made by Archer, but by Governor Lovelace in a letter to Verveelen. Is it possible that Lovelace provided the name?

27. Melick, *New-York Historical Society Quarterly* (January, 1948), p. 35; Riker, p. 255.
28. Paltsits, ed., *Minutes of the Executive Council*, I, 212-214.
29. Riker, p. 251.
30. Melick, *Manor of Fordham*, pp. 61-65; Paltsits, ed., *Minutes of the Executive Council*, I, 52, 52 n. 1, 214-219.
31. Melick, *Manor of Fordham*, pp. 65-66; Riker, p. 263.
32. Melick, *Manor of Fordham*, pp. 68-59.
33. *Ibid.*, pp. 69-73.
34. *Ibid.*, pp. 74-77.
35. *Ibid.*, pp. 78-81; Riker, p. 275; O'Callaghan and Fernow, eds., *Documents*, XIII, 459, 471; Paltsits, ed., *Minutes of the Executive Council*, I, 219-220.
36. Riker, pp. 278, 284, 294; Melick, *Manor of Fordham*, p. 80.
37. Theodore A. Leggett, *Early Settlers of West Farms: Westchester County, N.Y.* (New York, 1913), pp. 5, 26-27; *Collections of the New-York Historical Society for the Year 1892* (New York, 1893), p. 4.
38. O'Callaghan and Fernow, eds., *Documents*, XIII, 422.
39. *Records of...Eastchester*, I, 8.
40. Borough Town of Westchester, Record of Town Meetings, February 1, 1669/70, on microfilm, New-York Historical Society.
41. O'Callaghan, ed., *Documentary History*, IV, 136-138.
42. *Records of...Eastchester*, I, 2, 10, 12, 34.
43. *Ibid.*, I, 2, 3, 6, 10, 11.
44. O'Callaghan and Fernow, eds., *Documents*, XIII, 441.
45. This figure is extrapolated from the growth in population between the first known census in the area in 1698 and the second in 1703. See O'Callaghan, ed., *Documentary History*, I, 689, 691. Another indication of the population at the time is the tax assessment rolls of 1675 for Eastchester and Westchester, in which only 41 names are recorded. Of course, this list does not include women and children and those not taxed, and it does not include other areas of today's Bronx. See O'Callaghan and Fernow, eds., *Documents*, XIII, 488-489.
46. O'Callaghan and Fernow, eds., *Documents*, XIV, 602-603, 630.
47. "Thomas Pell," *Pelliana*, I (May, 1936), 23-36; Robert Pell, "Thomas Pell", *Pelliana* New Series, I (September, 1962), 52.
48. "Thomas Pell," *Pelliana* (May, 1936), pp. 20-22, 27; Robert Pell, "Thomas Pell," *Pelliana* (September, 1962), pp. 54, 63-65.
49. Robert Pell, "Sir John Pell," *Pelliana* New Series, I (October, 1963), 49-51.
50. *Ibid.*, pp. 51, 78-82; William A. Shaw, *The Knights of England*

(London, 1906) does not list John Pell as a knight.
  51. Robert Pell, "Sir John Pell," *Pelliana* (October, 1963), pp. 51-53.
  52. *Ibid.*, p. 53. *Pelliana* New Series, I (August, 1965) frontispiece shows a primitive painting of the house, which is probably fanciful.
  53. Robert Pell, "Sir John Pell," *Pelliana* (October, 1963), pp. 53-54.
  54. Lloyd Ultan, ed., "Document Relating to the Ursuline Convent at East Morrisania," *The Bronx County Historical Society Journal* VIII (July, 1971), 68-69; Bolton, *History of...Westchester*, II, 458.
  55. Bolton, *History of...Westchester*, II, 459.
  56. *Ibid.*, II, 458-459; Riker, p. 283.
  57. Bolton, *History of...Westchester*, II, 456-457.
  58. *Ibid.*, II, 259; Riker, p. 284.

CHAPTER VII THE DUTCH INTERLUDE

  1. Ronald D. Cohen, "The New England Colonies and the Dutch Recapture of New York, 1673-1674," *The New-York Historical Society Quarterly*, LVI (January, 1972), 60.
  2. E.B. O'Callaghan, ed., *The Documentary History of the State of New York* (Albany, 1849-1851) II, 91-92.
  3. E.B. O'Callaghan and B. Fernow, eds., *Documents Relative to the Colonial History of the State of New York* (Albany, 1856-1883) II, 572-573.
  4. *Ibid.*, II, 580; XIII, 474.
  5. *Ibid.*, II, 581.
  6. *Ibid.*, II, 590-591; *Records of the Town of Eastchester*, transcribed by the Eastchester Historical Society (Eastchester, N.Y., 1964- —) I, 14.
  7. Cohen, *New-York Historical Society Quarterly* (January, 1972), 60.
  8. O'Callaghan and Fernow, eds., *Documents*, II, 620-622.
  9. *Ibid.*, II, 632-633; *Third Annual Report of the State Historian of the State of New York, 1897* (New York and Albany, 1898), p. 160.
  10. *Third Annual Report*, pp. 160-161.
  11. O'Callaghan and Fernow, eds., *Documents*, II, 625-626.
  12. *Ibid.*, II, 638; Preston S. Valentine, "A Record of Some of the Valentine Family of The Bronx and Westchester," *The Bronx County Historical Society Journal* XI (Spring, 1974), 17.
  13. O'Callaghan and Fernow, eds., *Documents*, II, 708-709, 721.
  14. *Ibid.*, II, 631-632.
  15. *Ibid.*, II, 637-638.
  16. *Ibid.*, II, 643.
  17. *Ibid.*, II, 650-651, 691.
  18. *Ibid.*, II, 664.
  19. *Ibid.*, II, 684.
  20. Cohen, *New-York Historical Society Quarterly* (January, 1972), p. 54.
  21. O'Callaghan and Fernow, eds., *Documents*, II, 659.
  22. *Ibid.*, 703.
  23. *Third Annual Report*, pp. 164-167.

24. O'Callaghan and Fernow, eds., *Documents*, II, 665-666.
25. *Ibid.*, II, 673-674.
26. *Ibid.*, II, 696.
27. *Ibid.*, II, 709.
28. James Riker, *Revised History of Harlem (City of New York.)* (New York, 1904), pp. 316-317.

CHAPTER VIII FROM RIDING TO COUNTY

1. E.B. O'Callaghan and B. Fernow, eds., *Documents Relative to the Colonial History of the State of New York* (Albany, 1856-1883) III, 215.
2. Borough Town of Westchester, Record of Town Meetings 1665-1691, July 9, 1678, on microfilm, New-York Historical Society. Part of this entry is printed in Robert Bolton, *The History of the Several Towns, Manors and Patents of the County of Westchester* (New York, 1881) II, 295.
3. Borough Town of Westchester, Record of Town Meetings, July 9, 1678, on microfilm, New-York Historical Society.
4. *Ibid.*, January 9, 1679; Bolton, *History of...Westchester*, II, 298; *Records of the Town of Eastchester*, transcribed by the Eastchester Historical Society (Eastchester, N.Y., 1964- —) II, 19. According to the Julian calendar then in use in England and her colonies, the year began in March. Therefore, January, 1679, as recorded in the documents, would be January, 1680, on the modern calendar.
5. Borough Town of Westchester, Record of Town Meetings, June 27, 1681, on microfilm, New-York Historical Society. This is also printed in Bolton, *History of...Westchester*, II, 298.
6. *Third Annual Report of the State Historian of the State of New York, 1897* (New York and Albany, 1898), pp. 160-161, has a list of seven male Quakers from Westchester who were required to sign a document affirming allegiance to the Dutch authorities on October 28, 1673, just after the Dutch recaptured New York.
7. Bolton, *History of...Westchester*, II, 315; *Records of...Eastchester*, I, Loose Sheet 20.
8. Borough Town of Westchester, Record of Town Meetings, entries from October 6 to 25, 1680, on microfilm, New-York Historical Society. Bolton, *History of...Westchester*, prints some entries.
9. *Records of...Eastchester*, I, Loose Sheet 20.
10. *Ibid.*, I, 24X
11. *Ibid.*, I, 39; II, 3 1/2.
12. *Ibid.*, I, 49.
13. *Ibid.*, I, KB O).
14. *Ibid.*, I, X-25.
15. *Ibid.*, I, 34; II, 6.
16. *Ibid.*, I, 34. The date is misprinted in the source.
17. *Ibid.*, I, 35.
18. *Ibid.*, I, 37.

19. *Ibid.*, I, 38.
20. *Ibid.*, I, 37-38.
21. *Ibid.*, I, 42, 45.
22. *Ibid.*, I, 45.
23. *Ibid.*, I, 46.
24. *Collections of the New-York Historical Society for the Year 1892* (New York, 1893), pp. 36-37.
25. *Records of...Eastchester*, I, Loose Sheet 18; O'Callaghan and Fernow, eds., *Documents*, XIV, 697.
26. O'Callaghan and Fernow, eds., *Documents*, XIII, 492-493.
27. *Ibid.*, XIII, 501; *Records of...Eastchester*, II, 23 1/2.
28. *Third Annual Report*, p. 389.
29. *The Colonial Laws of New York From the Year 1664 to the Revolution* (Albany, 1894) I, 99.
30. O'Callaghan and Fernow, eds., *Documents*, XIV, 692.
31. *Records of...Eastchester*, I, Loose Sheet 17.
32. *Ibid.*, XIV, 697-698.
33. *Third Annual Report*, pp. 416-417, 426; *Colonial Laws*, I, 98.
34. O'Callaghan and Fernow, eds., *Documents*, XIV, 705.
35. *Third Annual Report*, pp. 288-289; *Colonial Laws*, I, 97, 99.
36. O'Callaghan and Fernow, eds., *Documents*, XIII, 493-494.
37. *Ibid.*, XIII, 494-495.
38. *Ibid.*, XIII, 495-496.
39. *Ibid.*, XIV, 721.
40. *Ibid.*, XIII, 501; XIV, 734; *Records of...Eastchester*, I, Loose Sheet 21.
41. O'Callaghan and Fernow, eds., *Documents*, XIII, 488-489.
42. *Records of...Eastchester*, I, 16, Loose Sheet 19.
43. O'Callaghan and Fernow, eds., *Documents*, XIII, 574.
44. *Ibid.*, XIII, 483; Harry W.C. Melick, *The Manor of Fordham and Its Founder* (New York, 1950), p. 84. Melick believes the inhabitants of Fordham requested Archer to resurrect the court. Considering their past attitude toward Archer and his use of the court to quash any action against him, this is difficult to believe. It is more likely that Archer filed the petition on his own behalf.
45. James Riker, *Revised History of Harlem (City of New York.)* (New York, 1904), p. 326; *Third Annual Report*, pp. 377, 426-427; Melick, *Manor of Fordham*, pp. 84-85. Melick was unaware that the records of the Court of Assizes in this case, the originals of which have been lost, are printed in the *Third Annual Report*.
46. Riker, p. 326; Melick, *Manor of Fordham*, pp. 84-85; E.B. O'Callaghan, ed., *Calendar of Historical Manuscripts in the Office of the Secretary of State, Albany, N.Y.* (Albany, 1865-1866) II, 43. Melick confuses some dates in these incidents, particularly because he lacks knowledge of the published records of the Court of Assizes in this affair.
47. O'Callaghan, ed., *Calendar*, II, 50; *Third Annual Report*, pp. 388, 391.
48. *Collections of the New-York Historical Society for the Year 1894* (New York, 1895), p. 437.
49. *Ibid.*, p. 436; Melick, *Manor of Fordham*, p. 89.

50. Melick, *Manor of Fordham*, pp. 88-89; Bolton, *History of... Westchester*, II, 508-509.
51. O'Callaghan, ed., *Calendar*, II, 78-79; Melick, *Manor of Fordham*, p. 95.
52. Melick, *Manor of Fordham*, pp. 92-94.
53. *Ibid.*, pp. 85-89; Victor Hugo Paltsits, ed., *Minutes of the Executive Council of the Province of New York: Administration of Francis Lovelace 1668-1673* (Albany, 1910) I, 220-221. Melick, *Manor of Fordham*, p. 85 n. 23, discovered two copies of the deed, one in Albany and one in Westchester County. Noting a discrepancy in the dates, he believes that the date was really January, 1674, using the Julian calendar (January, 1675, in the modern calendar used throughout this book), arguing that the year given for the reign of King Charles is closer to the truth in the Westchester deed than in the Albany one. Yet, the reign year is incorrect in both documents. Furthermore, the Court of Assizes did not decide finally in Archer's favor on the ownership of the island of Paparinemin until October, 1675, and it is unlikely that the colonial governors would make a purchase of the land before the case was settled, or that Verveelen would not protest the matter, contending, as he did, that the island was his. In addition, the January, 1679, date is in accord with the beginning of the sale of land in Fordham in November, 1678.
54. O'Callaghan, ed., *Calendar*, II, 82-83; Riker, p. 370.
55. O'Callaghan, *Documents*, XIII, 498.
56. *Third Annual Report*, p. 326; *Records of... Eastchester*, I, Loose Sheet 17, Loose Sheet 18, Loose Page 22.
57. *Records of... Eastchester*, I, Loose Sheet 23.
58. *Ibid.*, I, 36, 37.
59. *Ibid.*, I, 40.
60. *Idem.*
61. *Third Annual Report*, pp. 288, 399-400, 403.
62. The course of this case may be followed in *Ibid.*, pp. 364-366, 421; O'Callaghan, ed., *Calendar*, II, 84; *Collections of the New-York Historical Society for the Year 1912* (New York, 1913), p. 5.
63. *Third Annual Report*, pp. 218-219.
64. Bolton, *History of... Westchester*, II, 462.
65. *Ibid.*, II, 517-518.
66. Details of this case may be followed in Riker, pp. 353-354, 366-369, 382-386; O'Callaghan, ed., *Calendar*, II, 90, 106.
67. O'Callaghan, ed., *Documents*, XIII, 542.
68. *Ibid.*, III, 328-329; Thomas P. Phelan, *Thomas Dongan: Colonial Governor of New York 1683-1688* (New York, 1933), pp. 35-36; Bolton, *History of... Westchester*, II, 298.
69. William Smith, Jr., *The History of the Province of New York*, ed., Michael Kammen (Cambridge, Mass., 1972) I, 55.
70. *Colonial Laws*, I, 111-116.
71. *Ibid.*, I, 121-123.
72. *Ibid.*, I, 125-128.
73. *Ibid.*, I, 141-142.
74. *Ibid.*, I, 137-141.

CHAPTER IX REBELLION

1. E.B. O'Callaghan, ed., *Calendar of Historical Manuscripts in the Office of the Secretary of State, Albany, N.Y.* (Albany, 1865-1866) II, 153.
2. *Ibid.*, II, 154.
3. *Ibid.*, II, 128.
4. Robert Bolton, *The History of the Several Towns, Manors and Patents of the County of Westchester* (New York, 1881) II, 463.
5. James Riker, *Revised History of Harlem (City of New York.)* (New York, 1904), pp. 391-392.
6. *Ibid.*, p. 392.
7. William Smith, Jr., *The History of the Province of New York*, ed. Michael Kammen (Cambridge, Mass., 1972) I 139, 139 n.
8. This can be easily traced by carefully reading Colonel Lewis Morris's will printed in Bolton, *History of...Westchester* II, 464-466.
9. *Idem.*; Smith, *History*, I, 139-140.
10. Richard B. Morris, ed., *John Jay The Winning of the Peace: Unpublished Papers 1780-1784*, associate ed., Ene Sirvet (New York, 1980), p. 714.
11. *The Colonial Laws of New York From the Year 1664 to the Revolution* (Albany, 1894) I, 146-147, 152, 169, 175-176.
12. E.B. O'Callaghan and B. Fernow, eds., *Documents Relative to the Colonial History of the State of New York* (Albany, 1856-1883) III, 361.
13. O'Callaghan, ed., *Calendar*, II, 169.
14. Bolton, *History of...Westchester*, II, 315.
15. *Records of the Town of Eastchester*, transcribed by the Eastchester Historical Society (Eastchester, N.Y., 1964- —) I, 54; II, 8.
16. *Ibid.*, I, 54.
17. *Ibid.*, I, 55.
18. O'Callaghan, ed., *Calendar*, II, 153.
19. The Town Records of Westchester, on microfilm, February, 1685/6, May 27, 1686, August, 1686, October, 1686, microfilm reel TWC3, The Bronx County Historical Society Research Library. That few families owned more than one horse may be determined by the assessment rolls printed in O'Callaghan, *Documents*, XIII, 488-489.
20. *Records of...Eastchester*, I, 54.
21. Town Records of Westchester, March 9, 1686, March 10, 1686, microfilm reel TWC3, The Bronx County Historical Society Research Library.
22. E.B. O'Callaghan, ed., *The Documentary History of the State of New York* (Albany, 1849-1851) I, 164-165.
23. O'Callaghan, ed., *Calendar*, II, 167.
24. Bolton, *History of...Westchester*, II, 57-59.
25. *Ibid.*, II, 268-269. Grove Farm was located at today's Ferry Point.
26. *Records of...Eastchester* I, 49.
27. *Ibid.*, I, 54, 55.
28. Bolton, *History of...Westchester*, II, 289-290.
29. *Records of...Eastchester*, I, 57; Town Records of Westchester, April 18,

1687, microfilm reel TWC3, The Bronx County Historical Society Research Library.
    30.   Town Records of Westchester, copy of letter to the governor, May 3, 1687, microfilm reel TWC 3, The Bronx County Historical Society Research Library.
    31.   *Ibid.*, copy of letter to the governor, May 3, 1687, meeting records, May 2, 1687, May 3, 1687, microfilm reel TWC3.
    32.   *Records of...Eastchester*, I, 57.
    33.   Bolton, *History of...Westchester* II, 290.
    34.   Harry W.C. Melick, *The Manor of Fordham and Its Founder* (New York, 1950), p. 103; Riker, p. 389. Bolton, *History of...Westchester*, II, 516, says Archer died in October, 1685. This is impossible. Archer's son petitioned for an administrator for his father's estate on March 1, 1684 (now, March 11, 1685).
    35.   O'Callaghan, ed., *Calendar*, II, 108; Riker, p. 389.
    36.   O'Callaghan, ed., *Calendar*, II, 108.
    37.   Riker, p. 389, claims Archer owed Steenwyck £933 18s.; Melick, *Manor of Fordham*, p. 105 n. 5, states that Archer owed Steenwyck the staggering sum of £38,800 19s., while his son owed the merchant £89 3s. No matter which sum is correct, how Archer ever expected to repay such a huge amount remains a mystery.
    38.   Melick, *Manor of Fordham*, pp. 100-101.
    39.   Bolton, *History of...Westchester*, II, 510-511; *Collections of the New-York Historical Society for the Year 1893* (New York, 1894), p. 415; Hugh Hastings, ed., *Ecclesiastical Records of the State of New York* (Albany, 1901-1905) II, 888-889.
    40.   *Collections of the New-York Historical Society for the Year 1892* (New York, 1893), p. 168.
    41.   Hastings, ed., *Ecclesiastical Records*, II, 890; Harry W.C. Melick, "The Fordham 'Ryott' of July 16, 1688," *The New-York Historical Society Quarterly*, XXXVI (April, 1952) 210-211.
    42.   O'Callaghan, ed., *Calendar*, II, 140.
    43.   Bolton, *History of...Westchester*, II, 511; Melick, *Manor of Fordham*, p. 106.
    44.   Melick, *Manor of Fordham*, pp. 106-107 n. 9.
    45.   *Ibid.*, p. 106.
    46.   *Idem*.
    47.   Melick, *New-York Historical Society Quarterly* (April, 1952), p. 213.
    48.   O'Callaghan and Fernow, eds., *Documents*, III, 536, 537.
    49.   Records of the Town of Westchester, April 17, 1688, microfilm reel TWC3, The Bronx County Historical Society Research Library.
    50.   *Ibid.*, May 19, 1688; Melick, *Manor of Fordham*, pp. 111-112; Melick, *New-York Historical Society Quarterly* (April, 1952), p. 213.
    51.   Records of the Town of Westchester, May 19, 1688, May 21, 1688, May 25, 1688, microfilm reel TWC3, The Bronx County Historical Society Research Library; Melick, *Manor of Fordham*, pp. 112-113.
    52.   Melick, *New-York Historical Society Quarterly* (April, 1952),p. 213.
    53.   *Ibid.*, pp. 213-214.

54. *Ibid.*, pp. 214-217.
55. *Idem.*
56. *Idem.*
57. *Idem.*
58. *Ibid.*, pp. 217-218.
59. William S. Pelletreau, ed., *Early Wills of Westchester County New York From 1664 to 1784* (New York, 1898), p. 388.
60. O'Callaghan, *Calendar*, II, 171; Melick, *New-York Historical Society Quarterly* (April, 1952), p. 218.
61. Melick, *New-York Historical Society Quarterly* (April, 1952), pp. 218-219; Hastings, ed., *Ecclesiastical Records*, II, 960, 1035.
62. Melick, *New-York Historical Society Quarterly* (April, 1952), p. 219; Melick, *Manor of Fordham*, pp. 415-416.
63. Records of the Town of Westchester, September 10, 1688, microfilm reel TWC3, The Bronx County Historical Society Research Library.
64. *Ibid.*, September 27, 1688.
65. *Ibid.*, November 29, 1688.
66. *Ibid.*, March 25, 1689
67. *Ibid.*, April 3, 1689.
68. O'Callaghan and Fernow, eds., *Documents*, III, 572.
69. *Ibid.*, III, 591.
70. *Ibid.*, III, 573-576.
71. O'Callaghan, ed., *Calendar*, II, 128.
72. O'Callaghan and Fernow, eds., *Documents* III, 591; *Collections of the New-York Historical Society for the Year 1868* (New York, 1868), pp. 246-247.
73. O'Callaghan and Fernow, eds., *Documents*, III, 591.
74. *Ibid.*, III, 573-576; *Collections of the New-York Historical Society for ...1868*, pp. 259-260.
75. Smith, *History*, I, 71.
76. O'Callaghan and Fernow, eds., *Documents*, III, 594-595.
77. *Ibid.*, III, 601.
78. *Ibid.*, 595, 601.
79. *Ibid.*, III, 596.
80. *Idem.*
81. *Ibid.*, III, 597.
82. O'Callaghan, ed., *Documentary History*, II, 400.
83. *Ibid.*, II, 23-24.
84. O'Callaghan and Fernow, eds., *Documents*, III, 605, 606, 658.
85. O'Callaghan, ed., *Documentary History*, II, 45.
86. O'Callaghan, ed., *Calendar* II, 185, 186, 188; O'Callaghan, ed., *Documentary History*, II, 48, 49, 347.
87. O'Callaghan, ed., *Documentary History*, II, 50.
88. *Ibid.*, II, 53-54; O'Callaghan, ed., *Calendar*, II, 191.
89. O'Callaghan, ed., *Documentary History*, II, 55, 60; O'Callaghan and Fernow, eds., *Documents*, III, 656.
90. Records of the Town of Westchester, April 30, 1690, microfilm reel TWC3, The Bronx County Historical Society Research Library.

91. O'Callaghan, ed., *Calendar*, II, 188; O'Callaghan, ed., *Documentary History*, II, 75 n.
92. O'Callaghan, ed., *Calendar*, II, 193; O'Callaghan, ed., *Documentary History*, II, 71.
93. O'Callaghan, ed., *Documentary History*, II, 183.
94. *Ibid.*, II, 71-72, shows the order sent to Kings County.
95. *Ibid.*, II, 352; O'Callaghan, ed., *Calendar*, II, 194.
96. Dixon Ryan Fox, ed., *Minutes of the Court of Sessions (1657-1696): Westchester County New York* (White Plains, 1924), p. 78.
97. Theodore A. Leggett, *Early Settlers of West Farms: Westchester County, N.Y.* (New York, 1913), pp. 8-11.
98. *Ibid.*, pp. 11-13; Fox, ed., *Minutes of the Court of Sessions*, pp. 75-79.
99. O'Callaghan, ed., *Documentary History*, II, 266.
100. *Ibid.*, II, 359.
101. This position is ably defended by Jerome R. Reich, *Leisler's Rebellion: A Study of Democracy in New York 1664-1720* (Chicago, 1953), pp. 25-26, 46-49, 92-93.
102. This position is expounded by Thomas J. Archdeacon, "The Age of Leisler — New York City, 1689-1710: A Social and Demographic Interpretation," in Jacob Judd and Irwin I. Polishook, eds., *Aspects of Early New York Society and Politics* (Tarrytown, N.Y., 1974), pp. 63-82.
103. Bolton, *History of... Westchester*, II, 464-469.
104. O'Callaghan, ed., *Documentary History*, II, 68.
105. Bolton, *History of... Westchester*, I, 583-584.
106. O'Callaghan, ed., *Calendar*, II, 199; O'Callaghan, ed., *Documentary History*, II, 354.

CHAPTER X CONSEQUENCES

1. E.B. O'Callaghan, ed., *Calendar of Historical Manuscripts in the Office of the Secretary of State, Albany, N.Y.* (Albany, 1865-1866) II, 203.
2. *Ibid.*, II, 202-203; E.B. O'Callaghan, ed., *The Documentary History of the State of New York* (Albany, 1849-1851) II, 360-361.
3. O'Callaghan, ed., *Documentary History*, II, 363.
4. Lawrence H. Leder, ed., "Records of the Trials of Leisler and His Associates," *The New-York Historical Society Quarterly*, XXXVI (October, 1952), 441.
5. *Ibid.*, pp. 443, 445.
6. *Ibid.*, pp. 448, 454-457.
7. O'Callaghan, ed., *Documentary History*, II, 366-367.
8. *The Colonial Laws of New York From the Year 1664 to the Revolution* (Albany, 1861) I, 255-257.
9. Lawrence H. Leder, *Jacob Leisler and the New York Rebellion of 1689-1691*, unpublished M.A. Thesis, May, 1950, New York University, p. 144; O'Callaghan, ed., *Documentary History*, II, 380-381.
10. E.B. O'Callaghan and B. Fernow, eds., *Documents Relative to the Colonial History of the State of New York* (Albany, 1856-1883) IV, 83.

11. *Collections of the New-York Historical Society for the Year 1868* (New York, 1868), pp. 333-334.
12. O'Callaghan, ed., *Calendar*, II, 227; O'Callaghan, ed., *Documentary History*, II, 415-416.
13. O'Callaghan and Fernow, eds., *Documents*, IV, 83.
14. *Collections of the New-York Historical Society for...1868*, pp. 333.
15. O'Callaghan and Fernow, eds., *Documents*, IV, 83.
16. *Collections of the New-York Historical Society for...1868*, pp. 336-337.
17. *Ibid.*, pp. 337-338.
18. *Ibid.*, pp. 339-340.
19. *Ibid.*, p. 348; O'Callaghan, ed., *Documentary History*, II, 435-437.
20. Dixon Ryan Fox, ed., *The Minutes of the Court of Sessions (1657-1696): Westchester County New York* (White Plains, 1924), p. 77.
21. *Ibid.*, pp. 77-79.
22. *Ibid.*, pp. 73-79.
23. Paul M. Hamlin and Charles E. Baker, eds., *The Supreme Court of Judicature of the Province of New York: 1691-1704* (New York, 1952) II, 25, 27, 317-318.
24. O'Callaghan, ed., *Documentary History*, II, 412-413.
25. Fox, ed., *Minutes of the Court of Sessions*, pp. 85, 86, 87-88.
26. Hamlin and Baker, eds., *Supreme Court of Judicature* II, 320-321; *Collections of the New-York Historical Society for the Year 1912* (New York, 1913), pp. 73, 81, 95, 106.
27. *Colonial Laws*, I, 262-267.
28. Fox, ed., *Minutes of the Court of Sessions*, pp. 67-68; O'Callaghan, ed., *Documentary History*, II, 330-331.
29. O'Callaghan, ed., *Calendar*, II, 220, 221; O'Callaghan, ed., *Documentary History*, II, 330-331.
30. Fox, ed., *Minutes of the Court of Sessions*, pp. 67-68.
31. *Collections of the New-York Historical Society for...1868*, pp. 333-334; Hamlin and Baker, eds., *Supreme Court of Judicature*, II, 289.
32. The Town Records of Westchester, on microfilm, November 23, 1693, microfilm reel TWC3, The Bronx County Historical Society Research Library.
33. Fox, ed., *Minutes of the Court of Sessions*, p. 85.
34. *Ibid.*, p. 97.
35. *Collections of the New-York Historical Society for...1912*, pp. 78, 87.
36. Fox, ed., *Minutes of the Court of Sessions*, pp. 102-103.
37. *Colonial Laws*, I, 224-225.
38. Town Records of Westchester, September 23, 1691, microfilm reel TWC3, The Bronx County Historical Society Research Library.
39. *Ibid.*, October 2, 1691.
40. Hamlin and Baker, eds., *Supreme Court of Judicature*, II, 4, 10, 11, 261-262, 282-284; Harry W.C. Melick, *The Manor of Fordham and Its Founder* (New York, 1950), pp. 115-116.
41. Hamlin and Baker, eds., *Supreme Court of Judicature*, II, 7, 9, 277-278; Melick, *Manor of Fordham*, p. 115 n. 15.
42. Town Records of Westchester, October 26, 1691, microfilm reel TWC3, The Bronx County Historical Society Research Library.

43. *Ibid.*, November 5, 1691.
44. Hugh Hastings, ed., *Ecclesiastical Records of the State of New York* (Albany, 1901-1905) II, 1035; Melick, *Manor of Fordham*, p. 116; Hamlin and Baker, eds., *Supreme Court of Judicature*, II, 284-285.
45. Hamlin and Baker, eds., *Supreme Court of Judicature*, II, 15, 16, 19, 20, 285; Melick, *Manor of Fordham*, p. 116; Records of the Town of Westchester, March 30, 1692, microfilm reel TWC3, The Bronx County Historical Society Research Library.
46. Records of the Town of Westchester, April 22, 1692, August 4, 1692, January 2, 1692, microfilm reel TWC3, The Bronx County Historical Society Research Library.
47. Hamlin and Baker, eds., *Supreme Court of Judicature*, II, 26, 31, 285, 301; Melick, *Manor of Fordham*, pp. 116-117.
48. Records of the Town of Westchester, July 23, 1693, microfilm reel TWC3, The Bronx County Historical Society Research Library; Melick, *Manor of Fordham*, p. 117.
49. Town Records of Westchester, August 21, 1693, microfilm reel TWC3, The Bronx County Historical Society Research Library.
50. *Ibid.*, October 2, 1693.
51. Hamlin and Baker, eds., *Supreme Court of Judicature*, II, 285-286; Melick, *Manor of Fordham*, pp. 117-118, 163-166.
52. Hamlin and Baker, eds., *Supreme Court of Judicature*, II, 287; Melick, *Manor of Fordham*, p. 118; Records of the Town of Westchester, April 30, 1694, microfilm reel TWC3, The Bronx County Historical Society Research Library.
53. Hastings, ed., *Ecclesiastical Records*, II, 1109-1112; Robert Bolton, *The History of the Several Towns, Manors and Patents of the County of Westchester* (New York, 1881) II, 511-512.
54. Hastings, ed., *Ecclesiastical Records* II, 117.
55. Melick, *Manor of Fordham*, p. 119.
56. Hastings, ed., *Ecclesiastical Records*, II, 1116-1117.
57. *Ibid.*, II, 1127-1128.
58. *Ibid.*, II, 1136, 1138-1139, 1158, 1162-1163.
59. *Ibid.*, II, 1168-1169.
60. *Colonial Laws*, I, 231-236.
61. *Ibid.*, I, 258-262, 272-279, 334-338, 339-342.
62. O'Callaghan, ed., *Documentary History*, III, 29.
63. *Colonial Laws*, I, 339-342.
64. O'Callaghan, ed., *Calendar*, II, 233-245.
65. *Colonial Laws*, I, 239-242, 258-262, 272-279, 282-286, 315-321, 334-338, 339-342, 344-345, 354-356, 358-359, 369-375.
66. *Records of the Town of Eastchester*, transcribed by the Eastchester Historical Society (Eastchester, N.Y., 1964- —) I, second pagination, 2.
67. *Ibid.*, III, 1.
68. *Colonial Laws*, I, 315-321, 334-338.
69. *Ibid.*, I, 352-354.
70. Records of the Town of Westchester, May 3, 1692, May 27, 1692, microfilm reel TWC3, The Bronx County Historical Society Research Library.
71. *Ibid.*, August 4, 1692; Bolton, *History of... Westchester*, II, 290-292.

72. *Colonial Laws*, I, 296-300.
73. *Records of...Eastchester*, I, second pagination 3.
74. Records of the Town of Westchester, February 6, 1693/4, microfilm reel TWC3, The Bronx County Historical Society Research Library.
75. Bolton, *History of...Westchester*, II, 292.
76. *Records of...Eastchester*, III, 5.
77. Records of the Town of Westchester, April 22, 1692, microfilm reel TWC3, The Bronx County Historical Society Research Library.
78. Fox, ed., *Minutes of the Court of Sessions*, pp. 66-77.
79. *Ibid.*, 70-72.
80. Records of the Town of Westchester, December 20, 1692, microfilm reel, TWC3, The Bronx County Historical Society Research Library.
81. Robert Bolton, *History of the Protestant Episcopal Church in the County of Westchester: From its Foundation A.D. 1693 to A.D. 1853* (New York, 1855), pp. x-xi.
82. *Records of...Eastchester*, I, second pagination 2.
83. Bolton, *History of...Westchester*, II, 315-316.
84. *Records of...Eastchester*, I, second pagination, 6; III, 2, 4.
85. Bolton, *History of the...Church*, pp. xi-xii; Fox, ed., *Minutes of the Court of Sessions*, pp. 81-84.
86. *Colonial Laws*, I, 328-331; Bolton, *History of the...Church*, pp. xv-xvi. Bolton, *History of...Westchester*, II, 316.
87. *Records of...Eastchester*, III, 3.
88. Bolton, *History of the...Church*, p. 5; Bolton, *History of...Westchester*, II, 315; Records of the Town of Westchester, May 7, 1695, microfilm reel TWC3, The Bronx County Historical Society Research Library.
89. Bolton, *History of the...Church*, p. 4 n.
90. O'Callaghan, ed., *Calendar*, II, 231-232; Bolton, *History of... Westchester*, II, 589-598.
91. *Collections of the New-York Historical Society for the Year 1892* (New York, 1893), pp. 181-182; William S. Pelletreau, ed., *Early Wills of Westchester County New York From 1664 to 1784* (New York, 1898), p. 12-14; Bolton, *History of...Westchester*, II, 464-467.
92. Will of Lewis Morris, 1671-1746, Morris Family Papers, New-York Historical Society; Kathryn Morris Wilkinson, compiler, *Some Descendants of Richard Morris and Sarah Pole of Morrisania with Many Collateral Lineages* (Milwaukee, 1966), pp. 32-33; *Collections of the New-York Historical Society for ...1892*, pp. 180-182.
93. *Collections of the New-York Historical Society for...1892*, pp. 192, 196. The total given here is only partial, as can be seen by carefully examining a copy of the inventory printed in full in Bolton, *History of...Westchester*, II 467-469.
94. *Collections of the New-York Historical Society for...1892*, p. 192; Will of Lewis Morris, 1671-1746, Morris Family Papers, New-York Historical Society; Wilkinson, compiler, *Descendants of Richard Morris*, p. 33.
95. Dixon Ryan Fox, *Caleb Heathcote: Gentleman Colonist* (New York, 1926), pp. 4-11. This is the only full-length biography of Caleb Heathcote.
96. Fox, *Caleb Heathcote*, pp. 12-13; O'Callaghan and Fernow, eds., *Documents*, IV, 119, 232; William Smith, Jr., *The History of the Province of New*

York, ed. Michael Kammen (Cambridge, Mass, 1972) I, 91.
  97. Fox, *Caleb Heathcote*, pp. 11-12; Fox, ed., *Minutes of the Court of Sessions*, p. 69.
  98. O'Callaghan and Fernow, eds., *Documents*, II, 27, 29; Fox, *Caleb Heathcote*, p. 47.
  99. Fox, ed., *Minutes of the Court of Sessions*, p. 69.
  100. Lawrence H. Leder, ed., "The Missing New York Assembly Journal of April, 1692," *The New-York Historical Society Quarterly*, XLIX (January, 1965), 11-24.
  101. Fox, ed., *Minutes of the Court of Sessions*, p. 72.
  102. Bolton, *History of...Westchester*, II, 304.
  103. Records of the Town of Westchester, March 3, 1695/6, microfilm reel TWC3, The Bronx County Historical Society Research Library; O'Callaghan, ed., *Calendar*, II, 250.
  104. Bolton, *History of...Westchester*, II, 301-310. Bolton misreads the name Hunt in the original for Stuart.
  105. Records of the Town of Westchester, May 19, 1696, microfilm reel TWC3, The Bronx County Historical Society Research Library.
  106. *Ibid.*, June 5, 1696.
  107. Bolton, *History of...Westchester*, II, 310-311.

CHAPTER XI PERSPECTIVE ON THE BRONX FRONTIER

  1. University of the State of New York, *State Library Bulletin No. 2* (Albany, 1899), p. 169.
  2. "The Census of 1698 for Mamaroneck, Morrisania, and New Rochelle, Westchester County, New York," *The New York Genealogical and Biographical Register*, LIX (April, 1928), 104-105.
  3. Robert Bolton, *The History of the Several Towns, Manors and Patents of the County of Westchester* (New York, 1881) II, 464.
  4. Borough Town of Westchester, Record of Town Meetings, May, 27, 1686, New-York Historical Society.
  5. "Census of 1698," *New York Genealogical and Biographical Record* (April, 1928), 104-105; "New York Colonial Manuscripts, Vol XLII, Page 60, New York State Library, Albany," *The New York Genealogical and Biographical Record*, XXXVIII (April, 1907), 129-135 and (July, 1907), 218-219.
  6. Bolton, *History of...Westchester*, II, 464-466.
  7. *Ibid.*, II, 465.
  8. "Census of 1698," *New York Genealogical and Biographical Record* (April, 1928), pp. 104-105; "New York Colonial Manuscripts," *New York Genealogical and Biographical Record* (July, 1907), p. 219.
  9. See Jacob Judd, "Frederick Philipse and the Madagascar Trade," *The New-York Historical Society Quarterly* LX (October, 1971), 354ff; Edgar J. McManus, *A History of Negro Slavery in New York* (Syracuse, N.Y., 1966), p. 28.
  10. *State Library Bulletin No. 2*, p. 156.
  11. *Collections of the New-York Historical Society for the Year 1892* (New York, 1893), pp. 256-257.

12. E.B. O'Callaghan and B. Fernow, *Documents Relative to the Colonial History of the State of New York* (Albany, 1856-1883) XIII, 488, 574; "New York Colonial Manuscripts," *New York Genealogical and Biographical Record* (April, 1907), pp. 129-134.

13. "Census of 1698," *New York Genealogical and Biographical Record*, (April, 1928), pp. 104-105; "New York Colonial Manuscripts," *New York Genealogical and Biographical Record*, (April, 1907), 129-135, and (July, 1907), pp. 218-219; Evarts B. Green and Virginia D. Harrington, eds., *The American Population Before the Federal Census of 1790* (New York, 1932), p. 92.

14. "New York Colonial Manuscripts," *New York Genealogical and Biographical Record* (April, 1907), 129-134, and (July, 1907), pp. 218-219.

15. Bolton, *History of...Westchester*, II, 465.

16. William S. Pelletreau, ed., *Early Wills of Westchester County New York From 1664 to 1784* (New York, 1898), pp. 382, 385.

BIBLIOGRAPHY

This bibliography concentrates on those works, whether published or unpublished, that have a direct relation to people and events in the history of The Bronx during the years covered in this volume. Consequently, those publications that focus primarily on events in Europe not generally known in the United States, and on the supposed, but erroneous, Danish origin of Jonas Bronck, are not listed here. Both, however, may be found in the notes, and scholars seeking to use these works are urged to find them there.

UNPUBLISHED ARCHIVAL AND MANUSCRIPT COLLECTIONS

DTB. Gemeentie Archief. Amsterdam.
Dutch Colonial Manuscripts. New York State Library.
Morris Family Papers. New-York Historical Society.
Notarial Archives. Gemeentie Archief. Amsterdam.
Patents, Indian Deeds 1642-1659 In Book GG in the Dutch Language in the Office of the Secretary of State at Albany. C.D. Westbrook, tr. The New-York Historical Society.
Vingboom Map of New York City, 1639. Map Collection. Library of Congress.
Westchester Records. James Riker Collection. New York Public Library.
Westchester, Borough Town of. Record of Town Meetings 1665-1691. On microfilm. The New-York Historical Society.
Westchester, Town of. Records. On microfilm. The Bronx County Historical Society Research Library.

PUBLISHED MANUSCRIPTS
AND COLLECTIONS OF DOCUMENTS

Calendar of New York Colonial Manuscripts Indorsed Land Papers; in the office of the Secretary of State of New York 1643-1803. Albany: Weed, Parsons & Company, 1864.
Collections of the New-York Historical Society for the Year 1868. New York: The New-York Historical Society, 1868.
Collections of the New York Historical Society for the Year 1869. New York: The New-York Historical Society, 1870.
Collections of the New-York Historical Society for the Year 1892. New York: The New-York Historical Society, 1893.
Collections of the New-York Historical Society for the Year 1893. New York: The New-York Historical Society, 1894.
Collections of the New-York Historical Society for the Year 1894. New York: The New-York Historical Society, 1895.
Collections of the New-York Historical Society for the Year 1912. New York: The New-York Historical Society, 1913.
The Colonial Laws of New York From the Year 1664 to the Revolution. Albany: James B. Lyon, 1894.
De Vries, David Peterson. *Voyages from Holland to America, A.D. 1632 to 1664.* Henry C. Murphy, tr. and ed. New York: Kraus Reprint Co., 1971.
Fox, Dixon Ryan, ed. *The Minutes of the Court of Sessions (1657-1696): Westchester County New York.* White Plains: Westchester County Historical Society, 1924.
Greene, Evarts B. and Virginia D. Harrington, eds. *The American Population Before the Federal Census of 1790.* New York: Columbia University Press, 1932.
Hamlin, Paul M. and Charles E. Baker, eds. *The Supreme Court of Judicature of the Province of New York: 1691-1704.* New York: The New-York Historical Society, 1952.
Hastings, Hugh, ed. *Ecclesiastical Records of the State of New York.* Albany: James B. Lyon, 1901-1905.
Henry Hudson's Voyages. Ann Arbor: University Microfilms, Inc., 1966.
James, Bartlett Burleigh and J. Franklin Jameson, eds. *Journal of Jasper Danckaerts 1679-1680.* New York: Charles Scribner's Sons, 1913.
Jameson, J. Franklin, ed. *Narratives of New Netherland: 1609- 1664.* New York: Charles Scribner's Sons, 1909.
[Johnson, Edward]. *A History of New England. From the English planting in the Yeere 1628. until the Yeere 1652.* London: Nath. Brooke, 1654.

Journal of the Votes and Proceedings of the General Assembly of the Colony of New-York Began the 9th Day of April, 1691; and Ended the 27th of September, 1743. New York: Hugh Gaine, 1766.

Morris, Richard B., ed. *John Jay The Winning of the Peace: Unpublished Papers 1780-1784.* Associate ed., Ene Sirvet. New York: Harper & Row, 1980.

Niles, Samuel. "A Summary Historical Narrative of the Wars in New-England with the French and Indians, in the several parts of the Country," *Collections of the Massacusetts Historical Society.* Third Series, VI. Boston: American Stationers' Company, 1837.

O'Callaghan, E.B., ed. *Calendar of Historical Manuscripts in the Office of the Secretary of State, Albany, N.Y.* Albany: Weed, Parsons and Company, 1865-1866.

———, abstractor. *Calendar of New York Colonial Commissions 1680-1770.* New York: The New-York Historical Society, 1929.

———, ed. *The Documentary History of the State of New York.* Albany: Weed, Parsons & Co., and Charles Van Renthuysen, 1849-1851.

———, ed. *Journal of the Legislative Council of the Colony of New-York Began the 9th Day of April, 1691; and Ended the 27 of September, 1743.* Albany: Weed, Parsons and Company,1861.

——— and B. Fernow, eds. *Documents Relative to the Colonial History of the State of New York.* Albany: Weed, Parsons and Company, 1856-1883.

Paltsits, Victor Hugo, ed. *Minutes of the Executive Council of the Province of New York: Administration of Francis Lovelace 1668-1673.* Albany: the State of New York, 1910.

Pelletreau, William S., ed. *Early Wills of Westchester County New York From 1664 to 1784.* New York: Francis P. Harper, 1898.

[Purchas, Samuel]. *Purchas. His Pilgrimes.* London: William Stansby for Henrie Fetherstone, 1625.

Records of the Town of Eastchester. Transcribed by the Eastchester Historical Society. Eastchester, N.Y.: Eastchester Historical Society, 1964- —.

Seymann, Jerrold, ed. *Colonial Charters Patents and Grants to the Communities Comprising the City of New York.* New York: The Board of Statutory Consolidation of the City of New York, 1939.

Smith, William, Jr. *The History of the Province of New York.* Michael Kammen, ed. Cambridge, Mass.: The Belknap Press of Harvard University Press, 1972.

Third Annual Report of the State Historian of the State of New York, 1897. New York and Albany: Wynkoop Hallenbeck Crawford Co., 1898.

Trumbull, J. Hammond, ed. *The Public Records of the Colony of Connecticut.* Hartford: Brown & Parsons, 1850.

University of the State of New York. *State Library Bulletin No. 2.* Albany: The University of the State of New York, 1899.

Van der Donck, Adraien. *A Description of the New Netherlands.* Thomas F. O'Donnell, ed. Syracuse, N.Y.: Syracuse University Press, 1968.

Van Laer, Arnold J.F., tr. *Documents Relating to New Netherland 1624-1626 in the Henry E. Huntington Library.* San Marino, California: Henry E. Huntington Library and Art Gallery, 1924.

———, tr. and ed. *New York Historical Manuscripts: Dutch.* Baltimore: Genealogical Publishing Co., Inc., 1974.

———, ed. *Van Rensselaer Bowier Manuscripts.* Albany: University of the State of New York, 1908.

[Welde, Theodore, or John Withrop?]. *A Short Story of the rise, reign, and ruine of the Antinomians.* London: Ralph Smith, 1644.

Winthrop, John. *Winthrop's Journal: "History of New England" 1630-1649.* James Kendall Hosmer, ed. New York: Charles Scribner's Sons, 1908.

Wolley, Charles. *A Two Years' Journal in New York and Part of Its Territories.* Cleveland, The Burrows Brothers Company, 1902.

DOCUMENTS AND MANUSCRIPTS IN PUBLISHED PERIODICALS

"The Census of 1698 for Mamaroneck, Morrisania, and New Rochelle, Westchester County, New York," *The New York Genealogical and Biographical Record*, LIX (April, 1928).

"Deed from the Indians to Thomas Pell," *Pelliana*, I (May, 1941).

Denton, Daniel. "A Brief Relation of New York, With the Places Therunto Adjoining Formerly Called The New Netherlands, &c.," *The Bulletin of the Historical Society of Pennsylvania*, I (March, 1848).

"Governor Winthrop's Aknowledgement," *Pelliana*, I (May, 1935).

Hershkowitz, Leo, ed. "Select Documents Relating to Jonas Bronck," *The Bronx County Historical Society Journal*, I (July, 1964).

Leder, Lawrence H., ed. "The Missing New York Assembly Journal of April, 1682," *The New-York Historical Society Quarterly*, XLIX (January, 1965).

———, ed. "Records of the Trial of Leisler and His Associates," *The New-York Historical Society Quarterly*, XXXVI (October, 1952).

"New York Colonial Manuscripts, Vol. XLII, Page 60, New York State Library, Albany," *The New York Genealogical and Biographical Record*, XXXVIII (April and July, 1907).

Ultan, Lloyd, ed. "Document Relating to the Ursuline Convent at East Morrisania," *The Bronx County Historical Society Journal*, VIII (July, 1971).

HISTORIES OF THE BRONX AND WESTCHESTER COUNTY

Bolton, Robert. *The History of the Several Towns, Manors and Patents of the County of Westchester*. New York: C.F. Roper, 1881.

Comfort, Randall. *History of Bronx Borough, City of New York*. New York: North Side News Press, 1906.

Cook, Harry T. *The Borough of the Bronx 1639-1913: Its Marvelous Development and Historical Surroundings*. New York: Harry T. Cook, 1913.

Fluhr, George J. *The Bronx Through the Years: A Geography and History*. Bronx, N.Y.: Aidan Press, 1964.

French, Alvah P. *History of Westchester County, New York*. New York: Lewis Historical Publishing Co., Inc., 1925-1927.

Griffin, Ernest Freeland. *Westchester County and Its People, A Record*. New York: Lewis Historical Publishing Co., 1946.

Jenkins, Stephen. *The Story of the Bronx*. New York: G.P. Putnam's Sons, 1912.

McNamara, John. *History in Asphalt: The Origin of Bronx Street and Place Names Borough of The Bronx New York City*. Bronx, N.Y.: The Bronx County Historical Society, 1984.

Scharf, John T. *History of Westchester County, New York, Including Morrisania, Kingsbridge, and West Farms*. Philadelphia: L.E. Preston and Co., 1886.

Shonnard, Frederic and W.W. Spooner. *History of Westchester County, New York: From Its Earliest Settlement to the Year 1900*. New York: New York History Co., 1900.

Wells, James L., Louis F. Haffen and Josiah Briggs. *The Bronx and Its People: A History 1609-1927*. New York: Lewis Historical Publishing Co., 1927-1935.

HISTORIES OF OLD BRONX MANORS, TOWNS, AND NEIGHBORHOODS

Ackerly, Lucy D. *The Morris Manor: Address Delivered at the Fifth Annual Meeting of the New York Branch of the Order of Colonial Lords of the Manor in America*. N.p.: No imprint, 1916.

Barr, Lockwood. *Ancient Town of Pelham: Westchester County, State of New York*. Richmond, Va.: The Dietz Press, 1946.

Hall, Edward Hagaman. *The Manor of Philipsborough*. Baltimore: The Order of Colonial Lords of the Manor in America, 1920.

Pell, Howland. *The Pell Manor*. Baltimore: The Order of Colonial Lords of the Manor in America, 1917.

Melick, Harry W.C. *The Manor of Fordham and Its Founder*. New York: Fordham University Press, 1950.
Tieck, William A. *Riverdale, Kingsbridge, Spuyten Duyvil: New York City*. Old Tappan, N.J.: Fleming H. Revell Co., 1968.
Walton, Frank L. *Pillars of Yonkers*. New York: Stratford House, 1951.

PUBLISHED BIOGRAPHIES, GENEALOGIES, AND FAMILY HISTORIES

Atkins, T. Astley. *Adriaen Van Der Donck: An address delivered before the Westchester County Historical Society*. Yonkers: The Statesman Print, 1888.
Bolton, Reginald Pelham. *A Woman Misunderstood: Anne Wife of William Hutchinson*. New York: Privately printed, 1931.
Collier, William Miller. *Casper, a Collier, Hallenbeck, Conyn Name with Memoranda as to Bearers of it and Incidental References to Colliers named Jochem (Jehoiakem), Michael and Isaac*. Auburn, N.Y.: Privately printed, n.d. (1951?).
Cornell, John. *Genealogy of the Cornell Family*. New York: T.A. Wright, 1902.
Curtis, Edith. *Anne Hutchinson: A Biography*. Cambridge, Mass. Washburn & Thomas, 1930.
Delafield, John Ross. *Delafield: The Family History*. N.p.: Privately printed, 1945.
Fox, Dixon Ryan. *Caleb Heathcote: Gentleman Colonist*. New York: Charles Scribner's Sons, 1926.
Leggett, Theodore A. *Early Settlers of West Farms: Westchester County, N.Y.* New York: Tobias A. Wright Press, 1913.
Phelan, Thomas P. *Thomas Dongan: Colonial Governor of New York 1683-1688*. New York: P.J. Kenedy & Sons, 1933.
Rugg, Winnifred King. *Unafraid: A Life of Anne Hutchinson*. Boston and New York: Houghton Mifflin Company, 1930.
Sheridan, Eugene R. *Lewis Morris 1671-1746: A Study in Early American Politics*. Syracuse, N.Y.: Syracuse University Press, 1981.
Sitherwood, Francis Grimes. *Throckmorton Family History*. Bloomingdale, Ill.: Pentagraph Printing and Stationary Co., 1929.
Smith, Samuel Stelle. *Lewis Morris: Anglo-American Statesman ca. 1613-1691*. Atlantic Highlands, N.J.: Humanities Press, 1983.
Van Loon, Hendrick. *Adraien Block: Skipper, Trader, Explorer*. New York: Black Hall, Inc., 1928.
Wilkinson, Kathryn Morris, compiler. *Some Decendants of Richard Morris and Sarah Pole of Morrisania with Many Collateral Lineages*. Milwaukee: Privately printed, 1966.

OTHER PUBLISHED WORKS

Atkins, T. Astley. *Indian Wars and the Uprising of 1655 — Yonkers Depopulated: A Paper Read Before the Yonkers Historical and Library Association.* Yonkers: the Society, 1892.

Bolton, Reginald Pelham. *Early History and Indian Remains on Throg's Neck Borough of The Bronx City of New York.* Bronx, N.Y.: Bronx Society of Arts and Sciences, 1934.

———. *Indian Life of Long Ago in the City of New York.* New York: Joseph Graham Schoen Press, 1934.

———. *Indian Paths in the Great Metropolis.* New York: Museum of the American Indian — Heye Foundation, 1922.

———. *New York City in Indian Possession.* New York: Museum of the American Indian — Heye Foundation, 1920.

Bolton, Robert. *History of the Protestant Episcopal Church in the County of Westchester: From its Foundation in A.D. 1693 to A.D. 1853.* New York: Stanford and Swords, 1855.

Comstock, Sarah. *Old Roads from the Heart of New York.* New York: G.P. Putnam's Sons, 1915.

Fagan, Brian M. *The Great Journey: The Peopling of Ancient America.* London and New York: Thames and Hudson, 1987.

Fleming, Alice. *Highways into History.* New York: St. Martin's Press, 1971.

Holbrook, Stewart H. *The Old Post Road.* New York, Toronto, and London: McGraw Hill Book Company, Inc., 1962.

Indian Archaeology of Long Island. N.p.: The Nassau Museum of Natural History Education Leaflet 17, n.d.

Jenkins, Stephen. *The Old Boston Post Road.* New York and London: G.P. Putnam's Sons, 1913.

Judd, Jacob and Irwin I. Polishook, eds. *Aspects of Early New York Society and Politics.* Tarrytown, N.Y.: Sleepy Hollow Restorations, 1974.

Kenney, Alice P. *Stubborn for Liberty: the Dutch in New York.* Syracuse, N.Y.: Syracuse University Press, 1975.

McManus, Edgar J. *A History of Negro Slavery in New York.* Syracuse, N.Y.: Syracuse University Press, 1966.

O'Callaghan, E.B. *History of New Netherland; or New York Under the Dutch.* New York: D. Appleton & Company, 1846-1848.

———, compiler. *The Register of New Netherland; 1626-1674.* Albany: J. Munsell, 1865.

Pierce, Carl Horton. *New Harlem: Past and Present.* New York: New Harlem Publishing Company, 1903.

Riker, James. *Revised History of Harlem (City of New York.).* New York: New Harlem Publishing Company, 1904.

Reich, Jerome R. *Leisler's Rebellion: A Study in Democracy in New York 1664-1720.* Chicago: The University of Chicago Press, 1953.

Rich, Oliver A. *Holland on the Hudson: An Economic and Social History of Dutch New York.* Ithaca, N.Y.: Cornell University Press, 1986.

Ritchie, Robert C. *The Duke's Province: A Study of New York Politics and Society, 1664-1691.* Chapel Hill: The University of North Carolina Press, 1977.

Ritchie, William A. *The Archaeology of New York State.* Garden City: The Natural History Press, 1965.

Ruttenber, E.M. *History of Indian Tribes of Hudson's River.* Port Washington, N.Y.: Ira J. Friedman Division, Kennikat Press, 1971.

Schoonmaker, Marius. *The History of Kingston N.Y. From Its Earliest Settlement to the Year 1820.* New York: Burr Printing House, 1888.

Skinner, Alanson. *Exploration of Aboriginal Sites at Throgs Neck and Clasons Point, New York City.* New York: Museum of the American Indian Heye Foundation, 1919.

Smith, Carlyle Shreeve. *The Archaeology of Coastal New York. Anthropological Papers of the American Museum of Natural History,* XLIII, part 2. New York: The American Museum of Natural History, 1950.

Sturtevant, William C., ed. *Handbook of North American Indians.* XV *Northeast.* Washington, D.C.: Smithsonian Institution, 1978.

Trelease, Allen W., *Indian Affairs in Colonial New York: The Seventeeth Century.* Port Washington, N.Y.: Ira J. Friedman Division of Kennikat Press, 1971.

Washburn, Wilcomb E. *The Indian in America.* New York: Harper & Row, 1975.

ARTICLES

Bolton, Reginald Pelham. "The Home of Mistress Anne Hutchinson At Pelham 1642-3," *The New-York Historical Society Quarterly Bulletin,* VI (July, 1922).

———. "A Pioneer Settler's Home on Spuyten Duyvil Hill," *The New-York Historical Society Quarterly Bulletin,* V (April, 1921).

Cohen, Ronald D. "The Hartford Treaty of 1650: Anglo-Dutch Cooperation in the Seventeenth Century," *The New-York Historical Society Quarterly,* LIII (October, 1969).

———. "The New England Colonies and the Dutch Recapture of New York, 1673-1674," *The New-York Historical Society Quarterly,* LVI (January, 1972).

Ellis, David. "'Upstate Hicks' versus 'City Slickers,'" *The New-York Historical Society Quarterly,* XLVIII (April, 1959).

Judd, Jacob. "Frederick Philipse and the Madagascar Trade," *The New-York Historical Society Quarterly*, LX (October, 1971).
Lopez, Julius. "The Milo Rock Site, Pelham Bay Park, Bronx County, N.Y.," *Pennsylvania Archaelogist*, XXVIII (December, 1958).
Melick, Harry W.C. "The First Real Estate Development in The Bronx," *The New-York Historical Society Quarterly*, XXXII (January, 1968).
──. "The Fordham 'Ryott' of July 16, 1688," *The New-York Historical Society Quarterly*, XXXVI (April, 1952).
"Mrs. Anne Hutchinson," *The Magazine of History*, XXII (January-February, 1916).
Pell, Robert. "Sir John Pell: Second Lord of the Manor of Pelham," *Pelliana*, New Series I (October, 1963).
──. "Thomas Pell: First Lord of the Manor of Pelham Westchester Co., New York," *Pelliana*, New Series I (September, 1962).
"Thomas Pell," *Pelliana*, I (May, 1936).
Valentine, Preston S. "A Record of Some of the Valentine Family of The Bronx and Westchester," *The Bronx County Historical Society Journal*, XI (Spring, 1974).
Wright, Langdon C. "Local Government and Central Authority in New Netherland," *The New-York Historical Society Quarterly*, LVII (January, 1973).

UNPUBLISHED WORKS

Edsall, Thomas H. "Notes on Samuel Edsall." Copied February 26, 1925, by Gertrude Nelson for Florence Edsall Bryant. Typescript in the Local History and Genealogy Room, New York Public Library.
Leder, Lawrence H. *Jacob Leisler and the New York Rebellion of 1689-1691*. Unpublished M.A. Thesis, May, 1950. New York University.
[Melick, Harry W.C.]. "Decendants of John Archer of Fordham." Typescript in the Westchester County Historical Society.
O'Callaghan, E.B. "Lists of Officials of the Province of New York 1630-1775." O'Callaghan Papers. New-York Historical Society.
Rhodes, C. Alexander. "Biographies and Geneologies of the Shuneman Family, Van Bergen Family, Bronck Family, Witbeck Family, Finch Family, Perks Family for 800 Years." MSS, 1915? Microfilmed November 7, 1941. New York Public Library.
Wilcox, U. Vincent. "Prehistory of the New York City Area." 1970. Typescript in the New York City — Antiquities Collection. Library of the Museum of the American Indian.

INDEX

Achter Col, 43
adzes, 4, 156
Africa, 18, 175
agriculture, 4, 5, 21, 47, 59, 179
Alaska, 6
Albany, 11, 17, 19, 105, 136, 138, 139, 141, 155, 166, 169, 180
Albany Crescent, 11
Albert the Trumpeter, 54, 55
aldermen, 72, 167-170
Aldrich, Peter, 114, 174
Algonquin, 6
Amsterdam, 16, 19, 23-27, 30, 33, 35, 36, 38, 39, 43-45, 49, 54-56, 60, 61, 64, 67, 71, 87, 171
Andriessen, Pieter, 27, 28, 36, 176
Andros, Edmund, 94, 97, 100, 103-105, 107, 111, 113, 115-119, 130, 134, 137, 138, 140
Anglican Church, 85
animals, 3, 8, 9, 20, 34, 111, 182
Anthony and Susannah, 114
Antill, Edward, 151
Antinomianism, 33
Antone the neger, 175
apples, 59, 178
Archer, John, 71, 73, 74, 73, 75-77, 79, 86, 89, 90, 97, 103, 107, 108, 109, 110, 115, 117-120, 128, 170, 173, 174, 176, 177, 178, 180, 182
Archer, Jr., John, 109, 128, 129
arms, 44, 55, 56, 58, 60, 88, 93, 108, 154, 179
arrows, 5, 8, 49
Ashton, Thomas, 110
Assizes, Court of, 76, 77, 81, 98, 103, 104, 107, 108, 114, 115, 117, 118, 119, 121
Atlantic, 6, 15, 16, 23, 24, 26, 27, 52, 134, 165
attorney, 38, 43, 45, 48, 67, 108, 114, 117, 129, 148-150, 152, 155, 163, 164, 167
Augsburg, 134
avenues. *See* streets
Avery, Edward, 157
awls, 4, 9
axes, 4, 8, 15, 20, 34

Bailey Avenue, 11
Bailey, John, 167
Bailey, Nicholas, 59, 61, 70, 80, 133
Bailey, Thomas, 151
Baltic Sea, 23
banishment, 94

223

bannerstone, 4
baptisms, 98, 100
Baptist Church, 31
Barbados, 85, 86, 90, 91, 113, 115, 174, 175
Barker, John, 61
barley, 29, 37, 178
Barnes Avenue, 11
Barnes, William, 98, 127, 129, 138, 146, 148-150, 152, 156, 158, 160, 167
barrels, 141, 175, 178
Barton, Elijah, 133
Barton, Roger, 110, 130-133, 176
Bartow-Pell Mansion, 54
Bassett, Robert, 59, 181
Bastiensen, 90, 92, 130
Baxter, Thomas, 127, 138, 148, 153, 156, 167
Bayard, Nicholas, 130, 132, 134, 135, 137, 141, 143, 151, 152, 154, 163, 179
Bayard, Balthazar, 91
Beado, Francis, 92, 93
beans, 4, 5, 8
bears, 4, 9, 37, 59
beaver, 20, 35, 39, 53, 59, 89, 91, 92, 179
bedding, 165
Bedford, 139
beef, 72, 178
beer, 29, 98, 169
bees, 59
Belgium, 19
Bergen, 39
berries, 8
Bess, 113, 114, 174, 175
Betts, Richard, 73
Betts, William, 60, 70, 71, 75, 76, 81
Bickley, William, 161- 163
birds, 4, 7, 9, 182
blacks, free, 175
blacksmiths, 38, 101, 124. *See also* smiths

blankets, 165
Block, Adriaen, 16-18, 133
blockhouse, 103
Bloomer, Robert, 148, 149
boatman, 101
books, 22, 23, 29, 90, 159, 181
Boston, 33, 41, 61, 84, 130, 132-134, 137
Bout, Jan Evertsen, 46, 47
Boyle, Joseph, 181
Brazil, 19, 25
bread, 8
Breda, 43-45, 49
breeches, 59, 131
bridges, 75, 76, 81, 84, 97, 110, 111, 117, 157, 161, 175, 177, 181, 183
Bridges, Charles and Sarah, 67, 70, 82
Briggs, John, 41
Broadway, 73, 76
Bronck, Jonas, 20-31, 35-39, 41, 42, 57, 62, 63, 69, 70, 115, 117, 121, 172, 174, 176, 178-182
Bronck, Mortan, 21
Bronck, Peter, 28, 36
Broncksland, 37, 63, 70-72, 76, 79, 82, 84, 85, 90, 91, 113-119, 122, 127
Bronx River, 4, 21, 42, 62, 67, 69, 71, 72, 76, 79-81, 110, 116, 127, 130, 132, 133, 137, 138, 150-153, 156, 181
Bronx Kill, 3, 115, 116
Bronxdale Avenue, 11
Brooke, Lord, 53
Brooklyn, 55, 136
Brouwersgracht, 23
Bryan, Ensign Alexander, 61
Burger, Engeltie, 117
Bussing Avenue, 11
Butler, John, 125, 128
butter, 27, 29, 37
Buys, Aert Pieterse, 130, 131, 133

cabbage, 38
Cage, Richard, 107, 110
Calvinists, 12, 44
Cambridge, 52
Canada, 44
Cannife, Jeremiah, 110
canoes, 10, 14, 49, 104, 105, 116, 172
Cape Cod, 17, 52
captains, 6, 17, 93, 135, 158
Caribbean Sea, 25, 85
Carles, Catherine, 71
carpenters, 84, 158
carting, 103
Casling, Samuel, 155, 158
Castle Hill, 11, 102, 179
Castle Hill Avenue, 11
Castle Island, 17
Catholics, 12, 119, 133, 134
Catskill Mountains, 14
cattle, 21, 22, 25, 26, 29, 33, 35, 37, 42, 49, 51, 54, 59, 68, 72, 75, 82, 103, 106, 107, 111, 116, 117, 123, 127, 156, 178
Chadderton, William, 146, 150
Chancery, Court of, 120
Charles I, King, 52, 85
Charles II, King, 60, 62, 64, 84, 87, 94, 124, 183
cherries, 59
Chesterfield, 164, 168
Chock, Peter, 149, 150
church, 31, 59, 71, 85, 100, 129, 130, 132, 133, 137, 141, 150-154, 158-160, 164, 166, 170, 177, 179, 183
Church of England, 159, 160, 164
church wardens, 159
cider, 156, 178
City Island, 69
Claessen, Valentine, 90, 132, 174
clams, 5, 7, 9, 34
clans, 7
Clarke, John, 102
Clason Point, 5, 42

clay, 4, 5
clergy, 22, 31, 33, 98
clergyman, 22, 98, 124
cloth, 20, 29, 163
clothing, 7, 9, 82, 114
Co-op City, 67
coins, 163
Colen Donck, 45, 48
Collier, Benjamin, 121, 132, 143, 150
Collier, Edward, 136, 138, 143, 153, 168, 174
Colman, John, 14
Columbus, Christopher, 12
Colve, Anthony, 88, 94
commerce, 13, 15, 18, 47, 81, 97, 111, 157. *See also* trade
Committee of Safety, 136
common councilmen, 167-170
Common Pleas, Court of, 146, 151, 165
Commons, House of, 146
Coninck, Captain Frederick de, 56
Concklin, John, 110
Connecticut, 5, 6, 16- 18, 24, 31, 37, 51-53, 55, 60-62, 64, 67, 69, 80, 82, 84, 102, 105, 130, 134, 135, 170, 176, 177, 180, 183
coopers, 175, 181
Copenhagen, 21, 23, 28
Copenhagen, University of, 21
Coppathwait, Hugh, 122
copper, 15
Corlear's Hook, 35
corn, 4, 5, 8, 14, 49, 82, 101, 133, 152, 178
Cornell, Thomas, 41- 43, 45, 49, 51, 54, 57, 58, 67, 172, 176, 180
Cornell's Neck, 42, 45, 49, 67-70, 82
coroner, 42, 169
Corson, Hendrick, 151
Corstianssen, Hendrick, 16, 17
Cotton, Reverend John, 33
Council, 6, 7, 24, 38, 39, 46, 51, 61,

Council *(continued)* 73, 77, 85, 88-93, 104, 105, 110, 115, 117-122, 124, 128, 134-141, 143-145, 148, 149, 154, 155, 160-165, 177
cows, 27, 29, 73, 106, 107, 116
Cromwell, Oliver, 53, 84
Cromwell's Creek, 76, 79
Croton River, 160
cup, 29
currants, 14
Curtis, John, 90
cutlass, 29

daggers, 29
Dam Square, 24
Dam, Jan Jansen, 31
Danes, 22, 28
dart points, 4
Davenport, Nathaniel, 92
Davis Strait, 13, 15
Davis, Andrew, 131
De Waagh, 56
De Brant Van Troyen, 25-27
De Kay, Teunis, 130, 131
deer, 4, 7, 9
deerskin, 9
Delaware River, 16, 20, 53
Demarest, David, 77, 108, 109, 117
Denmark, 22, 23
Dermer, Captain Thomas, 18, 171
Description of the New Netherlands, 48
Devonshire, 38, 134
Diana, 175
Dirksen, Jan, 79
docks, 69
dogs, 8, 34, 157, 175
Donck, van der, Adriaen. *See* van der Donck, Adriaen
Dongan, Governor Thomas, 119-121, 124-126, 128, 137, 138, 140, 167
doublet, 29
Doughty, Elias, 70, 71, 111, 160

Doughty, Mary, 44, 49
Doughty, Reverend Francis, 44
Drake, John, 126, 148, 155, 157, 159
Drake, Jr., Samuel, 103
Du Sauchoy, Marcus, 79
DuBois, Louis, 114, 115, 174
Dudley, Joseph, 144
duffel, 20
Dutch, 12, 13, 15-20, 22-24, 26, 28-31, 33- 39, 41-49, 51-62, 64, 65, 67, 69, 71-73, 75, 87-94, 97, 103, 107, 111, 113, 114, 117, 129, 130, 132, 133, 137, 140, 141, 150-154, 160, 166, 173, 174, 176, 177, 179, 182, 183
Dutch East India Company, 13, 15, 18
Dutch Reformed Church, 129, 130, 132, 137, 141, 150, 151, 153, 166, 177, 179, 183
Dutch West India Company, 18-20, 24, 34, 51, 52, 55, 62
Duyts, Laurens, 27, 37, 176
East River, 3, 16, 17, 26, 53, 61, 63, 127
Eastchester, 11, 67, 68, 70, 80-82, 84, 86, 88, 92, 97, 100-104, 106, 107, 111-113, 118-120, 124-128, 135, 139-141, 148-150, 155, 157-160, 164, 173, 176, 178, 179, 181
Eastchester bridge, 81
Eastchester Road, 11
Easttown, 57. *See also* Oostdorp
Edsall, Samuel, 39, 70, 72, 85
elk, 4,
Embree, John, 101
Emmaus, 28
Emott, James, 151
England, 15, 16, 23, 31, 33, 41, 42, 47, 52-56, 60-62, 64, 65, 67, 72, 82, 84, 90-94, 98, 102, 104, 105, 130, 133-135, 144, 145, 150, 152, 155, 158-160, 164, 165, 168, 169, 172,

England, (continued) 173, 176, 183
English, 12, 13, 16-19, 21, 24, 31, 34, 37, 38, 41-43, 45, 49, 51-60, 62, 64, 65, 67, 69-72, 79, 82, 84, 85, 87-92, 94, 95, 97, 100, 102, 111, 114, 115, 121, 133, 140, 141, 145, 149, 155, 160, 164, 169, 170, 173, 174, 176, 182, 183
Esopus, 39, 114, 136
Essex in New Jersey, 136
Europeans, 12, 17, 18, 20, 31, 39, 49, 71, 156, 171-173, 176
Eustis, James, 67
Evarts, James, 70
eviction, 79, 133

Fairfield, 53, 58, 60, 67, 82, 84, 176
fairs, 156, 157, 168, 170
farmers, 21, 22, 24, 25, 27, 28, 41, 47, 49, 58, 60, 72, 81, 98, 118, 161, 178, 179
farmhands, 27, 29, 70
Faroe Islands, 21
feathers, 9
fence, 28, 54, 79, 111, 113, 131, 133, 178
Ferris, John, 70, 80, 127, 128, 150, 152, 156
Ferris, Samuel, 167
ferry, 72, 75, 76, 81, 110, 111, 124, 161, 168, 170, 176, 177, 183
ferry to Long Island, 168
fiscal, 54-56
fish, 4, 5, 7
fishing, 5, 8, 9, 11, 13, 19, 159, 182
Flatbush, 136
Fletcher, Governor Benjamin, 144, 145, 147, 148, 150, 154, 158, 160, 161, 165-168, 170
flour, 8, 139, 140, 177, 178
Flushing, 44, 71, 93, 176
fluted projectile, 3
Fogg, Reverend Ezekiel, 100
Fordham, manor of, 77, 79, 97, 102, 103, 107, 110, 128, 129, 132, 133, 137, 141, 150, 153
Fordham village, 74
forests, 11, 82
Fort Amsterdam, 19, 35, 55
Fort Nassau, 17, 19
Fort Orange, 19, 20, 38
fortifications, 31, 39, 103, 106
forts, 19
Fortune, 16
Foster, Miles, 162
foxes, 16, 59
Franklin, Benjamin, 123
Freedoms and Exemptions, Charter of, 19
freeholders, 119, 133, 153, 159, 160, 167, 169
freemen, 61, 64, 168
French, 19, 44, 94, 134, 138, 139, 146, 154, 155, 165, 180
frogs, 7
fruit, 8, 59, 178
Fruit trees, 59
furs, 15, 16, 20, 44, 171, 177

game, 5, 9
German states, 134
Germans, 25, 28, 174
Gever, Jacob, 25, 36, 176
Gibbs, Thomas, 86, 90, 92
Gilliam, Edward, 124
ginger, 163
gloves, 29
goats, 38
Goding, Samuel, 101
gold, 29
Gold, Major, 135, 140
Grady, Henry, 38
Graham, Isabella, 163
Graham, James, 148, 150, 163, 167, 172
grain, 19, 27, 29, 36-38, 59, 79-81, 85, 98, 101, 104, 105, 156, 157, 178
grass, 42, 51, 59, 72, 73, 178

grazing, 33, 49, 51, 72, 106, 107, 116
Greenland, 13
grist mill, 100, 138, 157
Grove Farm, 126, 178
Gun Hill Road, 11, 76
gunpowder, 20, 44, 141
guns, 29, 44, 48, 55, 92, 104, 156, 157, 175
Gustavus Adolphus, 22

Hackensack Indians, 35
Hadden, John, 133
Haiden, Will, 101, 103, 106, 113, 126
Haiden, William, 70, 88, 125
Halve Maen, 13
harbors, 69
Hardewyn, Martin, 79
Harlem, 3, 14, 16, 17, 26, 31, 37, 63, 71-76, 79, 82, 86, 89, 93, 94, 115, 116, 117, 127, 128, 133, 140, 173, 177-179
Harlem River, 3, 14, 16, 17, 26, 31, 37, 71, 72, 74, 76, 115, 127, 128, 133
Harrison, Katherine, 80
Hartford, 52, 54, 55, 60, 61
Hartford, Treaty of, 52, 54, 55
hats, 15, 29
hay, 28, 29, 54, 64, 68, 70, 73, 76, 79, 108, 116-118
Headley, Richard, 103, 113
Heart, Jonathan, 148
Heathcote, Caleb, 147, 158-160, 164-170, 177, 182, 184
Heddy, John, 76, 81
Heerengracht, 23
Hell Gate, 5, 17, 18, 61, 104
Hellegat, 17
Hempstead, 176
Hendricks, Jan, 77
Hendrucks, Geertrien, 39
Hermans, Augustine, 67, 68

hickory nuts, 8
High Bridge, 76
Hitchcock, Samuel, 139
hoes, 5
hogs, 29, 76, 77, 80, 82, 157, 161, 175, 178
Hoit, John, 88, 92
Hoit, Moses, 102, 106, 113, 126
honey, 59
Hoorn, 16, 26
horses, 27, 29, 38, 59, 61, 75, 82, 94, 106, 125, 157, 159, 174, 178
Hubbard, Edward, 131, 132
Hudde, Andreas, 24, 25, 26
Hudson, Henry, 13, 14, 20, 64, 171
Hudson, Jonathan, 110
Hudson River, 3, 14, 15, 17, 19, 30, 20, 35- 39, 59, 62, 114, 118, 160, 180
Hudson, Robert, 132, 174
Huestis, Robert, 61, 130, 133, 153, 156, 167
Huestis, Jr., Robert 153
Huestis, Samuel, 167
Hunt, John, 98, 127, 148, 150, 152, 156, 160, 167, 179, 181
Hunt, Josiah, 153, 156, 167
Hunt, Robert, 125, 174
Hunt, Thomas, 67, 68, 79, 80, 89, 115, 117, 126, 178
Hunt, Jr., Thomas, 77, 79, 80, 89, 94, 117, 174
hunters, 4
hunting, 3, 5, 7-11, 49, 102, 104, 157, 159, 175, 182
Hunts Point, 125, 174
Hutchinson, Anne, 33, 34, 41, 42, 54, 57, 58, 171, 172, 176
Hutchinson River, 4, 35, 67, 68, 111
Hyde, Anne, 133

indentured servants, 25, 26, 28, 36, 85, 86, 90, 182

Indian wars, 35, 46, 47, 49
Indians, 11, 12, 14-16, 18, 20, 29-31, 33-37, 39, 42-45, 48, 49, 53, 54, 55-57, 59, 62, 67, 69, 71, 76, 77, 79, 102- 105, 108, 111, 114, 116, 121, 126-128, 138, 170-172, 174, 177
Ingoldsby, Richard, 139, 163
Ireland, 15, 23
iron, 54, 93, 118, 162, 163
iron works, 162
Irwin Avenue, 73

Jackson, John, 100, 101, 103
Jacobsen, Jan, 27, 28, 37
Jamaica, 82, 97, 116, 119, 123, 135, 180
James II, King, 124, 129, 133, 134, 139, 147
Jans, Ytie, 37
Jansen, Geesje, 37
Jansen, Gerrit, 27
Jansen, Michael, 46
Jay, John, 123
Jennings, John, 157
Jensen, Cornelis Laurens, 116
Jerome Avenue, 11, 76
Jessup, Edward, 61, 63, 62, 64, 69, 79, 172
Jeuriaens, Teuntie, 23, 28, 36
jewelry, 163
Jones, John, 38
Jones, Morgan, 100, 124, 176
Jones, William, 110
Jönköping, 21, 22
Joris, Burger, 117
Juet, Robert, 14
Kaller, Jochem, 25, 28, 36, 176
Kalmar, War of, 22, 23
Katskill, 43, 44
Keskiskeck, 45
Kieft, Director-general Willem, 30, 35, 42, 43
Kiersen, Henrick, 130

King's Bridge, 161, 175, 177, 181, 183
Kingsbridge Road, 11
King William's War, 154, 180
Kipp, Johannes, 130, 131
Knyfe, Captain William, 89
Komstad, 21
Korte Boomdwarstraat, 23
Krynsen, Lieutenant, 89
Kuyter, Jochem Pietersen, 26, 27, 31, 37

language, 1, 6, 21, 23, 105
Lawrence, John, 61, 91
Lawrence, William, 93
lead, 10, 12, 13, 18, 31, 33, 38, 44, 45, 48, 58, 84, 104, 123, 131, 141, 164, 178, 182
League of Augsburg, 134
Lee, Joseph, 143
Leggett, Gabriel, 80, 138, 139, 141, 146, 147, 149, 155, 174, 182
Legislature, 61, 144, 147, 154-157, 159
Leisler, Captain Jacob, 135-151, 154-156, 160, 165, 166, 168, 179, 180, 183
Lenape, 6
Lewis, Thomas, 71
Leyden, 43
Liberties and Privileges, Charter of, 119
library, 22, 28, 30, 181
Lievenssen, Jacob, 25
liquor, 59, 104, 169
livestock, 27-29, 36, 37, 56, 59, 72, 82, 84, 106, 107, 125, 140, 163, 177-179
logs, 34, 82
London, 13, 93, 124, 136, 137
Long Island, 3, 4, 6, 16- 18, 20, 28, 31, 33, 35, 36, 42-44, 52, 55-57, 59-62, 64, 69, 82, 87, 88, 93, 97, 98, 100, 104, 105, 115, 118, 119, 127,

Long Island, *(continued)* 130, 135, 139, 141, 168, 176, 177, 180
Long Island Sound, 3, 4, 16-18, 31, 33, 42, 43, 52, 69, 104, 115, 127, 168
Long Reach, 128
Lords, House of, 145
Louis XIV of France, King, 87
Lourens, Christiana, 91
Lovelace, Governor Francis, 73, 75-77, 79-81, 84, 108, 152
lumber, 28, 42, 177
lumbering, 106
Lutherans, 21, 22
Lynch, Gabriel, 101
Lyon, 31

magistrates, 31, 33, 41, 56-60, 71, 75, 88-90, 103, 135
maize, 27
malt, 29
Mamaroneck, New York, 120, 148
Manhattan, 3, 16, 19, 20, 26-28, 35, 37, 43, 49, 63, 72, 73, 81, 82, 104, 105, 118, 176, 177, 180
Manhattan Indians, 5, 6
Manning, Captain John, 87
Manning, Robert, 106
manors, 69, 70, 77, 79, 82, 84, 89, 92, 97, 102-105, 107-111, 119, 126, 127-129, 132, 133, 137, 140, 141, 150, 151, 153, 161, 177, 182, 183
mantle, 29
Marble Hill, 15
market, 72, 156, 157, 168-170, 177, 181
market house, 170
marriages, 98, 100
Marschalk, Andries, 151
marshes, 4, 33, 42, 51, 59, 72, 73, 178
Mary, Queen, 133-136, 140, 142, 144, 145, 148, 149
Mary of Modena, 134

masons, 84
Massachusetts Bay, 31
mastodon, 3
masts for ships, 45
Mather, Warham, 124, 160, 176
Matthijs, Clara, 26, 27
mattocks, 20
Mattysen, Nelis, 91
Mayor's Court in New York City, 108, 109, 114-116, 119
Mayor's Court in Westchester, 168
meadowland, 44, 45, 68, 70, 71, 76, 77, 79, 106, 108-110, 117, 125, 129, 150
meeting house, 158
merchants, 13, 15-19, 22, 23, 25, 57, 61, 67, 72, 85, 118, 125, 128, 130, 131, 135, 136, 160, 164, 166, 170, 171, 177, 183
Mexico, 4
Meyer, Adolph, 117
Michielsen, Ryer, 130, 131, 133, 137
Milbourne, Jacob, 144, 145
Milford, Connecticut 61
military, 6, 19, 23, 56-58, 62, 64, 134, 135, 137, 139, 146, 155, 158, 165, 180
militia, 57, 87, 93, 102, 103, 135, 138, 140, 141, 148, 154, 155, 158, 165, 166, 173, 179, 180
milk, 29, 37
miller, 81, 179
mills, 45, 81, 92, 100, 101, 138, 139, 140, 141, 157, 166, 167, 178
Mills, Richard, 60-62
ministers, 21, 44, 59, 98, 100, 124, 129, 154, 158-160
ministry, 33, 159, 182, 183
mink, 20
Minniwits, 61
Minville, Gabriel, 114
mirrors, 29
Mohawk River, 17

Mohawks, 35, 44, 122
Monmouthshire, 85
Morris, Colonel Lewis, 85, 86, 90, 91, 113- 116, 118, 119, 121, 123, 135, 140, 174, 175, 178, 183
Morris, Lewis, nephew of Colonel Lewis Morris, 85, 86, 90, 91, 113-116, 118, 119, 121-123, 135, 140, 161-164, 167, 170, 172, 175, 180, 181, 183
Morris, Mary, 162, 163, 175
Morris, Richard, 85, 90, 91, 175, 182
Mosholu, 11
Mott, James, 150
Mullineux, Thomas, 113
muskets, 14, 20, 29, 58
mussels, 5, 7

navigation, 14, 17, 19, 23, 29, 36, 48, 51, 53, 59
Navigation Act, 48
necklaces, 9
Ned, 174
needles, 4, 9
Nell, 175
Netherlands, The, 12, 13, 16, 17, 21, 23, 27, 28, 43, 45-48, 52-56, 58, 64, 65, 71, 88, 94, 134, 170, 173
New Amsterdam, 26, 27, 30, 33, 36, 38, 39, 43-45, 49, 54-56, 60, 61, 64, 67, 71, 87, 171
New England, 31, 42, 52, 53, 55, 56, 60-62, 67, 90-94, 98, 102, 104, 105, 130, 134, 158, 172, 173, 176, 183
New England, dominion of, 130, 134
New Hampshire, 130
New Harlem, 72, 73,
New Haven, 53, 61, 91
New Jersey, 3, 6, 35, 118, 130, 136, 162, 163, 167, 174, 180
New Netherland, 17- 20, 24, 25, 27, 29, 31, 33, 36, 38, 39, 42, 43, 46, 47, 48, 51, 53, 56, 57, 59, 60, 64, 65, 71, 88-94
New Netherland Company, 17, 18 75, 76, 79, 82, 89, 93, 94
New Orange, 88, 90, 92, 93
New Rochelle, 69, 141
New York, 6, 14, 63, 65, 69, 72, 74, 77, 82, 84-88, 97, 98, 100, 102, 104-106, 108-110, 114-116, 118, 119, 122, 124, 126, 128-137, 139-142, 144, 146, 148-154, 159, 161, 163, 164, 165, 167-170, 173, 177, 178, 183
New York Bay, 14
New York City, 72, 77, 82, 84, 88, 104-106, 108, 109, 114, 116, 118, 119, 122, 128, 130, 134-136, 139, 140, 144, 146, 148, 150, 152, 153, 159, 161, 163, 169, 177, 183
Newfoundland, 14, 15
Newman, Thomas, 71
Newtown, 100, 136, 176
Nicoll, William, 155
Nicolls, Governor Richard, 65, 68-70, 73, 76, 117, 152, 167
Nicolls, Matthias, 107, 129
Nicolson, Francis, 130, 134-136
Nieuhof, 71
Nieuw Kirk, 24
Nine Men, the, 46
North Pelham, 69
North Riding, 82, 97, 102, 109, 111, 114, 116, 118, 119, 122, 140, 141, 177, 183
Northwest Passage, 13- 15
notary, 38
Nuton, Captain Lieutenant Brian, 56, 58
nuts, 4, 8

O'Neale, Hugh, 49, 111
O'Neale, Mary, 49, 69- 71
Oakley, Miles, 100, 167

Index

Odell, John, 131, 151
Oldenberg, Germany, 27
onions, 59
Onrust, 17, 18
Oostdorp, 57-60, 71, 88
orchards, 59, 110, 178
Osborne, Captain Richard, 102, 103, 107, 117
otter, 20, 59
oxen, 82, 103, 106, 107, 178
Oyer and Terminer, Court of, 120, 122, 123
Oyster Bay, 91
oysters, 5, 7, 9, 34

Palmer, John, 107, 132, 133, 148, 150, 181
Palmer, Joseph, 80, 88, 127-130, 152, 153, 156
Paparinemin, 73, 75, 76, 81, 108, 110, 161
Paparinemin bridge, 812
Parcell, John, 37
parsonage, 158
patroon system, 19
patroons, 19, 20
patroonship, 19, 20, 36, 43-45, 47-49, 172
peaches, 59
peas, 29, 59, 77, 94, 178
Pelham, 4, 5, 54, 69, 126, 127, 140, 159-161, 163, 173
Pelham Bay Park, 4, 5, 54, 69
Pelham Heights, 69
Pelham, manor of, 126, 127, 140. *See also* Pelham and Pell's manor
Pell, Dr. John, 82
Pell, John, 82, 83, 84, 88, 92, 98, 103-105, 111, 113, 118-120, 126, 127, 130, 135, 140, 141, 144, 148, 156, 163-166, 170, 172, 181, 182
Pell, Thomas, 52-58, 61, 62, 64, 65, 67-70, 82, 128, 172, 176, 182
Pell's manor, 82, 84, 92, 104, 105, 111, 119
Pequot Indians, 53
Pequot War, 53
Philip, King, 102, 105, 109, 172, 180, 183
Philipsburgh, manor of, 161
Philipse, Frederick, 71, 104, 105, 134, 136, 160, 161, 175, 177, 183
physician, 109
pictures, 29
Piepowder, Court of, 157, 168
Pieter, Carsten, 25, 36, 176
pigs, 59, 106, 107, 111
Pilgrims, 52
Pinckney, John, 84, 149, 150
Pinckney, Philip, 67, 70, 101, 111, 113, 126, 128
Pinckney, Rachel, 84
Pinckney, Thomas, 155, 157
Pinhorne, Chief Justice William, 143, 150
Pinnet, James, 93
pistol, 55
Piters, Maritje, 23, 28
plates, 29
Plymouth, 19, 44, 102, 130
Plymouth Company, 19
Ponton, Joseph, 136
Ponton, Captain Richard, 57, 61, 71, 72, 80, 81, 87, 90, 127, 129, 130, 135, 138, 141, 144, 146-149, 153, 170, 173
Pope, the, 134
population, 24, 47, 58, 59, 72, 80-82, 92, 98, 106, 107, 169, 172, 175, 180-182
Port Morris, 91
pottery, 4, 5, 8
Privy Council, 124, 137, 144, 145, 148, 155
property, 9, 26-28, 37, 39, 42, 44, 45, 47, 49, 53, 56, 58, 65, 67, 69, 70, 71-73, 75-77, 79, 82, 84, 89-91, 93, 94, 97, 104, 105, 107-110, 113-

Index 233

117, 121-123, 125- 129, 131, 133, 138, 140, 141, 143, 145, 147, 148, 151-153, 156, 158, 160, 161-164, 167, 169
Protestantism, 12
Protestants, 19
Providence, 31, 42
Provoost, David, 38
Pudway, Joseph, 136
Pugsley, Matthew, 125, 174, 181
Puritans, 31, 33, 52, 53, 98, 158

Quakers, 85, 89, 98
Queens, 17, 122, 135, 141, 155, 159
Quinby, John, 70, 81

raccoon, 59
Randall's Island, 3
rapier, 29
Rattlesnake Brook, 68, 156
Rawson, Eleanor, 181
religion, 31, 33, 59, 89, 100, 122, 133, 158, 183
Remonstrance of New Netherland, 46, 47
Rensselaerswyck, 20, 36, 39, 43, 44, 176, 180
Reynderss, Jeuriaen, 23
Rhode Island, 17, 31, 33, 35, 41, 52, 93, 130, 134, 176, 180
Richardson, John, 62, 63, 69, 79, 80, 107, 115, 120, 127, 130, 132, 138, 150-152, 156, 157, 163, 178
Richardson, Martha, 140, 141
Richmond, 159
Rider, John, 79, 121
ring, 29, 123
Riverdale, 71
rivers, 16, 45, 160, 166
roads, 75, 81, 84, 157, 177
Rombouts, Francis, 92
Roosevelt Island, 37
Rostock, 23
rum, 93, 98

rye, 29, 37, 178
Rye, 125, 139, 156

sachems, 6, 7, 53, 62, 76, 105, 156, 172
salt, 4, 14, 29, 33, 42, 110
salt cellar, 29
Sandersen, Thomas, 38
Sands, Captain James, 34
Savoy, 134
saw mill, 45, 138
Saw Mill River, 45
Saybrook, 53
Saye and Sele, Lord, 53
Scandinavia, 13
Scandinavian peninsula, 23
Schenectady, 138
schoolmasters, 52, 60- 62, 100
Schoorteenveger, 36. *See also* Andriessen, Pieter
schout, 43, 88
Scotland, 23
scrapers, 8
Seabrooke, Thomas, 102, 179
seawan, 9, 109
Sedgwick Avenue, 11
Selyns, Dominie Henricus, 129, 130, 132, 150, 153
sergeant of the mace, 168
Sessions of the North Riding, Court of, 111, 114, 116
Setauket, 176
Seton Falls Park, 68
settlements, 19, 24, 31, 39, 49, 59, 80, 93, 118- 120, 141, 171, 172, 177, 179, 183
Sharp, John, 94
sheep, 82, 106, 107, 125, 157, 161, 170, 178
sheep pasture, 125, 157, 170
shellfish, 4, 5, 7
shells, 8-10, 20
shipping, 53, 87, 125
ships, 12-20, 23, 24, 25- 27, 31, 45,

ships, (continued) 47, 53, 69, 85, 90, 93, 123, 125, 137, 165, 175
shoemaker, 157
shooting, 14, 159
Shurmer, Frederick, 151
Shute, Richard, 100, 101, 103, 113, 124-126, 128, 158
Sigmund, Thomas, 101
silver, 15, 29, 154
Siwanoys, 5, 6, 17, 18, 20, 34, 42, 53, 57, 67, 128, 156
Skane, 23
skinning, 8
skins, 35, 39, 53, 59, 91, 179
slave trade, 175
slaves, 85, 86, 90, 93, 113-117, 157, 163, 172, 174, 175, 180, 182
Sloughter, Governor Henry, 139, 144, 163- 165
Smaland, 21-23
Smeeman, Harman, 39
Smith, Captain John, 13
Smith, William, 77, 92, 123
Smith, Thomas, 101
smiths, 81, 179. See also blacksmiths
soapstone, 4
soldiers, 56, 75, 94, 155
Soundview, 42
Southwyck, Sussex, 52
Spain, 12, 13, 18, 47, 52, 134
Spanish, 12, 13, 18, 19, 85
spear, 3-5, 7, 8
spear points, 4, 8
Spicer, Thomas, 37-39, 41
spoons, 29
sports, 158, 159
Spuyten Duyvil Creek 14, 20, 44, 45, 72, 73, 75, 79, 80, 90, 93, 105, 107, 108, 110, 115, 124, 129, 130, 133, 161, 170
squash, 4, 8
stadtholder, 88, 133
Stamford, 71, 105

Staten Island, 3, 136
States-General, 13, 16- 18, 31, 46- 48, 56, 58, 62, 88, 89
Statham, Thomas, 110, 132, 136, 138, 141, 143, 146, 149, 151, 174
steatite, 4
Steenwyck, Cornelis, 77, 89, 109, 110, 118, 128, 173
Steenwyck, Margarieta, 129
Stephenson, Nicholas, 130, 131
Stevens, Nathaniel, 110
Stille, Cornelis Jacobsen, 27, 28, 37, 176
sting ray, 9
stock, 27
stockade, 105
Stockholm, 23
Stoll, Jacob Jansen, 39
Stony Island, 91, 116- 119, 121, 122, 140, 179, 183
streets, 11, 26
sturgeon, 5, 7
Stuyvesant, Peter, 38, 45-48, 51-58, 60-62, 117, 179, 180
Suffolk County, 135, 139, 141, 155
Suffolk, England 84
suffrage, male, 169
sugar, 163
Supreme Court, 146, 147, 149-152, 154
surgeon, 52, 53
surveyors, 79, 127, 153
Sweden, 21-23, 25, 117, 134
Swits, Claes Corneliesen, 29

tailor, 81, 101, 179
Tallcot, Captain John, 61
tankards, 29
tanner, 157
Tauvert, Andrew, 136
tavern, 36, 41, 98, 102, 156, 159, 169, 179
Taylor, John, 101
tenants, 22, 69, 74, 75, 77, 79, 81,

86, 89, 110, 130, 151, 152, 170, 173, 179, 182
Texel, 13, 16, 26, 47
The Hague, 47
Theale, Joseph, 148
theology, 21, 22, 29, 33
Third Avenue, 11
Throckmorton, John, 31, 33-35, 41, 42, 54, 57, 58, 67, 171, 172, 176, 180
Throggs Neck, 4, 5, 18, 35, 67, 68, 70, 80, 97, 126, 150, 157, 178
Tibbett's Brook, 11, 44
Tiger, 16
Tilden Street, 11
timber, 69, 97, 98, 157, 177
Tintern, 85
Tippett, George, 71, 73, 75-77, 81, 92, 93
tobacco, 14, 27-29, 59, 71, 72, 178
Tomkins, John, 101
Tomkins, Nathaniel, 113, 126
Toney, 175, 178
tools, 4, 9-11, 34
Torbay, 134
Tourneur, Jacques, 131
town house, 125
town meeting, 41, 42, 54, 98, 100-102, 119, 155, 158, 159, 173, 181
trade, 4, 10, 13-21, 24, 26, 31, 44, 71, 82, 101, 134, 144, 145, 157, 165, 175, 177
Trade, Lords of, 165
trails, 10, 11
Tremont Avenue, 11
tribes, 5-7 10, 14, 16, 17, 20, 29, 35, 37, 38, 44, 64, 102, 103, 104, 105, 171
Turner, Daniel, 167
Turner, Perigreen, 137
Turneur, Daniel, 76, 79, 81, 115-118, 121, 122, 137
Turneur, Jacqueline, 116
turtles, 8

Underhill, Captain John, 37
Unionport Road, 11
University Avenue, 11

Vail, Thomas, 137
Valentine, Matthias, 137
Valentine family, 90. *See also* Claessen, Valentine
van Brugge, Carl, 58
van Clyff, Dirck, 91
Van Cortlandt Avenue, 11
Van Cortlandt Park, 49, 71
van Cortlandt, Oloff Stevenson, 61
van Cortlandt, Stephanus, 91
van Cortlandt, Stephen, 134-137, 140, 143, 163
van Couwenhoven, Jacob, 46, 47
van Curler, Arent, 36- 39, 41, 43
van der Donck, Adriaen, 43-49, 57, 69, 160, 171, 172, 174, 176-178, 180, 182
Van Dyck, Hendrick, 30, 49
van Elslandt, Claes, 54, 55, 57, 58
van Ruyven, Cornelis, 58, 61
Van Rensselaer, Kiliaen, 20, 36, 43, 44
van Schelluyne, Dirck, 38
Van Tienhoven, Cornelis, 31, 47, 54, 56
van Vleek, Isaac, 130
vegetables, 8, 178
Verplanck, Gelyn, 92
Verveelen, Johannes, 72, 75, 76, 81, 90, 93, 107, 108, 110, 111, 124, 161, 173, 177, 183
vestrymen, 159, 160
victualizers, 169
Virginia, 13, 14, 71, 87, 90, 93, 123, 176, 180
Vreedlant, 33, 34
Vreedlandt in the Netherlands, 27

Waddell, Thomas, 118
Waldron, Resolved, 93

Index

Walloons, 19
walnuts, 8
wampum, 9, 10, 20, 59, 77, 179.
  See also seawan
war, 6, 10, 12, 13, 18, 22, 23, 30, 31, 35, 44, 45, 47, 52-55, 58, 62, 64, 85, 87, 88, 94, 102- 105, 109, 134, 135, 138, 154, 155, 165, 172, 180, 183
Ward, William, 166
watchcoats, 165
watchmen, 104
Waters, Edward, 60, 70, 88, 107, 127, 128, 130, 136, 141, 153, 160
weapons, 8
weaver, 81
Webley, Walter, 91, 114, 115, 120, 174
Weckquasgeeks, 5, 6, 29, 30, 35, 49, 104, 105, 111
Well, Samuel, 98
Wells, Philip, 129
Wessells, Hartman, 109
Wessells, Werner, 77, 92
West 230th Street, 73
West 231st Street, 11
West 238th Street, 76
West Farms, 63, 62, 69, 70, 79-82, 115, 138
West Indies, 85, 87, 123, 175
West, John, 109, 129, 179
West Riding, 109
Westchester Board of Trustees, 127, 149
Westchester, borough and town of, 167, 170, 171
Westchester, constable and overseers of, 68
Westchester County, 5, 45, 54, 67, 69, 71, 120- 125, 129, 132, 133, 135, 136, 137, 140, 141, 143, 144, 146-148, 150, 151, 155, 156-166, 172, 174-183
Westchester Creek, 4, 51, 54, 59, 97, 100, 157, 166, 167, 178

Westchester, Mayor of the borough of, 167- 170
Westchester town, 127, 158, 174
Westchester village, 54, 58
Westchester Path, 72
Westminster, treaty of, 94
whaling, 13, 20
wharfs, 69
wheat, 29, 82, 94, 101, 108, 116, 126, 133, 140, 152, 163, 177, 178, 179
Wheeler, Lieutenant Thomas, 55-57
White, John, 152
White, Thomas, 149
wigwams, 7, 38
Willett, William, 70, 167
William III, King, 134, 139, 145, 146, 149, 154, 180
William and Mary, king and queen, *See* William III, King and Mary, Queen
Williams, Roger, 31, 33, 52
Williams, Thomas, 136, 138-141, 143-148, 182
wine, 55, 169
Winthrop, Jr., Governor John, 62
witch, 80, 81
wolf pits, 98, 157
wolves, 7, 8, 98, 157, 158
wood, 4, 8, 33, 98, 177, 178
Wood, Ann, 100
Wood, Consider, 100
wool, 82, 178
workmen, 84
Wright, James, 101

Yonkers, 45, 63, 69, 73, 84, 104, 105, 111, 120, 124, 129, 159, 160, 175, 181
Yonker's land, 45, 49, 69, 71, 77, 81, 103, 111, 119

Zuyder Zee, 13, 26

ABOUT THE AUTHOR

LLOYD ULTAN is a professor of history at the Edward Williams College of Fairleigh Dickinson University in Hackensack, New Jersey. He served as president of The Bronx County Historical Society from 1971 to 1976, and has written articles and books on Bronx and American history, including the highly acclaimed *The Beautiful Bronx, 1920 – 1950*. He also is the author of *Legacy of the Revolution: The Story of the Valentine-Varian House* and *Presidents of the United States* and is founding editor of *The Bronx County Historical Society Journal*.

THE BRONX COUNTY HISTORICAL SOCIETY

The Bronx County Historical Society was founded in 1955 for the purpose of promoting knowledge, interest and research in The Bronx. The Society administers The Museum of Bronx History, Edgar Allan Poe Cottage, a Research Library, and The Bronx County Archives; publishes a varied series of books, journals and newsletters; conducts historical tours, lectures, courses, school programs, archaeological digs and commemorations; designs exhibitions, sponsors various expeditions, and produces the *Out Of The Past* radio show and cable television programs. The Society is active in furthering the arts, in preserving the natural resources of The Bronx, and in creating a sense of pride in the Bronx community.

Members of The Bronx County Historical Society receive:
A subscription to
The Bronx County Historical Society Journal
published semi-annually
The Bronx Historian Newsletter

Free admission to
The Museum of Bronx History
3266 Bainbridge Avenue at East 208th Street
The Bronx, New York

The Edgar Allan Poe Cottage
Kingsbridge Road and Grand Concourse
The Bronx, New York

♦

Invitation to
The Society's Annual High School Valedictorians Dinner, Historical Tours, Lectures, Exhibitions and other Educational Programs.

For additional information, please write or call.
THE BRONX COUNTY HISTORICAL SOCIETY
3309 Bainbridge Avenue
The Bronx, New York 10467
Telephone: (718) 881-8900

The Bronx County Historical Society is supported in part
with public funds and services provided through:
The Department of Cultural Affairs
The Department of Parks and Recreation of the City of New York
The Office of The Bronx Borough President
The Bronx City Council Delegation
The New York State Council on the Arts
The New York State Office of Parks, Recreation and Historic Preservation
The New York State Library
The Institute of Museum Services

PUBLICATIONS OF
THE BRONX COUNTY HISTORICAL SOCIETY

The Bronx in the Frontier Era: From the Beginning to 1696
   by Lloyd Ultan
The Bronx in the Innocent Years 1890-1925
   by Lloyd Ultan and Gary Hermalyn
The Beautiful Bronx 1920-1950
   by Lloyd Ultan
The Bronx It Was Only Yesterday 1935-1965
   by Lloyd Ultan and Gary Hermalyn
The Bronx County Historical Society Journal
   Published twice a year since 1964
The Bronx in Print: An Annotated Catalogue of Books and Pamphlets about the Bronx
   Edited by Candace Khuta and Narcisco Rodriquez
The Bronx Triangle: A Portrait of Norwood
   by Edna Mead
Genealogy of The Bronx: An Annotated Guide to Sources of Information
   by Gary Hermalyn and Laura Tosi
History in Asphalt: The Origin of Bronx Street and Place Names
   by John McNamara
History of the Morris Park Racecourse and the Morris Family
   by Nicholas DiBrino
Legacy of the Revolution: The Valentine - Varian House
   by Lloyd Ultan
McNamara's Old Bronx
   by John McNamara
Morris High School and the Creation of the New York City Public High School System
   by Gary Hermalyn
The South Bronx and the Founding of America: An Activity Book for Teachers and Students
   by Lisa Garrison
Edgar Allan Poe: A Short Biography
   by Kathleen A. McAuley
Poems of Edgar Allan Poe at Fordham
   by Elizabeth Beirne
Edgar Allan Poe at Fordham Teachers' Guide and Workbook
   by Kathleen A. McAuley
The Signers of the Constitution of the United States
   by Brother C. Edward Quinn
The Signers of the Declaration of Independence
   by Brother C. Edward Quinn
Presidents of the United States
   by Lloyd Ultan
Elected Public Officials of The Bronx Since 1898 (Updated Annually)
   by Laura Tosi and Gary Hermalyn
Landmarks of The Bronx
   by Gary Hermalyn and Robert Kornfeld
350th Anniversary of The Bronx Commemorative Issue
   The Bronx County Historical Society Journal
Bicentennial of the United States Constitution Commemorative Issue
   The Bronx County Historical Society Journal